101+ Ways God Speaks

— And How To Hear Him —

Sandy Warner

SOS Publications® • PO Box 7096 • Eugene, OR • 97401

101⁺ Ways God Speaks
— And How To Hear Him —

BY SANDY WARNER

Published by: SOS Publications®
PO Box 7096 • Eugene, Oregon 97401

All rights reserved. No part of this book may be reproduced or transmitted in any form or by any means, electronic or mechanical, including photocopying, recording or by any information storage and retrieval system without written permission from the author.

Copyright © 1984, 1995, 1997, 2000 by Sandy Warner.
Printed in the United States of America. First printing 1997, second edition 2000, third printing 2001, fourth printing 2002.
ISBN 0-9656768-0-3

Scripture quotations marked (TLB) are taken from *The Living Bible* © 1971. Used by permission of Tyndale House Publishers, Inc., Wheaton, IL 60189. All rights reserved.

Scripture taken from the NEW AMERICAN STANDARD BIBLE(R), © Copyright The Lockman Foundation 1960, 1962, 1963, 1968, 1971, 1972, 1973, 1975, 1977. Used by permission.

Scriptures marked (KJ) are taken from The King James Version. Public domain.

Scripture quotations marked "NKJV" are taken from the New King James Version. Copyright © 1979, 1980, 1982 by Thomas Nelson, Inc. Used by permission. All rights reserved.

Scriptures marked "AMP" are taken from the Amplified® New Testament, © Copyright The Lockman Foundation 1954, 1958, 1987. Used by permission.

All scriptures *(except TLB & AMP)* were taken from BibleWorks™ for Windows™ © 1992-1997 by Michael S. Bushell.

Some images from Zedcor, Inc. DeskGallery Collection © 1996. Used by permission.

Cartoons © 1997 John Warner. Used with permission.

Greek & Hebrew definitions were taken from Strong's Exhaustive Concordance of the Bible, © 1890 by James Strong, Madison NJ. Public domain.

If any acknowledgment of copyrighted material used in this book has been inadvertently omitted or miscredited in the footnotes, receipt of such information would be appreciated.

TABLE OF CONTENTS

101⁺ Ways God Speaks
— And How To Hear Him —

PART ONE - HOW HE SPEAKS

CHAPTER 1.
THE BOTTOM LINE
OF THE WHOLE KIT AND CABOODLE

1. He adds life to ordinary words (Quickening) 11
2. He uncovers truth (Revelation) 13
3. Separating mixture (Discernment) 13

PART TWO - WHERE HE SPEAKS

CHAPTER 2.
HE SPEAKS THROUGH THE BIBLE

4. Concordance definitions 18
   Strong's Concordance instructions 19
5. Dictionaries & encyclopedias 20
   Bible dictionaries 20
6. Different versions of the Bible 21
7. Cross references 21
8. Headings, margins and underlining 24
9. His Words on cassette tapes 25
10. Types & examples 25

CHAPTER 3.
HE SPEAKS THROUGH ALLEGORIES & PARABLES

11. Hidden allegories in our daily lives 28
    What we are doing at the moment 29
    Our job assignments 31
12. Our blOOpers 32
13. His promises 32
    The process of His promises 33
14. Allegorical stories 34
15. Parables 35
    New Testament Parables 35
16. Movie themes 36
17. Commercials & advertisements 38
18. Traffic signs & other signs 39
19. Headlines 40
20. Animal allegories 41
21. Creation facts 42

CHAPTER 4.
HE SPEAKS THROUGH OUR PERSONALITIES

22. Where our eyes glance 45
23. What we say 46
    Joyous emotions 47
24. Creative force: spoken faith 48
25. What we pray 49
26. What we sing 49
27. Anointed hands 50
28. Directing our thoughts 51
    Impressions 51
    An inspired flash of insight 52
29. Recurring thoughts and scriptures 53
    Recurring songs 53
30. Our yearnings 53
31. Soul dreams 54
32. Weakness 55

CHAPTER 5.
HE SPEAKS THROUGH PEOPLE

HE SPEAKS THROUGH GIFTS OF THE BODY OF BELIEVERS
- 33. The gift of service 58
- The gift of hospitality 59
- 34. The gift of exhortation 59
- 35. The gift of giving 60
- 36. The gift of ruling 61
- 37. The gift of mercy 62
- 38. The gift of helps 62
- 39. The gift of government 63
- 40. The musicians 64
- 41. The craftsmen 65
- Fresh creativity 65
- 42. The children's gifts 66
- Children's words 66
- 43. The seniors 67
- 44. The intercessors 68
- 45. The missionaries 69

HE SPEAKS THROUGH THE APPOINTED GIFTS
- 46. The apostles 71
- 47. The prophets 71
- 48. The evangelists 73
- 49. The pastors 74
- 50. The teachers and the gift of teaching 76

SHARING THE GIFTS
- 51. Using common sense 79
- 52. His super on our natural 82

CHAPTER 6.
HE SPEAKS THROUGH THE HOLY SPIRIT

53. His still small voice 85
    1st person 86
    2nd person 87
    3rd person 88
    4th person 89
    His inner audible voice 90
54. He speaks in visions 91
    Pictures 91
    Gazing wonders 93
    Carrying away 97
    Visions have a purpose 97
55. Holy Spirit dreams 98
    Dreams have a purpose 99
56. Opening our literal eyes 100
57. Opening our literal ears 101
58. Opening our literal smell 101
59. Opening our literal touch 102
60. Opening the sense of taste 102
61. Being transported in the Spirit 102
62. Falling under His power 104
63. Trembling in His Presence 107
64. Angels 108

HE SPEAKS THROUGH THE GIFTS OF THE SPIRIT
65. The word of wisdom 110
66. The word of knowledge 111
67. The gift of faith 114
68. Gifts of healing 114
69. Working of miracles 115
70. Prophecy 117
71. Discerning of spirits 118
72. The gift of tongues 119
73. Interpretation of tongues 123

PART THREE - WHEN HE SPEAKS

CHAPTER 7.
HE SPEAKS IN AND OUT OF TIME

74. Give Him time 124
75. Wait for confirmation 126
76. Seasons in our lives 131
77. Synchronizing of God's people 132
78. Circling through time 133
79. His Timeless Words 135
80. Numbers and clocks 136

CHAPTER 8.
HE SPEAKS IN A FAVORABLE CLIMATE

THE CLIMATE OF OUR HEART
81. When we have faith 139
82. When we abide in Jesus 141
83. When we let Him lead 143
84. When we yield 144

THE CLIMATE OF OUR DECISIONS
85. When we are at rest 145
    When we pause 146
86. When we ponder His Words 148
87. When we follow our conscience 149
88. When we do not strive 151
89. When we limit fleeces 153

THE CLIMATE OF OUR ACTIONS
90. When we pray 154
91. When we worship 155
92. When we make holy choices 157
93. When we seek counsel 157
94. When we fast 158

PART FOUR - WHAT HE SPEAKS

CHAPTER 9.
UNDERSTANDING WHAT HE SPEAKS

BUILDING A LANGUAGE
- 95. Common reference points 163
- 96. Puzzling together mystery words 164
- 97. Applying details 166
- 98. Puzzling together accumulated knowledge 167
- 99. Balancing knowledge with quickening 167
- 100. Building definitions 168
  - Finding definitions 169
  - List of definitions 171
- 101. A list of God's attributes 179

CHAPTER 10.
DISCERNMENT - SEPARATING THE WHITE, BLACK AND GRAY

- Pursuing the supernatural 184
- Making decisions about the supernatural 185
- Discerning the gifted vessel 187
- Separating the gray of the vessel 189
- Giant and flesh list 191
- Giants, thoughts and the enemy 195
- Rebuking enemy thoughts 197
- Discerning counterfeit spirits 198
- Prayer over unclean paraphernalia 200
- Discerning enemy dreams & visions 200
- Discerning misunderstanding 202
- Discerning the message 204
- Summary of how to discern 207

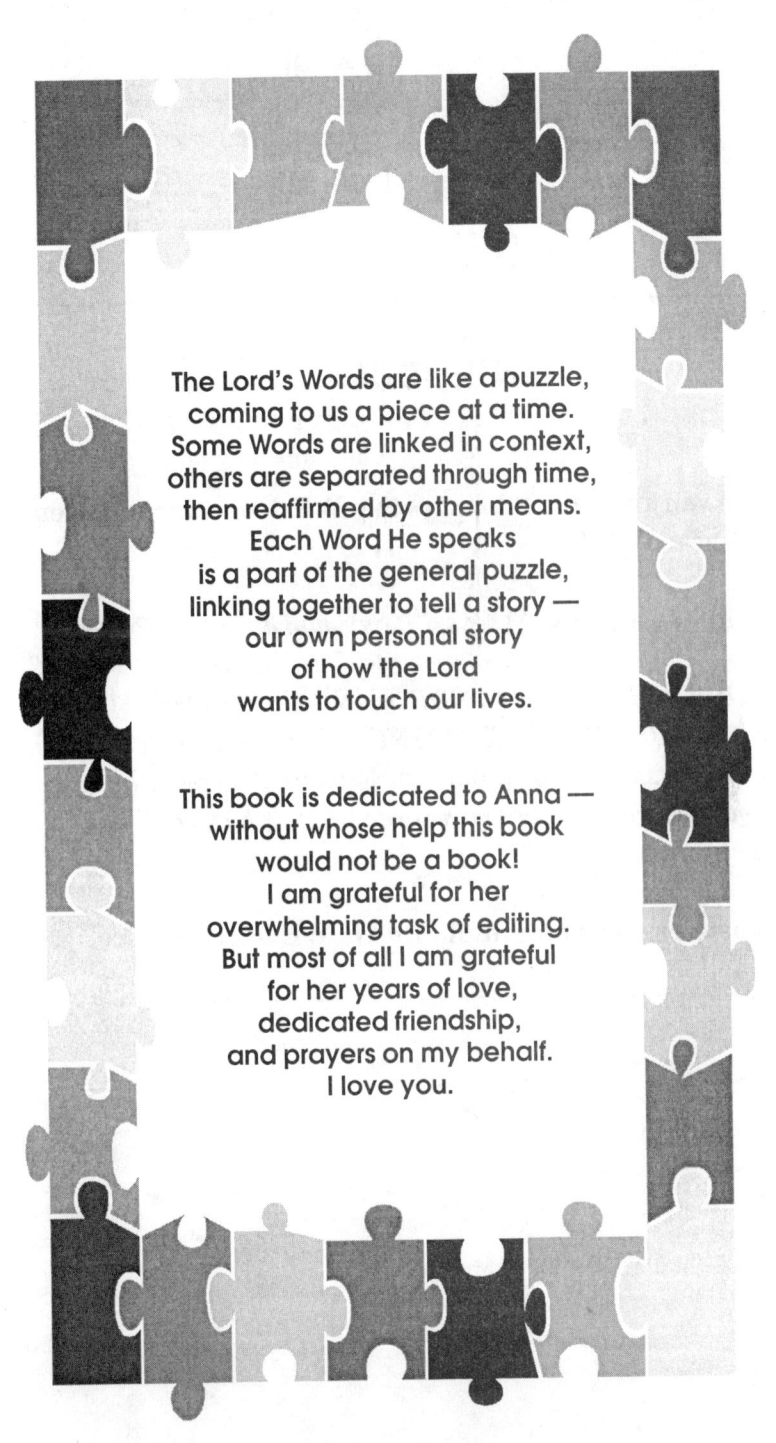

The Lord's Words are like a puzzle,
coming to us a piece at a time.
Some Words are linked in context,
others are separated through time,
then reaffirmed by other means.
Each Word He speaks
is a part of the general puzzle,
linking together to tell a story —
our own personal story
of how the Lord
wants to touch our lives.

This book is dedicated to Anna —
without whose help this book
would not be a book!
I am grateful for her
overwhelming task of editing.
But most of all I am grateful
for her years of love,
dedicated friendship,
and prayers on my behalf.
I love you.

INTRODUCTION

Did you know the Bible says that WE determine the extent we hear God?

Mark 4:23-25 (NAS) says, "If any man have ears to hear, let him hear. And He was saying to them, TAKE CARE WHAT YOU LISTEN TO. BY YOUR STANDARD OF MEASURE IT SHALL BE MEASURED TO YOU; and more shall be given to you besides. For whoever has, to him shall more be given; and whoever does not have, even what he has, shall be taken away from him."

That verse is a mouthful. It says WE have a choice.

CHAPTER 1:
THE BOTTOM LINE OF THE WHOLE KIT AND CABOODLE

The first time the Lord spoke to me — I will never forget it! I knew He spoke to Bible heroes and occasionally to pastors and missionaries, but definitely not to me. I was in my late teens and driving to a Christian conference. After getting tired of listening to the radio, I decided to worship the Lord through singing and praying. I sang as many songs as I could remember, then I started praying for everything I could think of. Finally I switched back to singing. Several hours had passed and now I was in the conference town. Having no idea of the church's location, I looked for a gas station to get directions. In the process I asked the Lord to lead me and as soon as I asked, WOW! Very exact directions entered my thoughts!

Was I ever astonished. Did the Almighty God just talk to ME??? When I asked for His help, I certainly didn't expect to hear Someone talk back. The Lord had actually talked to me! I wondered why! And I wondered if I would always have to work so hard to hear Him. That was a lot of worship, and my voice was hoarse by the time I had driven into town.

Now years later, I know Him more intimately, and don't have to become exhausted to hear Him. Our Heavenly Father really wants to have a personal relationship with us - not a stuffy, ritualistic, ceremonial obligation, but a real live friendship with Him. Jesus came to earth as a man and sometimes we forget that "down to earth" fact.

We all ask, "How do I know if it is really God speaking to me?" This entire book pursues that one question. This chapter contains the **prerequisites** of how God speaks to us. They are a vital link to applying all the other ways He speaks. In other words, <u>in every way we hear God, these three experiences recorded in this chapter must be present.</u>

1. HE SPEAKS THROUGH ADDING LIFE TO ORDINARY WORDS (QUICKENING)

"It is the spirit that quickeneth;[1] the flesh profiteth nothing: the words that I speak unto you, they are spirit, and they are life." (John 6:63 KJ)

All the Lord's Words, no matter what form we hear them, must be <u>quickened</u> by His Holy Spirit. The Bible says, only what is quickened by His Spirit will give life. Quickened is an obscure Biblical word, but without its power, our relationship with Him is limited to a dead language. The literal Greek meaning of the word quicken is to "make alive, or give vitality." We can go through life reading words and looking at signs, but **words are just words until they are quickened and we finally realize they apply to us.**

I remember hearing a story about a woman who brought her shy, unbelieving husband to church. He quietly listened to the entire sermon. Many things he heard related to his personal life *(were quickened)*. Later, when confronting his wife, he said how embarrassed he was that she had told the pastor all about his personal problems. She was astonished because she hadn't said anything.

Quickening happens when you hear a story, etc. and all of a sudden it connects with your personal life. His quickening power says, "Listen to this, I'm talking to you!"

His quickened Words are like a puzzle piece that perfectly fits the shape of your life — You could have a need, or be in a set of circumstances, or whatever, and when the Lord quickens something it becomes applicable, it has a niche — a place to fit. Quickened Words from the Lord are always relevant.

Sometimes a puzzle piece will appear to have the right shape and size but when you apply it, it is not a perfect fit. Quickening is not what appears to fit. Quickening is a realization that it <u>does</u> fit. **When it fits, your heart knows it.**

There are other times when God's Words can be like a dormant seed. What He has said may remain buried, hidden in the ground, for many years. When the time is right, He takes that Word and quickens it with life. Many years ago the Lord told me about a man who lived south of me but the Lord never shared his name. For a long time, I wondered who it was, then finally I just forgot about it. It wasn't until long after I'd met this person, that I remembered what the Lord had told me, and sure enough, that person fulfilled exactly what the Lord had said. The knowledge was dormant and for all purposes dead, until the Holy Spirit brought it to memory and quickened it with life.

2. HE SPEAKS THROUGH UNCOVERING TRUTH (REVELATION)

The two disciples were walking on the road to Emmaus, thoroughly preoccupied with recent events. They did not recognize Him when He walked with them and discussed the scriptures. Moved and touched (quickened) by what He said, they asked Him to stay with them.

"[Stay] with us, for it is toward evening, and the day is far spent." And He went in to stay with them. Now it came to pass, as He sat at the table with them, that He took bread, blessed and broke it, and gave it to them. Then their eyes were opened and they knew Him [revelation]; and He vanished from their sight. (Luke 24:29-31 NKJV)

As the Lord speaks, He suddenly "reveals" that He is the One speaking. Revelation is the sudden awareness of the Lord's Presence or Word. It is the realization, "OH! That was God speaking to me!" The Lord sometimes hides the fact <u>He</u> is saying something to you, then suddenly it "dawns" on you, it is HIM. Revelation[2] in the Greek Strong's Exhaustive Concordance Dictionary means to disclose, reveal, make manifest, appear, to lighten [as in illumination or to bring to light].

"OH it's Him!" cannot happen with logical facts. **His Words become obvious only by His Presence.** We cannot teach His Presence, but we can identify it. Learning to recognize His Presence through revelation is important in building a common language with Him.

3. HE SPEAKS BY SEPARATING MIXTURE (DISCERNMENT)

"But solid food is for full-grown men, for those whose senses and mental faculties are trained by practice to discriminate and distinguish between what is morally good and noble and what is evil and contrary either to divine or human law." (Hebrews 5:13,14 AMP)

As a baby grows, eventually he or she comes off pure milk and needs solid food and meat to grow strong and healthy. During the breakdown of food in the stomach the particles separate. The good part is sent to the cells, the waste is sent away.

Discernment[3] is similar to the process of digesting various Words from the Lord, through an impure or a mixed source, including our own distorted perceptions. First we separate what we hear by pondering it in bite size pieces. After we swallow, the food unravels or separates mixture: nutrient vs. waste. The nutrient feeds our relationship with the Lord, and the waste is unused and discarded.

Sometimes discernment requires genuine, thought-provoking

thought. As an example of this lengthy discernment process, I went through a long blind season when I couldn't see what the Lord was doing in my life. At first I questioned what was happening, and the Lord told me it was a season of *"winging it on in."* Having little idea of what that meant, I continued to plod through my days. The season stretched on and on and I began to doubt if I heard the Lord about the season and if I was in His will. I was at a loss and could not discern the answer. Prior to this time, I had received a little bird house for Christmas. The inscription said, "Wing on in." So when the Lord had said, *"Wing on in,"* I thought of that birdhouse. I interpreted it to be something like, "Fly by the seat of your pants!" That didn't sound too great to me. It was solid food, (strong meat) and I wasn't sure I liked chewing it.

Later I began to complain about being so blind and without understanding, and finally His 3-fold answer came to me. One night I was watching *Star Trek* about Diana Troy who had lost the gift of her unique intuition. She said it was as though she had lost her sight and had become blind. (That grabbed my attention because I had been complaining how blind I was to the Lord.) They said her loss was an opportunity to develop her other assets and make them stronger. So my first answer was "OK, He has put me in a blind season to help me develop other capabilities."

That night as I was pondering this answer, I flipped through some magazines[4] and read two stories. The first one was about a student who was painstakingly learning to write the alphabet. The letters seemed almost perfect to the student. He held his breath waiting for the instructor's feedback. "No, no, you are trying too hard!" the instructor said in exasperation. "There is no feeling." He took the student down the hall into a darkened classroom. "Now work here in the dark" and closed the door. Stunned, the student sat there fumbling with the pens. But gradually he began to relax and let his feelings rather than his eyes guide the pen. He began to let his *creative side* take over and felt the freedom of expression. He was no longer struggling to perfect his movements. He let the process flow.

I thought about how this applied to me. The words *wing on in, inner abilities and now creative side* seemed to have something in common. It still shouted *fly by the seat of your pants*! But what for? I thought, like the student writer, maybe I had been too uptight about discerning His will in my life. Maybe He wanted me to learn to relax and trust that He was leading me on the inside, in my conscience. (Conscience is discussed in chapter eight.)

The last story was about a young girl who landed a small airplane because her father had a heart attack. Not knowing specifically how, but being a passenger many times in childhood, she operated the plane by a little knowledge and memories. When she approached the runway, she knew she was going too fast to make the landing in a difficult cross wind. She <u>closed her eyes</u> to all the dials and buttons and listened to the motor. At first she would slow down too much, then would readjust her speed. She finally heard the right pitch to the motor and subconsciously knew it was right and landed successfully.

Thinking through this second story, I again saw the connection with "wing on in, inner abilities and creative side" but <u>literally</u> added, "Fly by the seat of your pants!" However this time I realized the girl wasn't using just her instinct to come up with guesswork. She was NOT making uneducated choices. She had been trained and educated in past experience, she just hadn't realized it.

Finally the three stories came together and I realized He wanted some hidden training I'd had in my past to come to the surface and become stronger. That was enough for me! Realizing I was in the Lord's will, I was just going to have to tough it out and hang in there. I needed to stop struggling with this season, knowing He was silently with me in this sightless place, and I was to hang in there until it was over.

When I went through this process to unravel the three stories that night, (Diana Troy, the student writer, and the pilot) a crimson thread of blindness tied them together: lost insight, placed in a darkened room and flying with closed eyes. They matched my situation *(were quickened)* and I <u>knew</u> *(revelation)* the Lord was trying to answer my complaints. But the process of how I figured out WHAT He was saying was discernment. It was just like digesting the good parts of the stories that were pertinent to me, and discarding the rest. That process took effort on my part to think it through.

Digestion, using the helpful and discarding the waste, takes time. To run a long race you need the strength of muscle which is built by protein. Protein or meat is not quickly assimilated into the body. Meat takes longer to break apart and be assimilated, in order to release energy. In comparison to the quick burst of His quickening energy of something sweet, God gives us something to discern (meat to chew on) to give us strength to run the race.

When the Lord quickens solid foods, the energy received is not a quick burst as from milk, but a gradual process of increased strength. <u>Therefore the quickening and revelation of solid food is not as easily identified</u> as previously described in this chapter: the instant, "OH that fits!" and "OH, that's Him!" Solid food doesn't give a quick OH! Rather, it's an "OOOOOOOOOOOOOOH!" It's the same Holy Spirit, and the same quickening and revelation, but one takes longer!

In the previous example of the three stories, there is a difference between quickened "milk" Words from the Lord and quickened solid food from Him. The night I received the answer to my questions was milk - they were concepts, like blindness and instinct, that were quickened right on the spot. I knew (revelation) He was talking to me. Now that's the kind of Words we like to hear from Him all the time! Quick and easy.

However, the original Word from Him was, "Wing on in," and that was not quickened at the time, rather it caused me to question what it meant, and eventually whether it was actually Him speaking. "Wing on in," was solid food. I didn't like it. It took a long time of chewing (thinking about it and questioning) before I was able to finally "swallow" that Word from Him.

Solid food is sometimes a barrier to Christians. They are used to receiving milk from the Lord and assimilating it quickly. The fact that solid food requires time to chew and time to digest, causes some to spit it out because it is not a familiar process.

This chapter is meant to merely introduce the concepts of quickening, revelation and discernment. Because these concepts are so vital to every thing we hear, examples will continue to be woven through out this book. Hopefully by the time you finish, you will have a genuine grip on understanding the concepts if you have never experienced them before.

Footnotes are for your optional continued study
All footnote definitions are taken from the Greek and Hebrew dictionary in back of the Strong's Exhaustive Concordance. All quoted scriptures are from the KJ [King James], NKJV [New King James Version], TLB [The Living Bible], NASB [New American Standard Bible], or the Amplified Bible [AMP].

1 Quicken: to vitalize, make alive, and give life. [2227 Gk Strong's]
2 Revelation: disclosure, appearing, coming, lighten, manifestation, be revealed. [602 Gk Strong's]
3 Discernment: judicial estimation, discern, disputation. From: to separate thoroughly, withdraw, oppose, discriminate, decide, hesitate, contend, make to differ, doubt, judge, be partial, stagger, waver. [1252 Gk from 1253 Gk Strong's]
4 First story was paraphrased from Guideposts Magazine: "Then You'll Really Know" by Timothy R. Botts. Second story was paraphrased from Guideposts Magazine: "Everything He Taught Her" by Patti Sharp. Reprinted with permission from Guideposts Magazine. Copyrights © 1992 and 1993 by Guideposts, Carmel, NY 10512.

CHAPTER 2:
GOD SPEAKS THROUGH THE BIBLE

STOP, TAKE TIME, PONDER, LISTEN

The Lord speaks His Word and reveals Himself in many ways. The best way to know the Lord is to read the Bible, His Holy Word. "I rejoice at Your word As one who finds great treasure....Your word is a lamp to my feet And a light to my path..." (Psalm 119:162 and 105 NKJV)

What a wonderful gift He has placed in our hands - His Words written so long ago. It is amazing to me that it has bypassed language and cultural barriers, geographical location, and decades of time. Someday we will know the story of how the Lord preserved His Words throughout such a long history!

The Bible is the first and easiest way to hear from the Lord, and is to be our guideline. When we launch out and begin to hear Him in various ways, they must always conform to it.[1]

Some go through spiritually dry seasons when they lose their love for reading His Word. This is similar to what the Bible calls a season of famine of hearing His Word. *(Amos 8:11)* Quickened Words from Him become few and scattered, and finally far between. Intimacy with the Lord seems so far away. Weariness of life settles in, and one falls into a long winter's nap. When in spiritual slumber the appetite shuts down; the hunger pangs fade away. Without notice, the mouth becomes dry. However when awakening, thirst for Him becomes unquenchable and the appetite roars to be fed. Thus comes the strength, will and tenacity to find water and food, and reading His Word becomes a joy and a delight.

If you have been experiencing a famine and want to break out of it and become excited about reading His Word, just ask Him for help. Living the life He desires for us is impossible without His help. We simply cannot do it on our own. The Lord never intended us to live independently from Him; in understanding, hearing, pleasing, and knowing HIM.

Another way to get excited about reading the Bible is to apply a formula through out this book: **STOP. TAKE TIME. PONDER. LISTEN.** Without using our will and deciding to make these four choices, we become like a locomotive with no brakes. We build up steam, stay in one gear, and propel forward without taking time to view the scenery. Each rail zooms by as we become lost in our goal of reading and forget to look where we are going. Instead, we should try riding a children's train that has no particular destination in mind other than to look and be a part of the fun!

What is the fun? The fun is HEARING HIM! The love, the zeal, the joy in life is RELATIONSHIP with HIM. Finding the fun, is removing the locomotive race in our minds, and reading with the intent of listening to what He has to say. Yet without the decision to stop, and the desire to hear Him, reading the Bible becomes just another pursuit of knowledge. The key to doing anything in life is to do it WITH HIM.

This chapter is a list of some ways God has shown me to stop and view the scenery — ways He has spoken to me while reading the Bible. They have renewed my joy of reading His Word. However, none of them could have happened had I not been in the frame of mind to stop and listen.

4. HE SPEAKS THROUGH CONCORDANCE DEFINITIONS

Much of understanding in life comes from the ability to define issues. The foundation to all definition is in the meaning of words. Just a little word can open the door to a hidden idea.

Although I am not a Greek or Hebrew scholar, I have discovered a great way of finding the meaning of words in the Bible. I look up individual words in the *Strong's Exhaustive Concordance*. It contains the Hebrew and Greek dictionary in the back. This huge book is a treasure. The Lord continues to quicken its definitions to my ears. You may be very surprised as to its enlarged meaning. It is wonderful to hear the Lord this way!

If you have a promise from the Lord, it is very helpful to look up each prominent word in the Greek and Hebrew dictionary. As an example, one night I heard the Lord say, *"There will I make the horn of David to bud." (Psalm 132:17 KJ)* Immediately I saw a picture - vision of my young son's new tooth! In the morning, I looked up the word "horn" in the *Strong's Concordance*. A number is recorded beside the verse containing horn. (7161) I looked up this number in the Hebrew dictionary in the back, and it defines horn in that particular verse as: {a horn as projecting, a flask, cornet, elephant's TOOTH, corner, **mountain peak**, ray of light, power.} He was sharing with me I would bud forth, like a tooth, in the growth of His power; as in a process, not a one time experience.

In the same period, I was told a friend's dream in which she and I were on a journey to the Holy City. Along the way, we viewed a beautiful row of **mountain peaks**, in lovely color and in a perfect line. The Lord quickened to me the remainder of the promised verse: *"There will I make the horn of David to bud. <u>I have ordained a lamp for mine anointed</u>." (Psalm 132:17 KJ)* Ordained means {to set in a row, to array in orderly fashion, stretch in a straight line}. (6186 Heb.) I understood that my life would be set in a row, just like the mountain peaks she saw.

There would be order in my growing and budding forth.

A good book that companions with *Strong's* is *Gesenius*. *Gesenius* is a Hebrew-Chaldee Lexicon to the Old Testament numerically coded to *Strong's*. It is an optional companion to use with *Strong's*. An example of using *Gesenius*: One night I was given a vision of a wild bull. I was in heaven looking down upon a vast wilderness plain. All of a sudden I saw a wild bull running fast and strong. Its gait was graceful and free. Later He gave me the scripture, *"His burden shall be taken away from off thy shoulder, and his yoke from off thy neck, and the yoke shall be destroyed because of the anointing." (Isaiah 10:27 KJ)* I looked up the word anointing in *Strong's*. The number was 8081. Then I looked up the number 8081 in Gesenius. It mentioned that 8081 and Isaiah 10:27, were metaphors of a bull growing so big it breaks its yokes!

Over and over again, these two books have blessed my portion of hearing ears, simply because I have taken the time to look up words. Without them, I would not have found the depth of what I heard and saw in relation to His promises. It takes time and discipline to look up words. Yet, looking up words is related to DEFINITIONS which is what building a new spiritual vocabulary is all about. **The more extensive our understanding of definitions, the broader our hearing capacity will be.**

Instructions for looking up your own verses and finding the Greek and Hebrew definitions in *Strong's* are:
1. Look up the <u>word</u> (in your verse) alphabetically.
2. To the side of that verse is the number code of your Greek or Hebrew word.
3. That number for your word is then recorded numerically in the Hebrew and Greek dictionaries in the back of *Strong's*.
4. These dictionaries translate and define the Hebrew and Greek words in that verse.

In writing this book, I have enclosed my gleanings of words from the *Strong's Concordance*. The numbers recorded in the footnotes are the *Strong's and Gesenius* code for each Greek or Hebrew word. They are recorded to help broaden the understanding of various concepts. Within the definition lists, I do not list variations of the same word, literal and figurative meaning, intent, verbs, nouns, adjectives, punctuation or etc. In reading a dictionary, it can become very laborious. In other words, I have deleted the (), {}, lit., fig., adj., neg. particle, dim., adv., coll., pass., pl., etc.!

When reading my paraphrase of *Strong's* translations and synonyms, you may research them without being bogged down with the details. In this book, the footnoted definitions are given to broaden your understanding of general concepts. If you want a more specific study, you may read the numbers and look up the lists for yourself, complete with the proper punctuation and details that relate to anything specific.

5. HE SPEAKS THROUGH DICTIONARIES AND ENCYCLOPEDIAS

A dear friend of mine, Auntie Shirley,[2] heard the Lord say the Word, *"Candling."* Having been a farm girl, she knew this is what they did to eggs. She did more research at the library through a dictionary and encyclopedia and found that candling meant to examine eggs for freshness and fertility by holding them up to a bright light. The word also meant to hold a bottle of wine in front of a lighted candle while decanting it, in order to detect sediment and prevent its being poured off with the wine. (Decanting is carefully pouring liquid from one container to another so as not to disturb the sediment.)

When she shared this with me, I was reminded of the scripture about pouring wine from bottle to bottle to separate the sediment from the wine: *"Moab has been at ease from his youth; He has settled on his dregs, And has not been emptied from vessel to vessel, Nor has he gone into captivity. Therefore his taste remained in him, And his scent has not changed. "Therefore behold, the days are coming," says the LORD, "That I shall send him wine-workers Who will tip him over And empty his vessels And break the bottles."* (Jeremiah 48:11-12 NKJV).

In response, I wrote in my journal: "In context, the Lord can do this to us or we can cooperate and do it to ourselves. When the light makes those dark things in our lives manifest, we can cooperate and remove them or we can run. If we run, the Lord will cause us to wander and tip us from time to time to separate the sediment from our lives anyway. The first way is a whole lot easier!"

The entire concept on "candling" proved true to what the Lord was doing at that time in my life. Her research on the definition of "candling" gave me clear understanding and helped put things into a proper perspective. Later I realized "candling" was a Word for the body of Christ, as it was identifying the season in which He was doing the same thing on a larger scale. What was occurring made more sense, all because she had taken the time to look up "candling" in a dictionary and encyclopedia.

HE SPEAKS THROUGH BIBLE DICTIONARIES

During one season the Lord began speaking to me about the

feasts. They are celebrations of the Old Testament, yet have a symbolic significance for us today and our future. Reading the Old Testament didn't give me the organized information I needed to apply what He was sharing. I began studying the feasts in Bible dictionaries and His revelation began to connect.

6. HE SPEAKS THROUGH DIFFERENT VERSIONS OF THE BIBLE

"Study and be eager and do your utmost to present yourself to God approved (tested by trial), a workman who has no cause to be ashamed, correctly analyzing and accurately dividing — rightly handling and skillfully teaching — The Word of Truth." "The whole Bible was given to us by inspiration from God and is useful to teach us what is true and to make us realize what is wrong in our lives; it straightens us out and helps us do what is right..." (2 Timothy 2:15 AMP and 3:16,17 TLB)

Reading different versions on a particular subject will sometimes enlighten our understanding. Often the choice of a different translation of the same Hebrew or Greek word will quicken the mind to another realm of thinking. For study, I like King James because the peculiarity of the language encourages me to look up the Greek and Hebrew words.

For instance in 2 Corinthians 12:9 the King James says, *"And he said unto me, My grace is sufficient for thee: for my strength is **made perfect** [5048] in weakness. Most gladly therefore will I rather glory in my infirmities, that the power of Christ may rest upon me."* I asked myself, "what does 'made perfect' mean? How can strength be made perfect?" So I looked up 'made perfect' in the *Strong's Exhaustive Concordance* and one of the translations for this Greek word "teleioo" (5048) means "to add what is yet wanting in order to render a thing full." In other words, when we are weak and our cup is not full, He adds what we are lacking in order to provide a full cup of strength!

For reading, I find the *New Living Translation* a unique version. I usually study Bible details, rather than reading them, so the *New Living Translation* is a fresh approach for my personality because it is simple and readable. Its format is generic and I can read it with the overall context in mind. You may be the opposite and do a lot of reading with little study. In any case, I recommend trying different versions until you find one you are comfortable reading.

7. HE SPEAKS THROUGH CROSS REFERENCES

He can speak through cross references. Many Bibles have good ones. When I can't find the verse I'm looking for, sometimes the cross reference will tell me. After He is already sharing an idea, the cross references gives Him room to expand.

Having a Bible program on a computer is a wonderful way to do cross referencing. You can type in the word or words you are wanting to find, and a list of all the verses come on the screen. If you are looking for a computer program, be sure and get one with the Strong's Concordance Greek and Hebrew Dictionaries included. That way if you become curious as to what the original Greek or Hebrew word means, you can look it up along with the definition. It is so easy.

The Lord also speaks in cross references to me at night. Sometimes I will hear a Word or Words from Him, having common denominators with other Words He has previously spoken. Later, when I look them up in my journal, I see they are talking about the same issue, but He is expanding upon it, and circling it once again to bring something else to light.

I have an unusual example about the Lord speaking in cross references. I belong to a small group who share the Words we receive from the Lord on a monthly basis. We began to notice that sometimes He would say very similar things to us on the same day, even though we lived miles apart. Often some Words would be exactly to the point and we realized that what we were hearing were cross references. When we put them together they told a story. Sometimes the story would be an expanded version of the theme or perhaps a totally different thought would come out of the joining process.

When I was first catching onto this new way of hearing the Lord, I heard Him say, *"Dominoes."* Then I saw a picture-vision of the letters "P L A Y E R S." These letters were separated, then came closer together as in a word. Then I saw a hand draw a line between each letter as though to say these are individual letters being brought together to say something. As I saw this I thought of dominoes and how you bring them together to connect.

As an example, I have recorded an excerpt from an entry in our combined journals for 8/2/96. Previously, the Lord had spoken to me about a surprise as well as a package I would be receiving. Then one day I saw a picture-vision of a wrapped package sitting on my table. I heard Him say, *"You haven't opened your gift yet."* It was not until the following entry that He made the cross reference saying that the package I had seen before was also the surprise. As you study each separate column <u>down</u>, these are the individual Words that three people heard this night. (These entries were things that were heard in His still small voice.) Then as you study the rows <u>across</u>, notice the cross referenced Words that match or connect:

Friend #1 rhema for 8/2/96 HEARD:	Friend #2 rhema for 8/2/96 HEARD:	Friend #3 rhema for 8/2/96 HEARD:
***Surprise** package*	***Rather startling*** *Assurance. Nothing happens without My permission. Assurance.*	*I assure you*
Sweet success	*Every detail.*	*Full*

Do you see how the words line up across the row? This kind of cross referencing is a wonderful way of being confirmed as His Word says, *"By the mouth of two or three witnesses every word shall be established."* (2 Corinthians 13:1 NKJV) Not only does He speaks to us on the same night, but He also uses this cross referencing within a few days of one another. When this quickened cross referencing occurs, I often will write an inspired Word based on the common words or theme that connect. It has been fun to do, and I recognize His inspiration while I write them. Then perhaps months will go by and as I thumb through these "Combo Words" (which is what I call them) one will hit me between the eyes as totally relevant to a brand new situation I am in at the time. The characteristic of God's Word is that it is eternal and His inspiration stands outside of time.

COMBO WORD:

You have yet to open your package. Rather startled you will be, but I assure you nothing happens without My permission. Again I assure you. A third time, I assure you! Sweet success is in your horizon, and every detail to the fullest plan is mapped out for you.

This cross referencing can be a lot of fun once you catch onto the fact the Lord can speak this way. Now years later, since we have recorded so many Words in our journals, sometimes we come across others who unknowingly share things that cross reference ours. Several times, I have heard tapes of sermons from distant yet wonderful men of God, mention a date or some specific time when the Lord said something major in their life. I would look it up in our combined journals and sure enough the Lord was saying the same thing to us.

You may not be in a partnering kind of relationship with sharing Words, but the Lord can speak to you in the same kind of way in the Bible. When He gives you cross references either through anointed hands, or impressions for a page, or margins and underlining (all coming up later) often they will line up in an overall theme that He is wanting to bring out to let you think about and apply to your personal life.

8. HE SPEAKS THROUGH HEADINGS, MARGINS AND UNDERLINING

A theme is like a coat tree. Ideas are on the branches, but the main trunk is what gives those ideas stability to "hang" securely.

Headings help us find themes that are a framework where everything can be placed in order to make sense. Sometimes all He wants to share is an overall idea, because the details can be confusing until we understand His theme. Then once He enlightens the idea, He can bring His Word to us through many other sources without confusion.

Sometimes when I turn to a page, I search for something relevant (quickened) and I draw a complete blank. Then I remember to include the headings, themes and subheadings. Often one will be quickened, jump out at me as pertinent and the Holy Spirit helps me ponder and search its application to my life.

Margin explanations contain little "punch-lines" hitting the simplicity of the theme. Often He will use this punch-line approach to something He has been trying to say in many other ways.

A friend said she had been praying for me and my family and then turned in her Bible to "under watchful care." I felt so nurtured and protected to hear that the Lord had asked someone else to pray for me, and that He was reassuring her of His protection.

When you underline something, it is because you have read it and it hit home. If it hit home once, and you turn to it again, chances are the Lord is walking you around the block until it becomes a part of your daily life.

During one particular season I was suffering under an immense number of obstacles against my hearing the Lord. One day a gal was telling me where she "carries her stress." There were two places between her shoulder blades that were really sore. I mentioned that mine were on my shoulders. After the Lord removed the obstacles, I heard Him say, *"A vacation between your shoulders!"* ☺ I was chuckling at His Word, and felt like shouting Hallelujah! Then I turned in my Bible. There was only one scripture highlighted on the page: *"...make great mirth, because they had understood the words that were declared unto them." (Nehemiah 8:12 KJ)*

9. HE SPEAKS THROUGH WORDS ON CASSETTE TAPES

Purchasing the Bible on cassette tapes is a creative way to hear. When we hear His Word in this manner, the same locomotive principle applies. If you hear something that is quickened, put on the brakes. Stop the recorder, ponder and apply what you have just heard — before moving on. Listen to the Bible in the car, during lunch hour, as you go to sleep or awaken - any time you can work it in. *"So then faith comes by hearing, and hearing by the word of God." (Romans 10:17 NKJV)*

After reading some handout notes written by a pastor, I prayed for him to have an opportunity to prepare more as they were a nice addition to his sermons. Then I listened to that sermon on tape. I turned it on in the exact location when he asked the congregation to pray that he would have time to prepare more notes. I have often turned on a tape where it is exactly relevant to an issue.

One day I made a huge effort to begin walking. My health needed exercise desperately. I plunged into that awful moment, one foot in front of the other. Simultaneously I turned on my recorder and heard the pastor say: "Christianity is like aerobics. You start to exercise, do it every day and you will get in shape." I laughed and giggled all the way through my session.

10. HE SPEAKS THROUGH TYPES AND EXAMPLES

The Israelite's lives and stories were given to us as examples, and as types: "Now these things became our examples... Now all these things happened to them as examples, and they were written for our admonition, upon whom the ends of the ages have come." (1 Corinthians 10:6,11 NKJV) "who serve the copy and shadow of the heavenly things..." (Hebrews 8:5 NKJV) "...Which things are an allegory..." (Galatians 4:24 KJ)

The Israelite's lived their physical lives with the Lord intervening on their behalf. They also lived their historical lives as a spiritual parable of what the Lord is saying to us today. The Bible says those who live by faith are the children of Abraham and have been grafted into the vine with Israel. So in the places where the Bible mentions Israel, it applies to us as well.

Because we live in His kingdom in spirit and truth, we are grafted[3] into Israel's vine through the spirit. *(Romans 9:8)* When we walk out Israel's prophesies and Words, we walk them out in the spirit, as parables, allegories, examples and types. We walk them spiritually; natural Israel walks them physically. Not only will the Old and New Testaments be fulfilled physically to the last jot and tittle, but they will also be fulfilled spiritually to the minute detail. The following are examples of how God speaks through spiritual types in the Old Testament:

Abraham - *(Genesis 21)*
> Abraham + Sarah = Isaac, the son of promise. Abraham + Hagar = Ishmael, the son of bondage. Jumping the gun and forcing God's promise, will create an Ishmael you will have to live with for the rest of your life, (including the generations after you)!

Gibeonites - *(Joshua 9:14 KJ)*
> The Israelites ASSUMED the Lord's will *"...and asked not counsel at the mouth of the Lord..."* Thus they were deceived. Presumption causes "grave" error.

The Israelites vs the Red Sea - *(Exodus 14:15)*
> Sometimes He backs us into a corner with no place to go except forward... trusting Him for a miracle.

Jacob - *(Genesis 31:32 TLB)*
> He vowed with his mouth, *"But as for your household idols, a curse upon anyone who took them. Let him die!"* Jacob did not know it was his beloved wife who took the idols. She later died in childbirth. Our mouths can speak with creative force.[4] This force is why vows were so detailed and explained in the Old Testament. Jesus said we are not to make oaths at all. *(Matthew 5:33-37)*

Murmuring - *(Numbers 11:20)*
> They lusted for meat. God gave them just that, until they were sick of it.

Lot's life - *(Genesis 13 and 19)*
> An example of the fruit of compromise.

Joseph - *(Genesis 37:8)*
> *"Joseph...Until the time that his word came to pass, The word of the LORD tested him."* (Psalm 105:19 NKJV) Why? Because God had given him a future promise of leadership. He was a symbol of *"...'Well done, good and faithful servant; you were faithful over a few things, I will make you ruler over many things. Enter into the joy of your lord."* (Matthew 25:21 NKJV)

Evil associations - *(Numbers 33:55 NASB)*
> "But if you do not drive out the inhabitants of the land from before you, then it shall come about that those whom you let remain of them will become as pricks in your eyes and as thorns in your sides, and they shall trouble you in the land in which you live."

Pharaoh - *(Exodus 7:3)*
> The illustration of God hardening a heart, ultimately for His purpose and our benefit.

Achan - *(Joshua 7:13 TLB)*

The affiliation with sin causes an inability to stand against our spiritual enemies. *"...You can not defeat your enemies, until you deal with this sin..."*

Tower of Babel - *(Genesis 11:6 NKJV)*
The Lord said, *"Indeed the people are one..."* An example of the power of unity and the futility of man.

Offerings - *(Exodus 35:21,22 TLB)*
"Those whose hearts were stirred by God's Spirit returned with their offerings...all who were willing hearted..." The Lord's sheep don't need fleecing to give.

The spies report - *(Numbers 14:1)*
An example of how an evil report will discourage others.

Sabbath rest - *(Hebrews 4)*
Pressing in to inherit the land by removing all unbelief and thus enter His rest. *"How long will you put off entering to take possession of the land which the LORD, the God of your fathers, has given you?"* *(Joshua 18:3 NASB)* A promise is left to us of entering His rest when we trust Him.

The Old Testament is a gold mine of types and allegorical symbols. They can be found in plain sight, open and on the surface, or down deep where one must plunge to find them. If you have dug deep and found an allegory about some story, or even a minute detail, He's one step deeper and waits for you to dig! The "smaller" you think, the more possibilities there are in discovering something. Examples of "small" can be an individual word or an underlying theme.

1 Bible: 2 Timothy 3:15-17
2 Auntie Shirley is a dear friend of the family.
3 Grafted: Galatians 3:7 and Romans 11:1-32
4 Creative force: Chapter 4, #24 - Spoken Faith

CHAPTER 3:
GOD SPEAKS THROUGH ALLEGORIES AND PARABLES

Both allegories and parables are symbolic messages that actually speak something else.

I began to understand allegories and parables when the Lord started speaking to me through dreams and visions. It took an entire season to discover He wanted them to be interpreted spiritually, not literally. (That is not always the case.) When I discovered this, I realized I was hearing Him, but wasn't UNDERSTANDING what He was saying!

I said, "Lord, I can hear You just fine, why don't You just talk to me and tell me what You mean?" What He spoke was plain as day: *"Sweet One, I am not teaching you YOUR language, I am teaching you MINE."* Immediately I saw two separate picture-visions. Each picture contained two pillars in His temple. The first picture had "substance" to it and was on earth. The other picture was an identical pillar, but it was somewhat ethereal. It was the same copy, only in heaven. Then He said, *"I teach you one, so that you might know the other."* He shows us the physical allegory in our physical lives so we may understand the "Words" He speaks into our spiritual lives.

I soon discovered allegories were a delight! They put a bounce in my step and a smile in my heart. He amazes me the way He speaks His Words in exact details, large and small, placing them in orderly fashion in my life. I have included many personal examples in this book of how He speaks in allegories. Ask Him to open your ears to hear Him this way. You will receive such joy.

11. HE SPEAKS THROUGH HIDDEN ALLEGORIES IN OUR DAILY LIVES

The definition of allegory is "a story in which people, things, and events have a symbolic meaning, often instructive.."[1]

Speaking in allegories is an excellent teaching method. The astute teacher will pave a road for the student to follow. She will lead a student by the hand, bringing him all the way to a door, then will let him discover the answer for himself. There is great joy in discovery, and we remember better if we discover it ourselves.

We are surrounded by the allegories of hidden symbols in everyday life. Allegories are discovered through various symbolic circumstances in our daily life, which join together to tell a story. It is like putting words together to make sentences. God delights in speaking to us in allegories. He receives such joy when we become enlightened to this manner of His reaching out to us. Our daily lives are like symbols: they contain hidden stories, if we listen.

Allegories and parables are the twinkle in His eye and the smile on His lips. I remember hearing an allegory about a person who spent his whole life's resources: time, money and energy, to search for a buried treasure. When he arrived home years later, depleted, exhausted and hopeless, he found it had been buried in his own back yard. The Lord has given you the treasure of allegories in your own back yard... Enjoy digging.

As an example of hidden allegories, the following is an excerpt from my journal. It was written in a time where I was painfully waiting for the Lord to help me get this book launched: "The Dr. has me on some medication designed to take out the excess salt stored in my cells. This is supposed to be preventative therapy against headaches. For the medication to work it must be combined with drinking plenty of water. I can clearly see the allegory: if the Lord said we are the salt of the earth, (thus we are supposed to release both preservation and flavor) yet we are storing it (and not releasing it for others) then we develop an overbalance which builds up and eventually causes pain. However, in order to start releasing the salt, there needs to be a daily balance of hearing from the Lord (water) so that the person giving the salt does not become dehydrated and discouraged." The point of this allegory is that the Lord is drawing the salt out of me to write and share this book with others. To do this, He is giving me plenty of His personal Words (water) so that I do not become dried out in the process of writing or sharing.

He speaks His Word repeatedly, from the largest miracle to the smallest detail within our lives. His Word is so much larger than what we perceive. Often what people DO in life, from the smallest details to their general employment, are perfect symbols of His Words to them. Sometimes we do not see the overall picture of His tapestry until it is completed. The moment of "OH!" revelation does not come when He first spoke His Word. However, whether we understand or not, His Word was spoken with each thread, joining and weaving, being carefully placed where it belonged. Often we can look back over our lives and see allegories of past experiences and understand. That is the day we finally say, "Oh! I get it!"

HE SPEAKS THROUGH WHAT WE ARE DOING AT THE MOMENT

Listen to what you are doing during moments of the day - it might be an allegory of what He wants to say to you.

Listening with our hands, feet and eyes have to do with listening to the allegories of the moment in which we are involved. Sometimes these allegories speak louder than spoken words. I have a little pillow that I put under my neck at night. Over and over again that little pillow case would come off. When I'd make my bed in the morning there'd be that little cover. One day the Lord quickened to me the concept of the word "revelation." It means to take off the cover. I laughed at the allegory. He was confirming that He was revealing things to me at night.

Another time the Lord had an amazing "Word" through my painting a picture for a friend. I am an amateur painter and didn't paint it intentionally the way it turned out! Her name means "Bright Clearing" so I attempted to paint a forest with light streaming through the trees. Before she hung it up, she propped it up on her kitchen counter and turned off the lights in the living room. Suddenly the picture took on an amazing appearance! A little light above her kitchen stove and behind the painting, pierced the canvas where I had painted the light rays, and illuminated the trees and forest floor. The forest floor came to life and was a beautiful living portrayal of the message, "Bright Clearing." It was a precious confirmation from the Lord that her life was indeed a bright clearing amidst a dark world.

The idea of listening to allegories, no matter what form they come in, is the decision to stop - and reflect upon them. Sometimes the allegories can come in a negative form which is His merciful way of getting our attention so that we don't have to be spanked. They are kind warnings from a loving Father. The negative allegories are a means for us to understand and judge our own wrong doing. *("But if we judged ourselves rightly, we should not be judged. But when we are judged, we are disciplined by the Lord in order that we may not be condemned along with the world." 1 Corinthians 11:31,32 NASB)*

Here are a few questions to help you find allegories: What are you doing? What is the definition of what you are doing? What is its purpose? What is its function? Can you find patterns in your life? Many times when we define something, and then apply the definition spiritually, we arrive at an "OH!"

Below is a list of hypothetical situations, giving examples of how our daily lives speak allegories:

1. A mother stuck at home with complaining children: she ponders, discovering her children are a reflection of herself. She's murmuring to the Lord. She makes a decision to alter her course and change her attitude.
2. Someone who takes time to be kind to an animal finds he has a merciful heart toward the downcast.
3. A person impetuously buying on sale uncovers that he is impulsive and impetuous with the Lord's guidance. He says, "Next time Lord, I'll wait for You!"
4. Someone who argues, butting his head against others, shows he is more like a goat than a sheep. Gaining a sore spot from confrontations, he apologizes and makes a decision to let go of

the need to always be right.
5. Enjoying puzzles, he realizes he would enjoy functioning in a ministry coordinating details and fitting them together.
6. A person may interrupt incessantly and talk all the time. He comes to the realization he prays, but seldom listens. From now on, he will make an effort to listen to the Lord and to others.
7. People who like to sing or hum find they have the gift of encouragement to share.
8. Another may be stubborn and narrow-minded with little flexibility. He perceives it is the same way in his relationship with the Lord: he places the Lord in many boxes and small ones, thus he adjusts his thinking to be less resistant to the changes occurring around him.
9. Through the enjoyment of cooking for others, one discovers she/he has the nurturing heart of the Lord.
10. A man driving his car recklessly through yellows and reds, finds he does not yield his will to the Lord and does not stop when warned. Next time, he yields and sees an improvement in his life.
11. Those who enjoy rearing children are content in having a servant's heart.
12. Someone who takes time to ponder, realizes he is like Mary and has chosen the better way. *(Luke 10:42)*
13. One locked in self pity suddenly realizes he cannot see God's point of view because he is wrapped up in a self view. He decides to start reaching out to others in greater need.
14. The person who drives past the closest parking place leaving it for another, will find he has done it unto the least of these His brethren, thus unto Him. *(Matthew 25:40)*

The most important concept in discovering the Lord speaks this way is the power of His quickening Spirit. <u>Some could follow a long road of life's allegories, only to discover they followed the interpretation of their intellect.</u> He speaks life only through the power of His Holy Spirit, and the way He does this is through **quickening** allegories and parables. **There is a vast difference between a language of the head, and a language of His Spirit.**[2]

HE SPEAKS THROUGH OUR JOB ASSIGNMENTS

An example could be someone who pumps gas for a living. He also spends much time quietly praying for people. His assignment within the body of Christ would be to pump power into people's lives. Listen to what you are doing during moments of the day. Our actions speak louder than our words most of the time and the Lord uses them to speak to us!

12. HE SPEAKS THROUGH BLOOPERS

Our bloopers can be a link to Him if we recognize Him in the process. I enjoy hearing Him this way, as so often He uses my mistakes to talk to me humorously. Once I was seeking His input about Chapter Two, saying I wanted to stick my toe in the water about an issue. Later while editing Chapter Two, I typed "CHAPTER TOE, God Speaks Through The Bible." I didn't notice until later and had a splendid laugh.

Another time, as I was getting breakfast ready and reaching for a spoon, I heard the Lord say, *"Parable."* I thought, "I wonder what the parable is?" I walked around the counter to set my bowl, cereal and spoon onto the table. Finally I looked at the spoon I had grabbed from the drawer — it was a giant serving spoon! (Larger than a tablespoon.) I giggled and ate my cereal with the huge spoon. The Lord had again confirmed that He had given me a large meal to serve the body of Christ and I needed to enjoy His promises and just let them happen in His timing, not mine. After I finished, I was still chuckling about it. I love His sense of humor.

13. HE SPEAKS THROUGH HIS PROMISES

The following account is about a promise He gave me from the scripture: *"...he turned the intended curse into a blessing for you, because the Lord loves you."* (Deuteronomy 23:5B TLB) Have you ever gone through a season of lemons and sour pickles? When I went through such a season, it was so long I began to get very chaffed and sore. The Lord began sprinkling my life with confirmations of His allegorical promise and funny jokes. *"A happy heart is good medicine."* (Proverbs 17:22 AMP) But I was crabby, and laughing just didn't seem appropriate in the midst of the sour circumstances. At times I wondered if I would ever laugh again.

One night a friend was awakened by the Lord and He started talking to her about pickles. He told her life was funny, a sour pickle turned sweet, and then asked her if she ever had a sour, sweet, pickle! Now that may sound very strange, but I happen to know her very well and KNOW the Lord really did say that! She was very sleepy and so He told her good night. After she put her pen down and was almost asleep He said, *"Aren't you glad it wasn't a sweet pickle turned sour? Smile."*

When she shared this with me, I laughed delightedly and received this as a confirmation of His promised verse, *"He turned the intended curse into a blessing for you, because the Lord loves you." (Deuteronomy 23:5B TLB)* Some time later once again He spoke to her the same kind of message, only about turning sour lemons into sweet lemonade.

One day I was particularly sad. While slicing a pickle, the Lord interrupted me and said, *"Lemonade."* Forgetting her Word, I didn't know what that had to do with anything. Waiting upon Him to hear more, I suddenly remembered what He had told her, and He opened my eyes to the allegory I was doing: slicing a sour pickle. In His kind way, He was interrupting my despondency with His funny joke and reconfirming His sweet promise that sour circumstances would turn sweet. I was so crabby I said to Him, "Lord I don't even LIKE lemonade, it hurts my teeth. Now if You had said orange juice, I would like that!" Did that stop the Lord? The next thing I get is a Word in the mail from my friend. This is what she heard! *"Sweet lemonade. Now orange juice. Changed the name. OK."*

THE PROCESS OF HIS PROMISES

Then Mary said, "Behold the maidservant of the Lord! Let it be to me according to your word." (Luke 1:38 NKJV)

A most endearing place of relationship with the Lord is hearing His promises. He speaks them from the Bible and other sources described in this book. There are two important things to understand about promises. One, recognize that a promise is not an instant occurrence, it is a future happening and a process. Two, we may believe a promise but that does not mean we understand what it will look like when it comes to pass. Therefore we need to resist preconceived ideas which may lead to disappointment.

When He plants His Word as a promise, it is inevitable that it will go through certain stages towards fulfillment. God gives a promise to us in seed form. That seed goes through stages of growth: first the blade, (the growth that appears about His promise). Then comes the head, (the visible fruit of His promise, but not yet fully mature). Finally, there is the mature grain in the head, (a fully stuffed, mature fruitful promise). At last, the fruition of the promise is ready to be plucked for use. *(Mark 4:26-29)*

When you first hear a promise from the Lord, because of its lengthy fulfillment process, resist the temptation to jump to conclusions. Take time to ponder and understand His point of view. One time I heard His promise, but did not understand what He meant. I stood through the wind, the hot sun, the rain and the storms, only to find when the promise came to fruition it was not what I thought it would be. When I went back and checked all His Words and confirmations in my notebook, He had performed His Word exactly the way HE SAID. It was not the way I had assumed.

It is so important to walk before running. A promise comes a step at a time, in its stages of growth. Running away with His promise tucked in our heart, without taking the time to understand it from His point of view, may cause us to stumble. Let the promise be a seed and give Him time to bring you understanding. We do not know what a full fruition promise looks like until it is grown, prepared and ready, but He can give us a glimpse to carry in our heart.

The Lord gave me an assignment many years ago which He called, *"Waiting for the brethren."* Although I didn't fully understand what He meant at that time, I realized later that it was a type of promise, because it would take years to come to pass and be fulfilled. He repeated this promise in many forms throughout the years, giving me progressive understanding. One particularly relevant Word occurred while I was listening to a sermon while driving. It was a story about WW11 and how all the U-boats traveled together in one unit. The fastest boat only went as fast as the slowest boat. That way, the German Subs wouldn't be able to pick them off one by one. I understood that the reason the Lord wanted me to wait for much of what He had promised was for my own protection as well as others.

14. HE SPEAKS THROUGH ALLEGORICAL STORIES

The warmth of a story can touch hearts where nothing else penetrates. He LOVES to tell us stories — if only we would take time to ponder HE is the One speaking.

He can speak through children's stories and comics or anywhere there is a story line. I remember when the Lord gave me the allegorical promise that I was going to become a butterfly. I was so excited at the idea He had SPOKEN to me, I did not put much thought into what He meant by it! I was thrilled to see "butterflies" suddenly appear in my life by way of Birthday cards and presents, etc.

One day my young son asked me to read him a story about a butterfly. As I read the story, the process of the butterfly's growth was quickened to me. The butterfly begins as a small egg. It grows into a little caterpillar who does nothing but eat, growing bigger and Bigger and BIGGER. Then it spins a cocoon away from the view of the world, and slowly is transformed with wings to fly.

As I began this faith process, His Words to me were given in seed form. *("Who hath despised the day of small things?"* Zechariah

4:10 KJ) Throughout my daily routines, I began to hear Him in increasing portions. It was a time of my intense hunger for the Lord, and obvious growth. Then the next season came and the changes He made in me took place on the inside without visible sight. In the fullness of time I burst through with thoroughly prepared wings of faith. **The definition of what I was going through became a joy simply because He had loved me enough to give me understanding and confirmation through a story.**

15. HE SPEAKS THROUGH PARABLES

The dictionary defines a parable as "a short, simple story teaching a moral lesson."[3]

"Gem"

Gem was an ordinary oyster. He lived a normal life inside his secure little shell within the vastness of his water home. One day he noticed a small irritation; a tiny speck of sand bothered him. It was so small he just ignored it.

About the same time a school friend teased him about his name, but what's in a name? He decided it didn't matter. The days went on, and still the irritation remained. Finally, he could no longer ignore it. He kicked, struggled, fought, and it grew worse.

The school oysters noticed his grumpy attitude and encircled him with jests. "Gem is a gem! Just look at his beautiful mud-brown shell. He's sure to win a beauty contest with that one!" On they would tease.

It seemed everything was an irritation to him now: his name, his friends. Life within his secure little shell was a pain. He could bear it no longer, he cried out to his Maker and asked for help. His Maker replied, "It is I Who named you and indeed you shall be My very own Gem. You will be placed in My crown and carried there for eternity."

Seven long years passed, and enduring the pain, he hung onto His Creator's Words. The day came for His Maker to pluck him out of the sea. Gem's heart leaped at His Presence and openly bared his heart. Unknown to him, deep inside his heart was a lovely pearl... Seven years in the making, he had become his name and now his beauty would be exposed to the heavens. He truly became a gem in the Lord's crown. *(2 Corinthians 12:7B-10)*

HE SPEAKS THROUGH NEW TESTAMENT PARABLES

Jesus chose to speak to the world in parables. The world is not given to understand them, or even recognize their existence. "Then the disciples came to Him and said, Why do you speak to them in parables? And He replied to them, To you it has been given to know the secrets and mysteries of the kingdom of heaven, but to them it has not been given... But blessed - happy, fortunate and to be envied - are your eyes, because they do see, and your ears, because they do hear. Truly, I tell you, many prophets and righteous men - men who were upright and in right standing with God - yearned to see what you see, and did not see it, and to hear what you hear, and did not hear it." (Matthew 13:10,11,16,17 AMP)

    Jesus told them they were to know the secrets and mysteries of the kingdom, but those outside had their hearts waxed hard so they could not hear. He said, *"Do not give that which is holy - the sacred thing - to the dogs; and do not throw your pearls before hogs, lest they trample upon them with their feet and turn and tear you in pieces."* (Matthew 7:6 AMP)

    Our God is a Holy God. He speaks Holy Words, no matter what form. In the Old Testament, He did not allow the unclean to approach His inner courts. We of the New Testament are made clean through Jesus and now have access to approach and know the inner courts of His Words.

    One day I was reading about the Indian's and pioneer's use of salt. Both used salt as a preservative to keep meat from spoiling. (Salt kills bacteria) I remembered that Jesus called us the salt of the earth and I understood the Biblical parable. If we are the salt of the earth, then our prayers preserve the lives of those around us. Our presence, and therefore our angels, are literally standing in the gap, keeping the earth from its deserving wrath and judgment.

    "Should you not know that the LORD God of Israel gave the dominion over Israel to David forever, to him and his sons, by a covenant of salt?" (2 Chronicles 13:5 NKJV)

    "You are the salt of the earth; but if the salt has become tasteless, how will it be made salty again? It is good for nothing anymore, except to be thrown out and trampled under foot by men." (Matthew 5:13 NASB)

16. HE SPEAKS THROUGH MOVIE THEMES

    I have always enjoyed movies, because I love a good story. However, I did discover that when I fed upon non righteous themes, that it placed me in danger of wounding my conscience and limited my ability to hear the Lord. Therefore I try to choose carefully.

    The first movie I remember really having a significant impact upon me, might be a strange choice to others, but at the time it hit me so hard that it changed my life. That movie was the first of the series called, "Karate Kid." I was in a perfect "setup" to be watching it. The background to my thinking prior to this was that I so believed in the sovereignty of

God that I seldom prayed, I simply accepted that whatever came along was God's will in my life. Then, adding to that, I believed that the enemy (satan) existed but the further he and I were apart the better, and I simply ignored that evil could possibly want a "will" in my life. Neither did I apply that God gave man a "will" — which means that I had a choice in life and that there is a war going on between God and His angels vs. satan and his demons to get that choice onto their particular side. I didn't realize circumstances could change by my refusing enemy plans for my life. In the mean time, there was a little "prayer meeting" a few hundred miles away that continued to pray for me, "Lord teach her to fight and use her authority!"

They may have prayed that prayer for a good year, but in one week's time the Lord decided to answer it. First I was moving some logs around in our wood stove, and suddenly a blast of air came down and blew flames into my face. The sleeve on my nightgown melted and my eyebrows were singed. I lived in such a place of faith that I didn't think to fear, I simply said, "Thanks Lord for Your protection!" Then a few days later I was lighting the heater in our camping trailer and "Boom!" a blast of flame came out and knocked me on my seat. "Thanks Lord!" I thought nothing of it. Then the next day a car came off the road, through our hedge and landed in our front yard. I didn't like that allegory at all because we had always likened our hedge to an army of angels encircling our property. I started wondering what was going on?

Then my mind wandered back to another strange happening. While we were in the process of cutting wood, the chain saw bounced off the top of my head. I didn't feel a thing except the bounce, then I touched my head. That was a mistake. My hand was filled with blood and I cried out the name of Jesus! We were miles away from a hospital and all I could do was say His Name over and over. By the time I hiked back to the truck, the bleeding had stopped and I was fine, but shook. (When I finally had the courage to wash my hair a few days later, chunks of hair fell out in the shower.) As I was recalling all this, I suddenly realized my peaceful little bubble was being invaded. "Lord what's happening?"

Then we went to the movie *Karate Kid*[4] which was about a teenager who wanted to mind his own business, but his moving into a new territory placed him right in the center of some bullies. He insisted he didn't want to fight, but finally they gave him no choice. He learned karate to defend himself and not only learned it, but totally defeated his opponents. When we were driving home, things were clicking in my mind. I couldn't help but identify with that kid! We pulled in the drive way and the mess from the car accident was still there. As I looked at the mess, I said something that probably resounded in the heavens: "THAT'S

IT! WE'RE AT WAR!!!!!" I meant it with every fiber of my existence.

I suddenly realized God's choice was to give me good gifts and the enemy's choice was the opposite. I had the choice to swallow either position. If I had believed these negative circumstances were good gifts from God, then I would have swallowed a lie. My bubble had been invaded and I wasn't going to take it lying down. After I understood this, the Lord gave me a dream where I was given a tiny, pure gold gun, and as I looked at it I wondered what I was supposed to do with it. Then all of a sudden all these mean looking dudes started chasing me, seriously wanting my gun. I ran and ran and finally I was too tired to run any farther. I stopped, turned around and faced my opponents and thus my gun faced them. You should have seen the looks on their faces! Those meanies suddenly had fear in their faces as they stared at my gun. They showed immediate respect and I looked at that little gun wondering in awe at why they wanted it, and how it could cause such a change in their behavior. The interpretation began to fall into place and He taught me that the trigger in the gun was my will and the bullets were the authority He's given to all who believe in His Name. The Lord needed my will to fight the enemy. He had given me the gun and the bullets, but I was the one who had to pull the trigger.

17. HE SPEAKS THROUGH COMMERCIALS AND ADVERTISEMENTS

Viewing a particular TV commercial for the first time, I noticed it contained a bunch of confusing traffic signs. As I saw them, I was thinking about my book and how the Lord speaks through anything in life, including traffic signs, *if we would only recognize His quickening power* upon our heart. As I was applying the truth of the signs and thinking about the frustration of life's delays and congestion, I redirected my attention to the end of the commercial which said: "Remember life has a passing lane. GO." He quickened it to me that when things look impassable, He provides a way through the mess.

Sometimes billboards and advertisements are quickened. I have found delight driving down the road, realizing He has spoken to me through **where my eyes have glanced, especially about what I was just thinking.** As I was driving home after attending some out of town evangelistic meetings, I was thanking the Lord that I had made the extra effort to go, and thinking of all those who like myself had sacrificed to attend. Just as I was thanking Him, I looked up at a billboard and my eyes fell on the words: "Worth the drive!"

One time I had been praying about whether I should add one more responsibility to my schedule, and glancing up at a magnetic sign, (a local business thought for the day) I read: *"Protect your time and space to carry out your dreams."* Immediately I thought about saving some time for writing, as that was the Lord's promise to me. One little sign, and the Lord quickened it with His power punch.

Another day I turned on the radio while in the car and heard someone singing about whatever it takes to walk with the Lord. As I was thinking about what it takes to have a relationship with the Lord and listening to the chorus, "Whatever it takes, whatever it takes," I glanced up at a movie advertisement and read, *"It Takes Two."* I remembered what I had written in my book that it takes two to have a relationship - one who speaks and one who listens. I was tickled at this little moment in time when the Lord interrupted my thoughts with His precious Words.

18. HE SPEAKS THROUGH TRAFFIC SIGNS AND OTHER SIGNS

I have often driven down the road and a "yield" sign or a yellow light will be quickened to me to yield to the Lord what I was just thinking. Miscellaneous signs, also the prior creative advertisements, can be allegorical symbols. We can read the words, even understand what they say, but do we take the added step to ponder if the Lord has just shared something allegorically? I had a friend who after reading one of the first drafts of my book realized the Lord was speaking to her on a long drive through different signs on trucks, cars and billboards along the way. She recorded them in the order they were quickened and so I list them here for you. After I read them, the Lord gave me an inspired "Combo Word" which tied them all together into a story.

- "Swift Transportation Co." on a white semi
- "Knight Transportation" on a semi
- A van with "Completion Specialties"
- A semi with a big "Omega" in white letters
- Sign board with "Beacon" on it
- Sign board with "Power" on it
- Sign with "So Close You Can Almost Taste It"
- Sign with "Brooks"
- Sign with "Safeway"
- Sign with "Mt. Angel"
- Semi with "Silver Eagle" on the mud flaps
- Semi with "Younger Oil"
- White car with "Legacy Health Systems" on the logo
- Sign with "Real Taste Real Deal"
- Sign with "Changes Today For Changeless Tomorrow"

Combo Word

"Fear not, *Knight* of My Round Table. I am bringing things *swiftly* to *completion*. I *finish* that which I have begun. Do not let the past length of your journey discourage you. The *beacon* light of My *power* is *so close you can almost taste it*. Deep calls to deep at the noise of My water*brooks*[5]. Even though you do not understand My specific plans, I have provided a *safe way* for your journey.

Listen to those *silver* haired *eagles*[6] who have given their lives to sitting at My feet. In spite of the length of their journeys, they have learned the lesson of renewing their *youthful* strength and *health*. In quietness and confidence they hunger for and *taste* My Words. They have learned to be *flexible* in their days, because in their youthful training of hard knocks, they sought the One Who does not *change*. Their future is in the constancy of My Presence. So is yours."

So you can see by this example, that the Lord uses ANYTHING in life to speak to us. Just remember the foundation principal, that no matter what, the concept or the Word must be quickened in order to fit into your own life. The words mean nothing without His quickening power upon them to give them life and meaning.

It is worthy to note that at the time she recorded these signs, they were quickened to her as she thought of common reference points the Lord had previously shared. However when I read them, I had my own reference points and so I wrote the Word based upon what the Lord was quickening to my own ears. Someone else could read the same signs and hear something different. There are as many applications to God's Words as there are words.

19. HE SPEAKS THROUGH HEADLINES

Often I have opened a newspaper or magazine and a headline jumps out at me because it is an allegory of something else the Lord is saying to my life at the moment. For instance, I had been praying for two days that the Lord would speak to me via a headline so I could have an example for this book! I knew He had spoken to me in my past as I glanced at headlines; I just had not written them down, being caught up in the reading instead. (Sound familiar?) Now, when I needed one to write about, my mind was blank. So I prayed about it.

Then I decided that I would just look in the paper and not quit until one popped out at me. (Was quickened.) I sat down expecting it to take all day, and it took about two minutes. This is the headline: **"Quick Rehydration Takes Lots of Liquid."** Immediately I saw the allegory and was reminded of this scripture: *"Repent therefore and be converted,* *that your sins may be blotted out, so that times of* **refreshing** *may come from the presence of the Lord, and that He may send Jesus Christ, who was preached to you before, whom heaven must receive until the times of* **restoration** *[restitution KJ] of all things, which God has spoken by the mouth of all His holy prophets since the world began." (Acts 3:19-21 NKJV)* That scripture means that after repentance comes the times of refreshment from the Lord. The heavens are retaining (holding back) Jesus Christ's second coming[7] until the times of this restoration of all things takes place.

The word "**restoration**"[8] in the Greek means restitution or restoration and it **comes from a word meaning "reconstitute"**[9] (in health, home or organization - to restore again). The word "reconstitute" in the dictionary[10] means "**to restore (a dried or condensed substance) to its full liquid form by adding water.**"

Here ye, all raisins! He is going to restore our dried out wrinkles by adding the rain of His Presence upon us! Some synonyms for the word reconstitute are **restoration, returning, restitution, recovery, repossession, reestablishment, replacement, and rebuilding**. Wouldn't you say that is quite a list when you think about God doing some of those things in your life?

So the bottom line of the allegory of the headline, "Quick Rehydration Takes Lots of Liquid" is; the Lord will do a quick work in restoring His church. To accomplish this, it is going to take a lot of the rain of His Presence.

20. HE SPEAKS THROUGH ANIMAL ALLEGORIES

I enjoy watching animals and hearing stories about their behavior. They each have such distinct personalities, even among their own species. The Lord taught me a concept about "waiting upon Him" through Cally, our cat. She had a funny and independent personality. When she was in the mood for love, she'd run right up to you and want your touch. But when she was not, she'd meander up the walkway when you called her, but stop just short of your arm's reach. The problem was, either way, when I reached out to touch her, *she moved*. So I'd take one step forward, reach out and touch her and then she'd move back one more step. This went on and on!

I was thinking about Cally one day while writing about how it takes the Lord time to set up His Words to us, and how it is important to give Him time to answer our needs. When the Lord starts talking to us about issues, He prepares His Words to be ready for us as we need them. But what if we stop just short of receiving His Word? [As in requesting something from Him, then stopping short of hearing what He wants to give.] Or what if we come to Him gladly, letting Him touch us, and He wants to continue touching us right in the exact location we are in, but we move away. [As in hearing Him via sermon, and not staying in that same place of reception when the service is over — then walking out the church doors, missing the next Word that lines up exactly with what He is still saying.]

As I thought about this, I realized that was exactly what I was doing at the time. My jump up and skitter/scatter behavior towards sitting at the Lord's feet and really searching His Words to me had become erratic and I wasn't giving Him the time He needed to complete anything He started. I was making it very difficult for His Word to come through my rushing. I prayed for His help to remind me to be still and hear Him everywhere, and not to be caught up in my hurried surroundings. Thank you Lord. Thank you Cally.

Some time later I wasn't feeling well and stayed in bed and rested. I decided to read my journal notes of the Lord's various Words to me in all the delightful ways He speaks. I was really enjoying spending the time with Him, and I had my Bible, devotional books, notes, pens and markers, pillows and all my creature comforts spread out all over the bed. That night I had a dream about Cally. She did a miracle! She voluntarily climbed into my lap, was sprawled out and hanging all over me. I had such a wonderful time loving her and she really liked it! I was really tickled when I awoke and realized it was the Lord's way of saying He enjoyed my day as much as I did!!!

21. HE SPEAKS THROUGH CREATION FACTS

"The heavens declare the glory of God; And the firmament shows His handywork." (Psalm 19:1 NKJV) His creation: what a wonderful way to get to know Him, and how often do we listen to what He is saying? Everything in life tells a story if we could just pause long enough to ponder...

Solomon said, "I went by the field of the slothful, and by the vineyard of the man void of understanding;...then I saw, and considered it well: I looked upon it and received instruction." (Proverbs 24:30,32 KJ) The Lord opened Solomon's ears to receive instruction from creation.

Do you stop and listen to Him through His creation and the environment in which you live your daily life? Jesus may quicken your ears to hear a delightful revelation from Him! All of life tells a story if we listen while we live. Below are some facts about creation. Find the SPIRITUAL allegories hidden like gems inside the facts. (The scriptures are given not to explain the allegories, but to give insights into general concepts. The interpretations are open as they apply to the intimacy of our daily spiritual life.)

1. An abundance of salt in bread dough, slows the yeast growth. *(Galatians 5:9)*
2. If a diamond is held in the light, one can see the colors of the rainbow. *(Colossians 1:26,27)*
3. Pine cones "blossom" their leaves when they are heated. *(James 1:2-4)*
4. The pupils of the eye enlarge to see in the dark. *(Isaiah 45:3)*
5. Most seeds have some kind of hull that cracks before it sprouts. *(Hosea 10:12)*
6. The deeper the water table, the deeper roots must grow. *(Psalm 42)*
7. The postal carrier, to carry good news, has to carry mace! *(Daniel 10:13)*
8. The eye of the storm is always quiet. *(Isaiah 26:3)*
9. During the winter, nutrients in a plant are used for the roots and stalk, and storing up food for when the plant bears fruit. *(Ecclesiates 3:1)*
10. Children have small attention spans and little patience. They learn best by short excerpts, not long involved details. *(2 Corinthians 11:3)*
11. During a forest fire the animals congregate closely and seem to get along. *(Philippians 2:1-2)*
12. Spring cannot come until winter is through. *(Song of Solomon 2:10-13)*
13. Morning-glory is a difficult weed to kill. It is a fast grower, entangles and winds its way around other plants, and it spreads by a vast underground root system. *(Mark 4:18,19)*
14. In times of drought, the deep rooted shrubs survive. The shallow ones die. *(Job 14:7-9)*
15. Children cry when they feel like crying and laugh when they feel like laughing. *(Matthew 18:10)*
16. Pioneers survived public opinion and the elements, to occupy new land. *(Numbers 13:30)*
17. Children like to be around people. *(Hebrews 10:25)*
18. Most women who do not have enough body fat do not ovulate. In times of famine, fruitfulness subsides. *(Joel 1:12)*
19. How many businesses would fail if builders stop building homes? *(Ephesians 4:16)*
20. How did sand become fine and easy to sift? *(Amos 9:9)*
21. Of all the people sitting at the pool of Bethesda, Jesus healed only one. *(Romans 9:18)*
22. No one has to teach a child how to be naughty. *(1 Corinthians 15:22)*

23. The waves in the ocean come in cycles. *(Ecclesiastes 3:15)*
24. No two snowflakes are alike. *(Psalm 139)*
25. Trees lose their leaves in the fall because of less light, not because it's cold. *(Isaiah 9:2)*
26. Salmon swim upstream to find their home. *(Revelation 3:21)*
27. Birds don't worry. *(Matthew 7:26)*
28. Roads are not built without someone doing the work. *(1 Corinthians 3:10)*
29. Monarch Butterflies do not suffer winter; they fly south. *(Luke 21:36)*
30. Children learn better through praise and encouragement than through scorn. *(Matthew 19:14)*
31. A recipe is not complete without all the ingredients. *(James 5:7)*
32. Cancer cells are disobedient cells. *(Proverbs 5:11-13)*
33. Snakes don't talk, and they don't walk, but they sure cause a lot of commotion. *(Genesis 3:15)*
34. Watch the ducks and geese. The ducks are meek and lowly. The geese are loud and abusive, intimidating the ducks. *(Titus 3:2)*
35. The turtles carry their home wherever they go. It is a refuge from all the elements. *(Psalm 91:1-2)*
36. The mother eagle removes the feathers out of the nest when it's time for her young to fly. *(Deuteronomy 32:11)*
37. We can't see electricity but it sure works!   *(Mark 5:30)*
38. Without (A), then (B) could not happen. *(John 11)*
39. The mother of most species stays close and keeps a watchful eye on her young. *(Isaiah 49:15)*
40. Our body framework is made from bones, muscles and ligaments connected one to another, and cannot perform a healthy function without each other. *(Ephesians 4:16)*
41. Disease is spelled dis ease. *(1 Peter 5:7)*
42. Man and woman were meant to complement one another, not compete. *(Genesis 2:18)*

1   Allegory: Webster's New World® Dictionary © 1990, 1995 by Simon and Schuster Inc.
2   Chapter Nine, Understanding What He Speaks
3   Parable: Webster's New World® Dictionary © 1990, 1995 by Simon and Schuster Inc.
4   Karate Kid: © Artwork and Design 1985 RCA Columbia Pictures Home Video
5   Waterbrooks: (Psalm 42:7)
6   Eagles: (Isaiah 40:31)
7   Second coming: "Behold, He is coming with clouds, and every eye will see Him, even they who pierced Him. And all the tribes of the earth will mourn because of Him. Even so, Amen." (Revelation 1:7 NKJV)

8   Restoration (Restitution KJ): # 605 from #600 in Strong's Exhaustive Concordance Greek dictionary.
9   Reconstitute: #600 in Strong's Exhaustive Concordance Greek dictionary.
10 Reconstitute: Webster's New World® Dictionary © 1990, 1995 by Simon and Schuster Inc.

CHAPTER 4:
GOD SPEAKS THROUGH OUR PERSONALITIES

22. HE SPEAKS THROUGH WHERE OUR EYES GLANCE

"Blessed are your eyes for they see: and your ears, for they hear." (Matthew 13:16 KJ)

One day I went to meet my son at the mall earlier than we planned. As I was asking God where he was, my eyes fell on a poster advertising the small video arcade. I turned completely around and walked back to that location. Sure enough, he was happily zooming the joy stick.

Another time as I was listening to a car radio sermon, I heard a story about a man who was locked in prison with a ball and chain. When the king pardoned him, they were to weigh his ball and chain on the scales. He was to receive the weight of the ball and chain in 100 percent pure gold. Just as I was thinking how precious that was, I came to a stop light. I glanced at the license plate in front of me; it said, "GOLD RUSH." Suddenly that sermon was relevant *(quickened)* to me, and I realized the Lord was talking to ME! *(Revelation)*

The Lord uses this method of talking to us, especially when we are reading. Sometimes our eyes will tell us He is speaking even before our brains register what we are seeing or hearing. Once we know that He uses our eyes, then we can **tune in and take the "time to ponder" where our eyes have fallen.** If your eyes have been drawn toward a place on the page, take the time to LOOK WHERE YOU GLANCE. He may open your "spiritual" eyes to a surprise!

I was wanting to spend some time with the Lord rereading old journal notes that had been organized on the computer and printed out. As I turned to the table of contents my eyes fell on a certain title. I thought to myself, "No I don't want to read that one, I'll try something else!" So I turned to another section in the notebook. After noting the title, I quickly decided that I'd better read that page! It was the same one

I had ignored in the Table of Contents. After I read it, I repented and told the Lord He certainly knew better than I!

You may have a goal of looking for a particular verse in the Bible when He has already spoken what HE wants to share through where your eyes glanced. **Part of recognizing this is remembering what you are thinking while you are looking.** He so often talks to us this way and we miss it because we are lost in our pursuit. He wants relationship with us when we sit with Him. Slow down and enjoy Him.

The key to tuning into where we glance, is remembering what we were thinking at the time of the glance. That may sound simple, but our minds wander. When we practice remembering, we begin to realize just how much. However, with this new habit in place the Lord will open many avenues of hearing Him in our surroundings. It becomes a true joy of discovery.

23. HE SPEAKS THROUGH WHAT WE SAY

God often speaks to us through our mouths, therefore we need to listen to what we speak.

Once I was struggling with the fact that the Lord was telling me no about a certain situation. Yet I still was asking for His "yes" at every opportunity. After my approaching the Lord for the umpteenth time, my son came into the room and asked me for something. I had already told my son no. My voice was stern as I said, *"You are arguing with me."* The Holy Spirit allowed me to hear my words; I had been arguing with God.

God often speaks to us through our mouths, therefore we need to listen to what we speak. Sometimes He will even speak the answers to questions we have asked Him. During one particular time in my life, circumstances were happening which I did not understand. In my asking for answers, the Lord didn't reply. I didn't understand why He wasn't explaining. I knew two things about that season. One, I was in school, and two, it was a new school (spiritual school). Finally, my answer came.

My son had been attending first grade for about three weeks. I asked him, "Have you noticed the teacher doesn't give you answers, she waits for you to answer them yourself?" (He said no.) I said, *"Teachers try to help the children grow up by encouraging them to discover answers."* Immediately the Holy Spirit quickened to me this was MY answer also. The Lord was teaching me to search and find answers based on what He had already shared in my past.

A few years later as I was seeking to hear more from the Lord, my son was talking about learning how to draw comics through some comic books created by his drawing instructor. He said when he first started reading the comics, he read them so fast he missed a lot of details. I said, *"The sign of maturity is when you begin to analyze things."* Immediately I knew what I'd said was a quickened Word from the Lord to myself. If I digested and internalized what He had already given me, then I would be ready to hear more from Him.

HE SPEAKS THROUGH JOYOUS EMOTIONS

Sometimes the Lord speaks to us through what we say by way of our emotional reactions. My young son was taking his annual swimming lessons. He knew how to kick, reach and pull and float; he just didn't know how to do them all at once! This season was also a time in my life when the Lord was teaching me to stand against satan and tell him, "No." I was learning how to use the authority God has given to all believers. Sometimes I felt like I was barely keeping my head above water and that water looked too deep. (He would reassure me I had a spiritual life jacket on and that did help.)

As I was beginning to connect with what He was teaching me, I kept turning to the scripture, *"In that hour Jesus **rejoiced**[1] in the Spirit and said, "I thank You, Father, Lord of heaven and earth, that You have hidden these things from the wise and prudent and revealed them to babes."* (Luke 10:21 NKJV) Jesus said this to the Father when He sent His disciples out with His authority for the first time.

I was too busy keeping my head above water to pay much attention to the scripture. The reality of Jesus' joy over me had not yet touched my life when He so wanted to reach me with His joy and approval. One day at my son's swimming lessons a miracle happened. Suddenly I saw him swim! All his movements came together and he swam beautifully half way across the pool. It was an indoor pool in a confined area, and I stood to my feet shouting and clapping with great joy!

Yet the Lord's excitement over my own overcoming still hadn't touched my heart. He loved me so much, He kept trying to send me encouragement. Even though the Lord kept giving me this verse I was still in the doldrums feeling not at all up to par. One day I was thinking about how happy I felt about my son swimming. As I opened my Bible again, there was that scripture about Jesus' great rejoicing. I thought, "Is it possible the Lord is feeling that way about me?"

An hour later I went to church and the pastor shared a little story before the service. He had video taped his son's soccer game. He asked what we thought was the most outstanding part of the tape. Of course, we thought he was going to say his son! He said it was the cheering parents' voices. I cried, as the Lord's Word finally reached my heart.

24. HE SPEAKS THROUGH CREATIVE FORCE: SPOKEN FAITH

The Bible says our mouths have creative force. *"...whoever says to this mountain, 'Be removed and be cast into the sea,' and does not doubt in his heart, but believes that those things he says will be done, he will have whatever he says. (Mark 11:23 NKJ) "...If you have faith as a mustard seed, you will say to this mountain, 'Move from here to there,' and it will move; and nothing will be impossible for you." (Matthew 17:20 NKJ)* The key ingredient is faith.

People as a whole believe in all kinds of things, without realizing what they believe. An example is someone who has just been exposed to the flu. People are ill all around her, and she says, "I just know I'm next." Although she doesn't see the germ, she believes in its potent power and verbalizes through her faith she's going to get it. People frequently make negative confessions about themselves, about others, about life and circumstances, and they speak it with much faith. Listen to what you say. You may be dispatching the wrong forces. You might ask, what do I do if I've really GOT IT? If I "get it" I speak the truth: "I'm fighting a germ right now!" (The truth is I'm fighting the germ physically and spiritually through resistance in Jesus Name.) If I think I am coming down with something, I don't say, "I'm coming down with something" because that is a statement of faith saying I am receiving an illness. Rather, I again say, "I'm fighting a germ." The power of the spoken word is a very serious matter. Listen to what you speak.

Faith is the creative element that dispatches forces with assignment in the unseen world.

25. HE SPEAKS THROUGH WHAT WE PRAY

While in the shower, I prayed, "Thank You Lord for a home run!" I had no idea why I prayed that, it just popped out of my mouth! When I sought the Lord about it, I turned in my Bible to *'The answer of the tongue is from the Lord.'* Then I found out a friend had prayed away the fears of a dying man, who consequently died in peace. The Lord told her the man had hit a home run. My prayer was a confirmation to her.

Listen to what you pray - there will be times when without forethought, you will pray the Holy Spirit's desire. Something simply pops out of your mouth which you never expected or thought. Listen to those times and receive them as the understanding of what the Lord's will is concerning that issue.

26. HE SPEAKS THROUGH WHAT WE SING

So much of hearing is just that: listen to what you are doing.

While finishing this book, I started humming an old song, "Come on let's get happy, we're headed for the promised land." Then later as I was doing dishes and thinking about writing, I sang, "Come on and let's get ready, we're headed for the promised land! I was tickled as I realized that was what the Lord was saying to me about this book.

There was another time the Lord shared a funny joke through song. In a private setting, the Lord had shared with a small group of people some very personal things. He also said it was time for them to "wake up" from a spiritual sleep and really swallow what He was saying. To hear this was somewhat disconcerting to their sense of privacy and stretching their "comfort zones" to the max. However, since it was an intimate setting, it wasn't quite as difficult as it might have been. Following this, one of them awakened in the morning singing an old song from kindergarten days. The proper words are, "Good morning to you, good morning to you! We're all in our places with bright shiny faces." However when she sang it, the words were: "Good morning to you, good morning to you! We're all in our faces, with bright shiny places!" They laughed as that was exactly what had just taken place.

Listen to what you sing. He may give an answer to your quandaries in the very song you are singing. Listen to the words: listen to HIM. So much of hearing is just that: LISTEN TO WHAT YOU ARE DOING.

27. HE SPEAKS THROUGH ANOINTED HANDS

*"But you have received the Holy Spirit and He **lives WITHIN YOU**..." "...but as the same anointing teaches you concerning all things, and is true, and is not a lie, and just as it has taught you, you will abide in Him." "...Your body is the home of the Holy Spirit God gave you, and **He lives within you**...So use every part of your body to give glory back to God, because He owns it." (1 John 2:27 TLB, 1 John 2:27 NKJV and 1 Corinthians 6:19,20 TLB)*

Only What is Quickened

The Lord anointed my hands the night I turned to the two stories in #3 Discernment. When I opened to the student writer and the girl pilot, I turned to exactly what He wanted to say to me about hanging in there through a blind season.

We have anointed hands, because we are His temple. Often our hands will turn exactly to the place He wants us to read. It is not coincidence we happen to turn to something that hits home! It is a real joy to begin to realize He lives in and through our hands.

Once I was worrying about a letter the Lord inspired me to write. In prayer, I turned to my Bible two times. The first page I turned to, my eyes fell on the margin phrase: "writing of a letter." The second turn was a highlighted "needless fear." I was given perfect peace and I stood on that confirmation from God.

Remember Chapter One — When you hear the Lord through these different ways: **IT MUST BE QUICKENED, REVEALED AND DISCERNED!**

"OK Son, we're packed and ready to go. I'll spin the globe and where my finger lands, that's where we'll take our vacation."

"Sure Dad."

"What does it say?"

"Made in China"

© John Warner

28. HE SPEAKS THROUGH DIRECTING OUR THOUGHTS
Directing our thoughts is subjective and we have an active participation.

An example of this would be, "I wonder how so and so is doing. I think I'll call her." You call and crying she says, "I am so thankful you called!" The Lord often guides our thoughts in exact accordance to His will and we do not recognize it's Him because we have an active participation in it.

During Christmas vacation, my son had to work on a large project[2] from school. He had previously gathered the materials prior to the school break but did not have the necessary printout of the guidelines. The very same day he began his project, I looked at my desk, and thought I'd better file my "to be filed" pile. As I was sorting through my papers, my sons' needed printout of the guidelines popped forth! We have no idea how it got into my pile. And what was even more amazing was the fact that he had picked up the guidelines at a conference out of town, even prior to knowing he would be given the project at school. The Lord knew all of this and directed his thoughts to pick up the piece of paper at the conference and my thoughts to organize my desk at the moment of his need.

Hearing the Lord through our mind is separate from to our mind. When the Lord speaks to our thoughts (which is His still small voice in chapter 6), it is completely separate from our personality. We have no involvement in what is said. However, the way the Lord speaks THROUGH our thoughts is to DIRECT them. We are a part of the process while He gently steers us in the right direction.

Thoughts that go through one's mind, are subjective experiences. The more garbage the mind is fed by way of spoken words, written words, and visual sights, the more impure one's thoughts will be. The word fed should be emphasized. It's not necessarily what one is exposed to that creates impurity, it's what one FEEDS ON. One knows the difference without explanation. The change[3] of one's carnal mind into the mind of Christ[4] is a step by step process. The more we feed our thoughts on HIM, the sooner we will be transformed.

HE SPEAKS THROUGH IMPRESSIONS
"Draw me, we will run after thee..." (Song of Solomon 1:4 KJ)
"No one can come to Me unless the Father who sent Me draws him..." (John 6:44 NKJV)

Anna[5] and Auntie Shirley began hearing the Lord's still small voice speak numbers (amidst His Words) to them. On an inkling (impression of the Holy Spirit) one was drawn to look up the number definitions in the *Strong's Concordance.* To their astonishment, the definitions fit with what the Lord was saying to them.

Impressions of His Holy Spirit are not the Lord's still small voice (explained in Chapter 6.) **Impressions are similar to notions, senses, perceptions, inklings.** When pausing before Him as I read His Word, sometimes I turn to a certain book in the Bible and am impressed by a particular chapter or verse number. Sometimes I have a notion to read a small section in a devotional book. I sense page numbers and I have been blessed to read exactly what I needed. My joy of fellowship with the Lord was increased, because <u>I paused to give Him the opportunity to draw me</u> before reading His Word.

The Lord began talking to me about being an intercessor for others in my prayers. Later as I was thinking about it, I felt **impressed** to open my Bible and I turned to a section I had previously highlighted: So the children of Israel said to Samuel, *"Do not cease to cry out to the LORD our God for us, that He may save us from the hand of the Philistines. ...Then Samuel cried out to the LORD for Israel, and the LORD answered him."* (I Samuel 7:8,9 NKJV) I was encouraged that the Lord was not only serious about this position in my life, but that He was also giving favor to my prayers. As a result, I began looking for opportunities to pray because the faith He had planted in my heart <u>knew</u> that prayer makes a difference for others. I realized a prayer is the greatest gift we can give someone else. Soon the Holy Spirit was drawing me to pray for strangers as I drove down the street or as I passed them in the grocery store. I had the encouragement that things would break free in their life.

HE SPEAKS THROUGH INSPIRED FLASH OF INSIGHT

Often we have ideas and do not recognize them as separate from ourselves. Sometimes we think we had a brilliant flash of genius when it was really the Lord. He is wonderful to speak rational, logical ideas into our lives. They are like short power-packed sentences.

Our history is founded upon inventors' sudden flashes of genius. They awakened in the morning with new ideas. Or when they least expected it, they found answers in a simple thought, perhaps while doing something else. Brilliant and simple people alike have been inspired by the Holy Spirit with genius ideas. It is comforting to know the Holy Spirit is bigger than an IQ!

One day I was praying about needing another filing cabinet, the problem was that we had no practical space for one. My husband said,

"Why don't you just clean out the ones we have?" Brilliant idea! Would you believe after 20 years of collecting, I threw away a 4 foot pile of paper? Not only did I find the answer to my filing needs, but in the process of throwing things away, I found some important material I needed for publishing my book. Thank You Lord for inspired insight.

29. HE SPEAKS THROUGH RECURRING THOUGHTS AND SCRIPTURES

Be sensitive to **recognize thoughts that keep coming back to you.** It's a possibility the Holy Spirit is speaking to you. Sometimes their recurrence is a call to pray over them until they are resolved. Sometimes they are accompanied by a stronger yearning, and the Lord is wanting you to take an active part in resolving them.

He will bring scriptures to your mind in the same manner. If He brings a verse to your memory more than once in a certain time period, then He is really wanting to get His message planted in your life. In ministry situations, He may bring a recurring verse until you release yourself to share it.

HE SPEAKS THROUGH RECURRING SONGS

Have you ever noticed the song you sing in church will sometimes go over and over in your mind? Listen to the message. You may be delighted to discover He is speaking His response to your worry or question of the moment.

After a time of personal and difficult death to self will, the Lord brought a melody to mind I hummed for days. Having forgotten the words, I finally found the song and listened to the words: "He didn't bring us this far to leave us. He didn't teach us to swim to let us drown. He didn't build a home in us to move away. He didn't lift us up to let us down." (By Joni Erickson Tada) In His wondrous way, He brought me needed encouragement.

30. HE SPEAKS THROUGH YEARNINGS

Yearnings are a stronger feeling that the thoughts need to be resolved.

Thoughts through our mind, occurring with what I call strong drawing power, are also a way the Lord speaks to us. It is a strong yearning, a calling and a feeling that the thoughts need to be resolved. When I was attending an out of town meeting, I had a very strong feeling to go over to a man I knew and give him a big hug and ask him how he was. As I asked, "How are you?" and he replied, "Fine," I asked him again, "Really?" He was basically telling me he was fine but the yearning in my heart was telling me differently. Later, during a break, he came over and shared a few things. He was terrible! As soon as he finished sharing, I could hardly wait to pray for him, as that yearning was still there. I prayed a very long prayer over him until the yearning stopped. Those around agreed with me and the Holy Spirit accomplished His work.

People experience this drawing within a ministry situation, when they are being called upon by the Holy Spirit to pray, say, write, meditate, act, etc. upon what they are thinking. The Psalmist said, *"I was dumb with silence, I held my peace, even from good; and my sorrow was stirred. My heart was hot within me, while I was musing the fire burned: then spoke I with my tongue." (Psalm 39:2-3 KJ)* If you experience this, discern which power is drawing you. The Lord's drawing power, above all motives, is always LOVE.

31. HE SPEAKS THROUGH SOUL DREAMS
The Lord uses dreams of the soul to confront truth. (Psalm 16:7 and 17:3A KJ)

Dreams of the soul relate to each personality, and are unique to that person simply because not everyone has the same personality. They are not enemy dreams, nor are they Godly dreams.

It is the Holy Spirit's position to make darkness manifest.[6] Darkness likes to hide and derives much of its power by staying hidden. When the Holy Spirit penetrates the soul of man, He brings light to those places that do not glorify Him. The Holy Spirit will manifest our very thoughts and motives, for we cannot overcome darkness unless we know what it is and where it is. The first step to recovery is to recognize the problem.

If we listen, the Holy Spirit can use dreams of the soul to penetrate those dark areas. He will then encourage us to deal with those exposed truths in our daily circumstances. He is very persistent and will not give up on us. If you find yourself having recurring dreams of some type or another, it is a possibility the Holy Spirit is knocking on your door to help you grow and overcome.

There are other reasons for soul dreams. Sometimes, a person is unable to resolve a situation in real life. (Other words for "resolve" are to conclude or settle.) He has been physically removed from the circumstance and is unable to overcome the situation first hand. Then soul dreams can be a way of resolving circumstantial conflicts second hand.

The human soul only finds freedom from the inside out. Thus, the core of resolving any situation in life is the inward "contentment level." When the Lord provides the freedom of resolution, He works on our places of discontentment. We cannot be content with unforgiveness, greed, lust, anger, resentment, etc. within our hearts, for they are issues that always cry for resolution. The only way we become content from the inside out is to let go of those attitudes and issues that do not glorify Him.

Dreams of the soul can become our barometer in registering our progress of overcoming situations of discontentment. The Lord may use them to encourage us by allowing us to see this progression. Sometimes we are so busy fighting the inner issues during the day, we aren't in a stopping place to receive encouragement.

For instance, someone has soul dreams on a continual basis of running away from enemies. Perhaps that person has a problem in real life dealing with confrontations and will avoid them at any cost. The Lord wants to strengthen that person's stand and through the consistent dreams at night of running away, finally gets through to that person what is occurring in his life. Then maybe the very day the person takes a stand on something, that night he dreams he didn't run away when pursued.

The Lord has no desire to browbeat us with our weaknesses. He will not send us gifts that condemn and make us feel that there is no hope. He will bring us truth and help us to see it; in the overcoming process He will set us free.

He never wants us to be badgered by soul dreams. Satan loves to use these dreams to twist and turn them as a knife into our heart. He is a tormentor, accuser, and twists truth. Satan can influence dreams of the soul to destroy our progress instead of building it. It is up to the individual dreamer to discern and choose the truth and challenge of the soul dream. A soul dream can also be used to build and bring health. However this only relates to the dreamer's ability to hear, see, and understand what the Lord is saying and how he can be helped. Truth can set us free in Jesus. It can also destroy, without Him.

32. HE SPEAKS THROUGH WEAKNESS

"For you see your calling, brethren, that not many wise according to the flesh, not many mighty, not many noble are called: But God has chosen the foolish things of the world to put to shame the wise; and God has chosen the weak things of the world to put to shame the things which are mighty... that no flesh should glory in His Presence... that as it is written, He who glories, let him glory in the Lord." (1 Corinthians 1:26-27,29,31 NKJV)

I read a precious testimony of a gal who had a radical conversion experience. After she became a Christian, she had many wonderful experiences with the Lord. Her pastor asked her to give her testimony. Being timid, she prepared and prayed but when she stood at the podium, she could not speak. Being shy in the first place, this was embarrassing to her; try as she could, no words came. Tearfully she yielded her inability to the Lord, and soon the Holy Spirit filled that place. Even though she never said a word, there was repentance and conversions all over the sanctuary. Through her weakness, the Lord did what her testimony could not.

Paul said in 1 Corinthians 2:2-3 *"...When I first came to you I didn't use lofty words and brilliant ideas to tell you God's message. For I decided that I would speak only of Jesus Christ and his death on the cross..* **I came to you in weakness — timid and trembling. And my preaching was very plain**, *not with a lot of oratory and human wisdom,* **but the Holy Spirit's power was in my words...**" *(The Living Bible)*

The Lord created us human beings, not supermen. And we **are** weak. We have a tendency to feel we are either too tall, too short, too fat, too skinny, too tired, too hyper, too bold, too shy, too dumb, too ugly, too smart, too funny, too serious, too old, too young... (ETC!) to be that perfect person to hear Him, to be used by Him, or to feel worthy of His touch. The truth is we can do nothing to be worthy of the Lord. Just accept what you consider your weakness, and let Him touch you, and let Him touch others through you. The following is an excerpt from my devotional book,[7] *"Words to Ponder"* which explains perfectly His heart on the Power of Weakness:

— The Power of Weakness —

In My kingdom, I send the mouth of babes to still the avenger. I empower the foolish to confound the wise. The cowards are given holy boldness. The meek are raised to possess the spoils of war.

I do not intend weakness to shame. Rather, weakness is a mark of honor. For only through weakness can My full complete power rest upon your life. If I place you in an environment of weakness, it is because there is an assignment for you that will be hindered any other way.

The strength of flesh has no might in the unseen world. The enemy lies, telling the world there is strength in control, intimidation, debate, intellect, mastery. He puffs up man with these false securities, for darkness is desperately afraid of weakness. Weakness that empties self in any form leaves one vulnerable to depend upon Me. Within that dependence I am released to work greater victories to defeat the realm of darkness.

Rejoice in weakness. It is not something to fear. Rather glory in it, that My full miraculous power may be dispatched without hindrance.

"My grace is sufficient for thee: for my strength is made perfect in weakness."
[2 Corinthians 12:9 KJ]

1. Rejoiced: to jump for joy, be exceedingly glad, exult. [21 Gk Strong's]. Jesus was absolutely delighted.
2. John's project for Future Business Leaders of America won first place in state. ☺
3. Mind of Christ: (Romans 12:1,2)
4. Mind of Christ: (1 Corinthians 2:16)
5. Anna is what we call my Mom. She received her name when my son was too young to pronounce his grandma's name, Nana. He called her Anna instead. Shortly after that I heard the Lord call her that and I knew He was naming her after Anna in the Bible.
6. Darkness manifest: (Mark 4:22)
7. Devotional book: a flyer is in the back of this book, also an order address.

CHAPTER 5:
GOD SPEAKS THROUGH PEOPLE

HE SPEAKS THROUGH THE GIFTS OF THE BODY OF BELIEVERS

"For just as we have many members in one body and all the members do not have the same function, so we, who are many, are one body in Christ, and individually members one of another. And since we have gifts that differ according to the grace given to us, let each exercise them accordingly: if prophecy, according to the proportion of his faith; if service, in his serving; or he who teaches, in his teaching; or he who exhorts, in his exhortation; he who gives, with liberality; he who leads, with diligence; he who shows mercy, with cheerfulness." (Romans 12:4-8 NASB) *"Now you are the body of Christ, and members individually. And God has appointed these in the church: first apostles, second prophets, third teachers, after that miracles, then gifts of healings, helps, administrations, varieties of tongues."* (I Cor 12:26-27: NKJV)

Knowing the Lord through the gifts in His body of believers is designed to be an earthly example of God living among man. Each gift represents a portion of Who God is, and is His tangible means of reaching out to people. When we examine what each gift means and its proper function, we see how God intended it to be.

The task of hearing the Lord through a gift becomes difficult when we place our eyes on imperfect mankind rather than God's perfect gift. The fact that God chose to make Himself available to us and actually dwells within us is amazing. But when coupled with the stumbling block of who we are and how inadequately we represent Him, it is astounding.

The Lord places each one of us in His body, the church, according to His divine will and pleasure. We do not all have the same gifts, but we are created to join together, to function as a complete unit. Each gift emanates a certain part of Jesus Christ so that He may dwell with us. He speaks to us through each of His gifts if we would hear.

There are many members in the Lord's body. He fills each with His grace and power to do the given assignment. He bestows different gifts to different people in direct relationship to the various tasks at hand. *"Now God gives us many kinds of special abilities, but it is the same Holy Spirit who is the source of them all. There are different kinds of service to God, but it is the same Lord we are serving: The Holy Spirit displays God's power through each of us as a means of helping the entire church."* (1 Corinthians 12:4,5,7 TLB)

33. HE SPEAKS THROUGH THE GIFT OF SERVICE

This gift of service[1] (ministry) is the ability to see and do the things that are necessary. It gives assistance and meets practical needs.

This gift can be likened unto a waitress in a restaurant. A good waitress oversees her tables, foreseeing needs before they occur. Being quick to respond to the task, she also asks if anyone needs anything she might have overlooked.

People who have the gift of service enjoy doing the nitty-gritty things, being practical and down-to-earth. Their ministry is a gift to people in physical need. They also liberate others to be able to stay in the realm of prayer and ministry of the Word. Because those with the gift of service feel great zeal and satisfaction in giving their gift, they need to be sensitive to the Holy Spirit if He should desire to say no. It could be the Lord's will for the needy person to receive in another way, at another time. Also the giver's own family should not be neglected. It should be considered that people with the gift of service often suffer burnout because the human body is vulnerable and weak. A proper assessment of the gift, how it is to be given and how much to give, needs to be in balance, always in accordance with His will.

I know a precious gal who has the gift of service. She has a true servant's heart. I sat beside her during a service and because it was going to be an especially long one, I'd brought my little step stool to rest my feet upon and some water to drink. When I arrived, I placed my things under my chair, and went off to visit. Finally I sat down at my chair and she made sure my stool was right there, and my water was accessible. I mentioned that she had the gift of service, and I'm not sure what she thought. A little while later the guest speaker needed a glass of water. Guess who jumped from her seat so fast that no one else had time to even think about it? I laughed and said "SEE???" She looked surprised as though to say, "Well maybe I do at that." Then during one particular time I got a little teary. It took about 2 seconds and she had a Kleenex in my hands. I said, "SEEEEEEE???????" I think she finally agreed. The point to this story is that her gift is so imbedded inside that it is merely an extension of her personality. That is the true nature of having Jesus inside us. Much of what we have to give seems like just our normal personalities, but it really is Jesus. We can see how out of the ordinary this precious gal's heart is, but she had a difficult time visualizing it. May the Lord open our eyes to our own gifts and to the beautiful gifts of others. May we see Jesus.

• *Within Jesus' body of believers, the gifts of service are His hands and feet. A gift cannot be appreciated unless it is received. Next time your arms are full and someone opens a door for you, consider that it may be the Lord reaching out to you. He so desires to lighten your load.*

HE SPEAKS THROUGH THE GIFT OF HOSPITALITY
Be hospitable to one another without grumbling. As each one has received a gift, minister it to one another, as good stewards of the manifold grace of God. (1 Peter 4:9 and 10 NKJV)

Along the same lines of the gift of service is the gift of hospitality.[2] The above verse says for everyone to be hospitable. However there are those who are gifted with this, and have a special yearning to open their home and provide a warm welcome for those in need of lodging. I have often been in the homes of these people who are the first to recognize your need and make their resources available.

• *The Lord speaks to us through these people by saying, "Even though I have called you to be like strangers in a foreign land, I will provide all your needs as You trust in Me."*

34. HE SPEAKS THROUGH THE GIFT OF EXHORTATION
The gift of exhortation[3] is the ability to inspire someone to move forward from the past. It can touch a heart to begin again and move into action. It gives hope and encouragement to see beyond the difficulties and onto a brighter future.

I know a special lady who has a vivacious personality, and loves to talk to people. Throughout the years she's had a "ministry" to people who are sick. Visiting often, calling and sending cheer, she has been a real uplift to many people. Whether she has ever thought of it as a ministry, I do not know. My guess is that she just considers it a part of her own personality and natural life. But it is obvious that her gift of cheer is God-given and is a wonderful uplift.

For some, this gift needs the balance of patience. An exhorter has the ability to foresee the desired result and is greatly motivated towards helping one obtain it. His zeal is so fervent he needs patience to slow down to the pace of the downhearted one. Someone having this wonderful gift to encourage and motivate others may often seem insensitive to the pain of the moment, being misconstrued as a lack of compassion. Yet, the Holy Spirit has so touched the one who has the gift to exhort, there is great motivation to do something about it.

• *The gift of exhortation within Jesus' body is His heart, saying, "I believe in you." Next time someone reaches out with a smiling touch of words, listen for the Lord's great zealous heart to motivate you away from the "mully-grubs." Understand that He waits to see your tear sparkled eye look up and say, "OK Lord, I dare to try again."*

35. HE SPEAKS THROUGH THE GIFT OF GIVING

The gift of giving[4] is the motivation to meet physical, financial, material, and spiritual needs:
Physical: Luke 10:33-35
Financial: Acts 4: 34-36
Material: Luke 3:11
Spiritual: Romans 1:11

The Word says, "Take heed that you do not do your charitable deeds before men, to be seen by them...do not sound a trumpet before you...But when you do a charitable deed, do not let your left hand know what your right hand is doing: that your charitable deed may be in secret: and your Father who sees in secret will Himself reward you openly." (Matthew 6:1-4 NKJV)

I am reminded of one particular lady who has always been a "giver." When she was affluent, she gave of her finances and gave an over abundance of expensive gifts to those around her. Then when difficult times came, (one time I found out her family had lived on potatoes for a week) she continued to give cards, a quick phone call, and hand made articles. When even harder times came, and she was out of work, she gave of her life's energy and helped clean, organize and paint a sickly person's home. Why did she do this? Because the gift to give was deeply entrenched in her heart. It was the most natural thing in the world to give of her substance, and when that was too small, she gave her labor. Her gift to give is an extension of the Lord's generous heart.

The best kind of giving is not with outward flashy show, but rather with humility as this gives grace and dignity to the one who receives. It also restrains pride in the giver.

A giver is to give without strings attached. Giving without expectation of anything in return will release the giver to give abundantly and with joy. If the giver has expectations of receiving, this road will lead to disappointment, unforgiveness, grudges, and finally bitterness. Expectations also hinder and restrain the receiver from the joy of receiving. Instead, the receiver is given chains and locks when the gift was meant to be a blessing.

• *The gift of giving is the substance carried in Jesus' hand. Next time someone imparts something to you, listen to the Lord's heart and purpose for giving it to you. He rejoices in being your Provider, and is so blessed when you tell Him, "Thank you."*

36. HE SPEAKS THROUGH THE GIFT OF RULING

The gift to rule[5] is similar to owning a business, but not necessarily working at the business location. This has the proficiency to chart a plan of action to sustain the business, but not necessarily the one to carry it out. He relies upon others to function and accomplish his plan.

The gift to rule has the ability to see the overall whole of where something or someone is going. I know a man who has this gift. He has the ability to see trends coming and going from a long way off, in people's lives, in politics, in spiritual issues, in the market place, and most any place in life. He always has had a unique ability to collect facts from miscellaneous places, and come up with something profound. He seems to collect it all, rolls it around a while, then comes up with a punch-line that grips the heart with understanding. It's as though his brain is this huge melting pot of interesting sources of information, then when the Lord would like to make something out of the melted glob, out pops the gift.

• *The gift to rule within Jesus' body is like having the mind of Christ. Next time someone gives you an insight of an overall trend, or perhaps purpose, listen, for it may very well be a gift from the Master. He is the Master Planner and receives great satisfaction in sharing His secrets. It is a double pleasure when we recognize Him as the Source.*

37. HE SPEAKS THROUGH THE GIFT OF MERCY

One with the gift of mercy[6] has the yearning to give kindness, love and tenderness to the downtrodden. This brings needed comfort, understanding, and sensitivity.

I experienced Anna's and the Lord's gift of mercy in an unusual way. One day I awakened particularly discouraged. It was so strong I called her and asked for her prayers. I had no idea how strong her mother's heart had been activated for battle. All day long she prayed and frequently bound the spiritual harassment of hopelessness and discouragement. She also asked that her "baby girl" (middle aged!) be given back her joy. While she was standing in line at Fred Meyers and still praying under her breath, someone said, "My baby girl." She knew it was the quickened voice of the Lord to her, that He had sent help and answered her prayers.

Meanwhile, I had been so caught up in my work I had completely forgotten I'd asked her for prayer. As I was working, all of a sudden I felt the Lord's comforting Presence very close. I had wonderful goose bumps, quickening, refreshing touches and because of His close Presence I fell into spontaneous worship while I was working at the computer. I was thrilled and continued working. Then all of a sudden it happened again. Then again! About this time, I said, "Lord I've missed Your refreshing Presence so much! How wonderful, and where have You been?" His touches came in wave after wave for about 4 hours. I was truly blessed.

At 5:00 P.M. Anna called and asked, "Did the angels show up yet?" She said she had been bombarding heaven, taking authority and really praying for me all day. I was very grateful, so touched by this love and mercy for my downtrodden feelings! This was "mercy" in action, and also an amazing confirmation to me of the power of prayer and it really encouraged me to pray more!

• *The gift of mercy is the tender place within the body of Christ. Next time someone reaches out to you with a prayer or a kind word of understanding, you can know the Lord's heart is yearning to touch your downhearted places. Minister to His yearnings, and reach out to Him by saying, "Thank you Lord." He feels your pain and so desires for you to receive His mercy.*

38. HE SPEAKS THROUGH THE GIFT OF HELPS

The gift of helps[7] is the ability to render assistance, (spiritual, physical, etc.). It is that place that works along side of another, like participating on a team laboring together for a common cause.

I saw a precious example of this in the hiring of the disabled. One day my husband and I stopped into a fast food restaurant for lunch.

The gal who took our order was sssooooooo slow. I observed her, wondering what age she was, and thinking she had an extremely precious spirit. I was surprised to see her at the front counter taking orders, especially at the noon rush. As she finally punched in the order and called it out back, I saw the little smiles on the sandwich makers, and I also saw the manager's grin as she peeked around her shoulder. From the back I heard, "Way to go Lori!!" She lit up like a light bulb with a huge smile. She put her hands in the air and said, "YES!!!" I laughed with her and asked, "Is this your first week?" She said, "I am really learning. I am learning really good. I am really learning this, and this is my 3rd week!" I was so touched by her innocence and pure spirit.

As I looked for a clean table, which is difficult to find during a rush, I immediately noticed that every empty table was spotless. I arranged our things and waited for my husband to bring our order. As I waited, I watched the cleanup gal. She moved so slow it was like watching everything in slow motion. She went from here to there, in no particular order, polishing things with her rag. As I was marveling at the fact this fast food franchise would hire these people at rush hour, I saw the true beauty of how each person's gift in the body of Christ is supposed to function. This precious cleaning lady did her job well, and I knew she was <u>fulfilled</u> in doing it. Someone else might really be stressed and unhappy doing it, but she was content. As I thought this, she wandered to the garbage can lid and started polishing it! (How many fast food restaurants have clean garbage can lids during rush?) Just then another person came out with his broom and swept a little place in back, then disappeared. And last, when the order arrived, a girl carefully read the number on the ticket, and announced it with obvious care. (How many times have you heard someone call out your number as though it was the most important number in the world?) I was so touched by this portrayal of kingdom ministry working in harmony and in a loving atmosphere.

- *The gift of helps links arms with others. Next time someone joins and aids you in a common purpose, consider it the Lord helping you in your task. He loves it when we value His gifts to us.*

39. HE SPEAKS THROUGH THE GIFT OF GOVERNMENTS

The gift of governments[8] is the ability to administer a plan.

The one with this gift of administration is like a manager who follows the direction of the one with the gift to rule. He shares the burden of that one who has the master plan, facilitating all the details.

The best gift of a manager is to find the most efficient way to **delegate** the operations to get the job done. However, I have noticed both in the business world and nonprofit organizations, that a good portion of managers work long, hard hours. Some of this is because of cutbacks and the streamlining of larger organizations, but some of it is because the managers have the tendency to do it all themselves. These managers are intelligent, have people skills, office skills, and jack-of-all-trade skills, and it is difficult for them to let go because it is faster and more organized to do it themselves! They want to delegate, but seeing the drain it would take to train others, they do it instead and consequently these people are working 50, 60, 70+ hours a week. It's the same with mothers who have the gift of administration. They are so organized and efficient, their children simply fall in line and take little responsibility in the family. The mother carries the whole load.

The way out for these poor overworked people with the gift of administration is to learn how to facilitate the resources available: people's skills and availability. Then perhaps the manager could restructure the job assignments to better fit the people, and better fit the overall goal. In the end, this relieves the manager so that he may facilitate the workers towards the goal instead of becoming buried in the details.

- *The gift of administration has the ability to see the need and dispatch others to fix it. He organizes and facilitates towards an overall goal. We can see the Lord's heartbeat surge through His body when His administrator dispatches life to all the cells. Next time you rub shoulders with an administrator, hear the strength of the Lord's pounding heart to reach the goal of delivering life. His power is mighty, and His flow is strong.*

40. HE SPEAKS THROUGH MUSICIANS

"...Seek out a man who is a skillful player on the harp; and it shall be that he will play it with his hand when the distressing spirit from God is upon you, and you shall be well." (1 Samuel 16:16 NKJV)

Music can communicate without words and penetrate hearts. When people have the gift of music, they have the ability to play their instrument in a way that encourages responses from the listeners. In other words, their music touches the heart and spirit. This warms the listener into a receptive place of worshipping the Lord as well as hearing His Words. Songs can often penetrate a heart with the Lord's message when the spoken word cannot.

Not everyone enjoys the same kind of music. In today's world, there is music for long hairs, short hairs, and even no hairs. Likewise, it is the same for worship music. There is no right or wrong way to worship the Lord, there are only different ways. The Lord is anointing new kinds of music to communicate His message to all mankind, not just a certain group.

I once heard a tape of a song that had people from all over the world worshipping the Lord in their own way. I could see that each portion of the song represented not only the people, but their culture. It was a token of themselves and their unique personalities worshipping the Lord. I was so touched by their expressions of heart, even though I didn't understand the words. The Lord used their worship through music to make me tender to His Presence and receive His touch.

• *Heaven resounds with music. When we hear music, we hear a touch of heaven declaring the glory of God.*

41. HE SPEAKS THROUGH CRAFTSMEN

"..and every willing craftsman will be with you for all manner of workmanship, for every kind of service..." (1 Chronicles 28: 21 NKJV)

I once observed two toddlers playing with "Lego" building blocks. The first one enjoyed building and rebuilding different toys with the same blocks. The second one liked playing with them only after they were built. The first became a student who enjoyed working with his hands. The second became a student who loved brain activities and computers. How can you compare apples and oranges? The fact is, the first had the gift of handy work, the second had other gifts.

Anyone with the creative ability to work with their hands is a craftsperson. Examples of these gifted crafts people are builders, painters and plumbers, florists, seamstresses, hairstylists, decorators, artists, etc. The Lord uses their handiwork to speak through the beauty of design and remind us of His creativity. Often the things fashioned are allegories of something He wants to say to and through the craftsperson's personal life.

HE SPEAKS THROUGH FRESH CREATIVITY

In these last days the Lord is going to use every available means to reach a multitude in His harvest. The old church ways are not going to look the same because He's going to use new means to reach a new generation. The Lord is inspiring "creativity" in the body of Christ in a greater way than ever before. Places the world has previously occupied, will be taken back by the church, and become new creative ways to share salvation to the lost. The Lord will be using dance, music, poetry, drama, and any number of other means, including ones not yet thought of, to bring the joy of the salvation message to the world.

I know a gal who has this creative gift of craft and art. First she decorated her church with huge wall mountings made of beautiful color and satin like material. My favorite is the banner of a life size lion saying, "The Lion of Judah." She later made shimmering flag like banners on poles that she began to use in worshipping the Lord, like David did in dance. Then she created worship instruments called glory rings that are similar to cheerleaders' pom poms, only these are shimmering and a different shape. People began to use these in joyful dance and expression of their praise to the Lord. Next she made some long, twirling type instruments that people twirl over their heads in beautiful motions of glimmer and color. Later, with her color laser printer, she began making prophetic crests for people of scriptures and symbols of the gifts in their lives. The list goes on.

There are many untapped ways to worship the Lord and many ways of sharing His message that we have yet to imagine. This gal's gifts are just a small rain drop of this amazing creativity the Lord is pouring out upon His people.

- *The Lord uses handiwork to open doors of the heart through looking upon beauty.*

42. HE SPEAKS THROUGH CHILDREN'S GIFTS
"Whoever receives one little child like this in My name receives Me. (Matthew 18:5 NKJV)

One season the Lord told me I would grow "holy bold." I considered my personality as a little church mouse who preferred to remain unseen and unheard. Cute mice and mouse stories popped into my life from everywhere.

My young son drew me a picture of a green Christmas tree with a HUGE mouse trying to hide in it. John's gift was a precious way for God to make His point: even if I stayed a mouse, I would grow so big I just couldn't hide! So many times my son would draw or color picture stories and give them to me in perfect timing with the Lord's Word.

HE SPEAKS THROUGH CHILDREN'S WORDS
"You have taught the little children to praise you perfectly. May their example shame and silence your enemies." (Psalm 8:2 TLB)

"Beware that you do not despise or feel scornful toward or think little of one of these little ones, for I tell you that in heaven their angels always are in the presence of and look upon the face of My Father Who is in heaven: Allow the little ones to come to Me, and do not forbid, or restrain, or hinder them, for of such {as these} the kingdom of heaven is composed." (Matthew 18:10 and Matthew 19:14 AMP)

      Children are gifts straight from heaven and His heart. I have been astonished by the direct Words of my Father that come through what they say and do. As I walked through a prolonged season of wavering, seemingly on a spiritual swing set vacillating between two opinions, I would swing one way and think maybe the Lord meant such n' such, or I would swing the opposite. The Lord gave me a picture-vision of myself near the waves of the ocean. Every time a large wave (overwhelming circumstance) would come close, I would scurry to the top of a very small and skinny tree. The bottom trunk was about four inches in diameter. When the wave would hit, the tree bent way over to one side and then the other, bouncing back and forth!

      It was a perfect allegory of what I was doing during that season. Isaiah 35:3 says, *"...confirm the feeble knees."* My knees were anything but confirmed, they felt more like rubber legs, just like that tree trunk! I felt so sifted and tired of wavering. One day as I was thinking about wavering back and forth with rubber legs and feeling very condemned, my very young son interrupted my thoughts. He said out of nowhere, "Mama, I am worried my knees might break." Regaining my composure, I explained that when we bend and exercise our knees, it is good for them for it makes them strong! That was one of many times I remember his little voice penetrating my thoughts and bringing me encouragement from the Lord. I am now trained to know and believe that good gifts come in small packages!

• *God speaks very clearly through children's mouths, we only have to listen.*

43. HE SPEAKS THROUGH THE SENIORS

"Listen to your father who begot you, And do not despise your mother when she is old. Buy the truth, and do not sell it, Also wisdom and instruction and understanding." (Proverbs 23: 22-23 NKJV)

      Sitting in a mall I was watching toddlers play in a central playground area. Their little muscles and mouths were going 90 miles an hour — not a still moment in the whole group. Their exhausted parents and grandparents were sitting on the benches patiently (and not so patiently) settling squabbles and kissing owies. Meanwhile, the toddlers were running in every direction. I was exhausted just watching it all and thinking how nice it would be to have that much energy!

That set my mind to thinking about how we are born with a bank account of so much energy and by the time we are seniors we've spent most of it. Then I started thinking about how much life changes for the older ones, where pieces of life fall away and life's priorities change. Have you ever noticed that most the seniors don't have great worldly ambitions in which they pour their every waking moment? What matters most to them is people — sitting at the feet of others and enjoying conversation and relationships. Seniors love loving.

Jesus said <u>love</u> was to be everyone's priority — love the Lord with all our hearts and love others as we love ourselves. That's all. He didn't say we had to accomplish anything, merely love. So why do we have to wait till we've spent most of our bank account of energy to get our priorities straight?

That day on the bench as I watched the older ones watch the children, I also thought that it was a parable of how we grow up in our relationships with the Lord. We start out so full of our own pursuits in serving the Lord. Our lives are filled with activities based around Him. The more mature we become, the less ambitious we become in our own pursuits. Spending time with Him is what matters most and we are content to sit at His feet and just enjoy Him.

• *When the Lord speaks to me through a senior citizen, He says, "<u>You</u> are what matters most in My life, and I want to be with you!"*

44. HE SPEAKS THROUGH THE INTERCESSORS

"Likewise the Spirit also helpeth our infirmities: for we know not what we should pray for as we ought: but the Spirit itself maketh intercession for us with groanings which cannot be uttered." (Romans 8:26 KJ)

When it comes to deep intercession, there is a place in God that few of the body of Christ know exist. This is a place beyond the bless-me prayers where an empty vessel becomes filled with God's life pulsing heart for His people. These sacrificial people spend hours in prayer, not minutes. They long for God's Presence, His help, His touch, and are literally praying His kingdom to earth. The Lord deposits a portion of His burdens upon them and He uses them as vessels to bring to birth that which He wants to bring forth on earth.

In these last days, it is not unusual for intercessors to be touched in a physical manner with various expressions of groaning and crying. Regardless of gender, their "womb" area may actually contract and bear down as though a woman in travail. *"Ask now, and see, Whether a man is ever in labor with child? So why do I see every man with his hands on his loins Like a woman in labor, And all faces turned pale?" (Jeremiah 30:6 NKJV)* In the contracting process, some may even groan as though pushing forth a baby.

Other intercessory actions may be like signs communicating God's Word. For instance, one lady who had been a faithful and devout church attendee for over 30 years suddenly stood up in a service and crowed like a rooster. The pastor respected this devout and normally quiet lady, but was shocked and asked her after the meeting why she did that. She sincerely said that the Holy Spirit had impressed her to crow like a rooster as a sign to the congregation that it was time to wake up from spiritual slumber, because the Lord was birthing a new day!

I was in a meeting when there was a sudden pause during worship with a total hush in the congregation. I heard the Lord whisper to me, *"Get ready, here it comes!"* Then immediately a shy intercessor sitting next to me sang forth as loud as she could, the sound of a trumpet announcement, like a fanfare. Signs like these are a signal that the whole earth is preparing for the birth of what the Lord is bringing forth in these last days.

I heard a testimony about a man who was disturbed seeing these kind of things happen in his meetings and asked the Lord what was going on. Then he heard a panther scream in his bedroom. With his hair standing on end, he finally realized it happened in the spirit and asked the Lord, "What was <u>that</u> for?" The Lord told Him that all of creation was groaning for what He was bringing forth:

"For the anxious longing of the creation waits eagerly for the revealing of the sons of God. For the creation was subjected to futility, not of its own will, but because of Him who subjected it, in hope that the creation itself also will be set free from its slavery to corruption into the freedom of the glory of the children of God. For we know that the whole creation groans and suffers the pains of childbirth together until now." (Romans 8: 19-23 NASB)

• When the Lord speaks through an intercessor, He is saying, "I have placed My heart and My Word as a deposit in this person's life. Listen to what My Spirit is crying!"

45. HE SPEAKS THROUGH MISSIONARIES
"...and not only this, but he has also been appointed by the churches to travel with us in this gracious work, which is being administered by us for the glory of the Lord Himself..." (2 Corinthians 8: 19 NASB)

Missionaries are pastors in a foreign land. They have left the comforts of their own homes and family and chosen to adopt God's children of another land. The Lord has gifted them with the ability to learn a foreign language and culture. They have learned to be flexible in such surroundings and trust the Lord for their supplies.

I heard of a missionary wife who was having a difficult time explaining how Jesus was nailed to a cross, for the people did not understand what a nail was, never having seen one. She happened to open a can of peaches sent from home, and inside was a rusty nail. The Lord provides in mysterious ways. The missionaries are often the first ones to see Him provide in these unusual yet tangible ways.

• *When we hear the Lord through a missionary, we hear Him say, "I care enough to reach you at your own level of life, and I care enough to live among you, My people."*

HE SPEAKS THROUGH THE APPOINTED GIFTS

"And His gifts were {varied; He Himself appointed and gave men to us,} some to be apostles (special messengers), some prophets (inspired preachers and expounders), some evangelists (preachers of the Gospel, traveling missionaries), some pastors (shepherds of His flock) and teachers." (Ephesians 4:11 AMP)

Each appointed gift has been called, chosen and empowered by God to equip and perfect[9] the saints to do the work of the ministry of building up His body. The appointed gifts are given for the repairing, furnishing and building the members toward wholeness. *"...until we all attain oneness in the faith and in the comprehension of the full and accurate knowledge of the Son of God; that {we might arrive} at really mature manhood - the completeness of personality which is nothing less than the standard height of Christ's own perfection -* **the measure of the stature of the fullness of the Christ,** *and the completeness found in Him." (Ephesians 4:13 AMP)*

The focus of this verse and the purpose for the appointed gifts is Jesus Christ. There are many sermons, teachings, doctrines and precepts that can be found in the Bible, but they are not meant to be the focus. The Old and New Testament both point to one mark: Jesus Christ. Biblically accurate sermons and teachings are not wood, hay, and stubble. However when they do not place the people's heart and focus on relationship with Jesus Christ, and becoming LIKE HIM, they only clutter our focus.

Leaders need to reevaluate on a continuing basis what is taught and why it is taught. This will give needed adjustments, as sometimes a joint pops out of place.

46. HE SPEAKS THROUGH APOSTLES

The apostles[10] are sent as God's messengers. They are like pioneers, breaking ground for new territory not yet possessed.

Receiving their direction and message straight from God, places them in the front line of courage to give forth His message. They face the obstacles of blazing a path at the very beginning of their mission. Public opinion and the inflexibility of people to venture into new territory are obstructions against the mission. Nevertheless, because they are sent by God, they are given the grace to stand and bring forth God's message.

Paul was a good example of this. Until Paul, the disciples were sent to the Jewish people. But the Lord wanted salvation for the Gentiles so He commissioned Paul. Paul broke new territory and not only had public opinion to overcome, but the mindset of the previous apostles.

Likewise, the other apostles had the mindset of the Jewish faith to overcome, as Jesus fulfilled the law and started a new era of salvation through faith in Him rather than in Jewish laws. And again even after he had preached Jesus, Peter was reminded by the Lord that eating Kosher was no longer necessary. People's mindset is a major obstacle in being on the front lines of introducing new territory.

• *Hearing the Lord through apostles, is hearing a portion of His message, His nature, and His character. The gift they offer the body of Christ is God's agenda. The apostle says: "God is going somewhere, let's put away our mindset and join Him!"*

47. HE SPEAKS THROUGH PROPHETS

The prophet[11] operates in four main functions: he foresees, and he foretells. He also keeps watch for the safety of the wall, and raises his hands in intercession in the time of battle.

In the Old Testament the prophet was called God's watchman.[12] The Israelites had watchmen that stood in the towers keeping watch for any good or bad news that approached the welfare of the city. So when God called His prophets "watchmen," the people understood what that meant in relation to spiritual issues.

The watchman's most important gifts are his eyes, ears and mouth. *"Go, set a watchman, let him declare what he sees."* (Isaiah 21:6 NKJV) The prophet sees and hears and then dispatches what he understands, receiving inspiration to speak God's announcements. The inspiration to speak is not necessarily for public ears. Sometimes, it is given in prayer with the authority to speak God's Word to be fulfilled on earth. An example is when the Lord commanded Ezekiel to speak to the dry bones: *"Again He said to me, "Prophesy to these bones, and say to them, 'O dry bones, hear the word of the LORD!"* *(Ezekiel 37:4 NKJV)*

Most of the prophet's gifts are received in private, not outwardly apparent to the body of Christ. *"...If there be a prophet among you, I the Lord will make myself known unto him in a vision, and will speak unto him in a dream."* *(Numbers 12:6 KJ)* Much of his training to hear and understand is through the privacy of visions and dreams.

The true prophet appointed by God is like an iceberg. The public only sees the very tip. The submerged gift is the time spent standing at his post. When the Lord directs him, it only takes a brief moment to declare what he has seen. Most of his assignment is in private, and only when the Lord commands does he come forth publicly to declare what he sees.

The prophet's post not only watches outwardly in the distance, but also looks inwardly toward the safety of the community. He makes up the hedge, and stands in the gap: *"And I sought for a man among them, that should make up the hedge,*[13] *and stand in the gap before me in the land..."* *(Ezekiel 22:30 KJ)*

For the Israelites, the watchman's post kept watch over the wall. If there was a breach or gap in the wall, vulnerable to enemy onslaught, he made sure it was repaired. The wall in spiritual terms was the spiritual hedge of protection surrounding the people from captivities, famines, wars, etc. When the Israelites resisted their conscience and disobeyed the Lord, they suffered the consequences of their wall being broken. This gave vulnerability to enemy attacks.

Today, if a hedge (wall) has been damaged, the Lord instructs and encourages the prophet how it will be repaired. Sometimes it will be repaired by outwardly confronting the cause of the breach. However, most of the time, standing[14] in the gap is the 99 percent of the unseen iceberg. God tells the prophet what's wrong, and then He tells him how HE is going to fix it. (God fixes it, not the prophet.)

When the Lord reveals how the breach will be fixed, the prophet is given inspiration and authority to delegate the repair. Nehemiah is a good example of the physical allegory of this concept. He was given the king's letter of delegated authority to dispatch supplies to rebuild the wall. *(Nehemiah 2:8)* The prophet's supplies are spiritual. The Lord reveals whatever is needed to spiritually repair the wall, then the prophet prays with authority what the Lord has spoken.

Sometimes during the repair of a breach, the enemy comes against the vulnerable places. As an example, the Lord rebuked the false prophets because they did not remain when there was a breach in the wall during battle. *"...those who prophesy out of their own heart... Woe to the foolish prophets, who follow their own spirit and have seen nothing! ... your prophets are like foxes in the deserts. You have not gone up into the gaps to build a wall ... to stand in battle on the day of the LORD." (Ezekiel 13:2-5 NKJV)*

The prophet stands with his spiritual hands raised, interceding on behalf of the warriors. He becomes an active part in the battle of anything coming against God's Words. Sometimes the battle will be lengthy. Yet, there comes a time when the Lord specifically tells him the battle is won in heaven. "It is finished!" Then the prophet's position becomes an active stand of faith, believing God has spoken victory. He expectantly watches and waits for the promised victory to be performed on earth as it was spoken and seen in heaven.

Standing and believing God for His promised victory is a rest from the heat of battle, but it still requires abiding, tarrying, enduring, continuing, being employed, and remaining. God sees the victorious end from the beginning and speaks before it comes to pass. He who stands in the gap no longer needs to command and speak God's Word in the battle. He rests from war and yet remains steadfast against circumstance that says the victory is lost. He hears and believes God according to God's spoken victory. He awaits with hopeful and active anticipation for His Words to come to pass. The breach will close, with the enemy in retreat as God has spoken.

When knowing the Lord through a prophet, (as well as the other appointed gifts) there is a tendency to have one's eyes on the man, and not the Lord. An example of this is looking to the prophet for guidance, or a special word from the Lord. This perspective is no different than going to someone with the gift of mercy and asking him if he has the gift of mercy for them today! God is the source, not the person. The prophet is merely the Lord's servant who dispatches what he sees and hears. He is completely vulnerable and reliant upon the Lord for His gifts just like everyone else. The prophet's eyes look to the Lord as his source, and so it should be with the people.

- *Knowing the Lord through a prophet, is seeing a special side of the Lord. His desire is to provide the encircling security of safety for those He loves. He keeps watch over all our ways and is ever before us, preparing His people for what's coming. When we have sinned and caused our hedge (wall) to be broken, the Lord sees that it is mended to completion. He is our intercessor in times of enemy onslaught.*

48. HE SPEAKS THROUGH EVANGELISTS

The evangelist's[15] gift is to communicate salvation in relevant terms to the lost. His gift is being Jesus' mouth. The Lord sends him as His trumpet to the lost world. He announces the great joy of salvation to those who will receive.

The Lord calls the evangelist to be a kind of intercessor for the lost. He will feel the groaning and yearning of the Lord's heart to reach the lost ones. The evangelist will be touched with their cries of loss, and the Lord's cries for His lost sheep. His prayers are filled with the desire that salvation be sent to those he loves. He is given that part of God's heart which has a great zeal for souls.

The evangelist recognizes there is a fullness of time for each individual to come to the Father, and speaks relevant words to those who are being drawn by Him. The evangelist's words are empty without the drawing power of the Father. Jesus said, *"No one can come to Me unless the Father who sent Me draws him."* *(John 6:44 NKJV)* The Lord knows the conditions of hearts and will not draw a hardened heart who is stubborn in his own ways, until He knows it is the fullness of time for that heart to melt.

The story of the prodigal son *(Luke 15:11)* describes much of the Father's heart toward the lost. In the fullness of time for the son to return home, the Father (looking for his son in the distance) ran to his side, greeted and kissed him. The ring, the robe, the fatted calf were his welcome home gifts so freely bestowed. The allegory of the ring is like a "promotion" of placement and assignment within the Father's household. The robe is the Father's "enduement" or mantle of authority. And the fatted calf is the spiritual meat provided for the son to celebrate new beginnings. The evangelist gives these good gifts as the Father's enfolding welcome home.

• *When we know the Lord through the gift of evangelism, we understand His great zeal and effort to go forth and seek the lost. The evangelist's home is where the lost are found. He travels far and wide to give His good news. Through an evangelist, the Lord calls, invites, and encourages lost ones to hope and believe in starting a new life.*

49. HE SPEAKS THROUGH PASTORS

The pastor[16] lives along side of and with his sheep, watching over them with God's care. He nurtures them into an abundant life. They need healing, feeding, protection and guidance.

Of all the appointed gifts, the pastor has the greatest variety of responsibilities. A pastor is similar to a shepherd who looks over all the sheep in his care, and becomes a nurturing father to them. He is their friend. In family life when a father's child has an "owie," the father takes great care to fix it properly, down to the last detail. If his child runs away from home, he does all he can to find his loved one. If the child is hungry, he gives forth a banquet from his heart. If the child is hungry, sick, or lost, his dad does not impose strict rules upon him, pressuring him to comply to rules and help with household tasks. Likewise, the nurturing shepherd is like the "dad" to his flock.

When a pastor bares his heart and becomes vulnerable to those he loves, he becomes one with them, living among, and identifying with their personal lives. With a closeness established he can be there to restore, feed, guide, and protect His own. The pastors are the heart of the body of Christ. *"Jesus said ...I have called you friends; for all things that I have heard of my Father I have made known unto you." (John 15:15 KJ)* Is a pastor to be any less to his sheep?

I was so touched by hearing a story in a radio sermon. The Lord told me years ago He was going to raise a new crop of nurturing shepherds, who were willing to truly nurture His sheep. Because of knowing this, I was particularly interested in this living example of the true heart and role model of what the Lord's pastor should be. The pastor said he was just getting on an airplane to go home from a conference when a lady started crying as he approached. He recognized her as having been in his congregation years earlier when she lived in his town. It turned out she was crying with relief because she knew help had arrived! She had been nervous about her six year old son flying all by himself and now she knew he would be safely guarded by her former pastor. So they made special arrangements for him to sit by her son during the flight.

On the flight, they played army with tanks and men, colored pictures and shared stories. He said it was the best plane flight he'd ever had. I was so deeply touched by this. He mentioned how tired of flying he had become. But this time he got to enjoy it through the boy's eyes of his first experience in flying. The boy was absolutely thrilled.

Besides the beauty of this man's willing heart to love a child, I thought his experience was also an allegory of the nurturing fathers enjoying the experience of those taking their first flight of faith in accepting Jesus as their Savior.

Visiting a church in another town, I witnessed a sight I will never forget. The pastor asked for a few minutes of testimonies. After a few were shared, a young fellow with long dirty hair, dressed in tattered clothing stood up in the back row. All he said was, "I have been away for a long time and I have come back to Jesus." The pastor, dressed in Sunday clothes, said nothing. There was a hush as he stepped away from the podium, and took the long walk down the aisle. When he approached the young man he threw his arms around this man and said, "Welcome home, my dear brother." I still get teary when I think of it.

- *The most important gift the pastor has to give to his flock is his heart. When* a dad becomes a friend to his family his children come home. When we hear the Lord through a pastor, we hear His Father's heart towards us.

50. HE SPEAKS THROUGH TEACHERS AND THE GIFT OF TEACHING

Teaching is the ability to impart knowledge and understanding on a relevant basis. It clarifies the hidden things, bringing them into focus.

The teacher's[17] position within the body is the pastor's right arm. He brings detailed understanding, in an overall manner, to concepts the Holy Spirit has taught. Teachers work in a smaller setting and have the opportunity to bring the intimacy of details to individual lives. The teacher is one who loves to study, research, and prepare specifics for presentation. He devotes the time it takes to bring a greater understanding of concepts the Holy Spirit is bringing to the flock. Teachers give details, bringing delight to others through offering the particulars. Jesus was a wonderful Teacher, using the details of the surrounding circumstances and environment to reveal the mysteries of God.

The Lord gives a teacher the gift to be able to communicate what he learns. Many times, when we hear the Lord through a teacher, there is a quickening of a little detail shared, maybe a definition, or an example that rings in our ears the rest of the day. The Lord delights to speak to us through the smallest, detailed gifts. Through the teacher, there is time for these intimate gifts of His Word to be planted in our hearts.

Paul warns *"Let not many of you become teachers, my brethren, knowing that as such we shall incur a stricter judgment." (James 3:1 NASB)* Like the other appointed gifts, the teachers are held accountable for how and what they teach His people. They are representatives of His message and need to act and teach accordingly.

However, in spite of this warning, the Lord needs people who are willing to become teachers. Many of you have been sitting on the sidelines with wonderful gifts yet untapped. The Lord needs <u>you</u> for His huge harvest. He has multitudes of children of all colors, shapes, sizes and age wanting to play with you! It's like a Mom who asks her son if he wants to watch the baseball game. He says, "Mom, I don't want to watch, I WANT TO PLAY!" She realizes she has slipped into the role of a watcher and not a player and is missing out in life because of it. If you have slipped into being a pew warmer, when the Holy Spirit nudges you, please consider getting into the game and sharing your life and time with others. *"...The harvest truly is great, but the labourers are few; pray ye therefore the Lord of the harvest that he would send forth labourers into His harvest." (Luke 10:2 KJ)*

- *The Lord speaks through teachers by stimulating us to look at the details and apply them in a personal way.*

When my husband and I were first married he used to build houses, in fact he built our own. I fondly watched him and also enjoyed the various stages of the construction process. In reflection, I can see an analogy that the appointed gifts are very similar to building a house:

- The apostle is the concrete foundation. It is the lowest structure of the house, and designed to carry much weight. The foundation determines the size, shape and dimension of the building. There is a great necessity for pouring a level foundation and not a crooked one.

- The prophets are the framework and the windows. The 2 x 4 framework of the walls are not visible when the house is finished. The framework stands in the breaches of the house until the walls are formed. The windows are the watchman's post to view beyond the walls.

- The evangelist is the exterior color and environment of the house. His message as someone passes by, is "Welcome." He is a gift clearly visible that proclaims the beauty of the overall package.

- The teacher fills the house with color and comfort, like the furniture, carpet and drapes. But the lovely things to fill the home belong to the members. Each is a chosen vessel, with a chosen gift to add beauty and warmth to the home.

- The roof is the pastor. He shelters and protects his house and provides a covering from the elements that rage against it.

I heard a cute idea of portraying the gifts in the body of Christ, which I have expounded upon: <u>The way you tell a person's gift is to watch how he responds to any given situation.</u> Pretend a little boy is carrying a glass of water, trips and spills the water. Each response is the person with their own particular gift to share:

The gift of Ministry: "Are you all right? Here, let me get the mop and broom!"

The gift of Hospitality: "Come to my home, and I will be happy to share something to drink and cookies."

The gift of Exhortation: "I know you're going to be just fine. We'll just wipe off those pant legs and you'll be on your way! Next time you'll do better."

The gift of Giving: "I'll go get you another glass of water."

The gift of Ruling: "Who designed these steps any way? We need to redesign them so this doesn't happen again."

The gift of Mercy: "Oh Sweetheart, I'm so sorry! I know exactly how you feel. The same thing happened to me."

The gift of Helps: "Let me carry your water for you."

The gift of Governments: "I'll find a builder to rebuild this step according to the new design."

The Musician: "Let's all worship the Lord in spite of a tough day!"

The Craftsman: "I'm going to build a water stand in the back so they won't have to carry the water so far."

The Children: "Ouch! Would you like my balloon with the smilie face?"

The Senior: "My my, dear one, come sit on my lap and I'll tell you a story about the little boy who spilled his water."

The Intercessor: "Little one, I will pray for you that the Lord will keep you safe and keep you from falling."

The Missionary: "I know of a land where they carry water in a different manner. Let me tell you about it!"

The Apostle: "I found a place where we can get you a new glass of water. Here, let me show you the way."

The Prophet: "Always walk carefully as though you carry a glass of water in your hands, and beware of stumbling blocks in your way."

The Evangelist: "There is someone thirsty over in the corner. Will you take some water to him?"

The Teacher: "May I teach you how to walk with a glass of water in your hand? If you were to hold your hand just so, making sure your thumb is placed... And did you know that the Greek word for glass comes from the word..."

The Pastor: "Here, let me help you up, and let's make sure you're OK!"

— SHARING GIFTS —
51. HE SPEAKS THROUGH COMMON SENSE IN GIVING GIFTS

The gifts in Romans 12 and 1 Corinthians 12, are various manifestations of the Holy Spirit the Lord has deposited within His people. Together, as a whole, they make up His body. How often we take for granted these gifts and forget to hear His touch. He has placed the gift of His Presence within His people because of His strong love and desire to reach out in a tangible way. What a miserable world it would be without His precious gifts through His people!

When one has a gift to give, common questions are asked, "How do I know I'm supposed to give it? Or how do I know when or how?" This section expresses the idea of giving as a cooperating process:

"If you are really eager to give, then it isn't important how much you give. God wants you to give what you have, not what you haven't. Of course, I don't mean that those who receive your gifts should have an easy time of it at your expense, but you should divide with them. Right now you have plenty and can help them; then at some other time they can share with you when you need it. In this way, each will have as much as he needs. Do you remember what the scriptures say about this? "He that gathered much had nothing left over, and he that gathered little had enough. So you also should share with those in need." (2 Corinthians 8:12-15 TLB) The equality spoken of in this passage has to do with teamwork. This is not one person doing all the work, but all contributing as they are able.

The key to being used by the Holy Spirit for any giving is being available. The Bible records guidance standards in giving gifts. The first is giving in relation to one's ability. *"Every man shall **give as he is able**, according to the blessing of the Lord your God which He hath given you."* (Deuteronomy 16:17 KJ) *"For if there is first a willing mind, it is accepted according to what one has, and not according to that he does not have."* (2 Corinthians 8:12 NKJV) We cannot give what we do not have.

Secondly, as seen in the above verse, (willing mind), we do not give out of obligation. All giving requires man's free will. God does not give through an unwilling vessel. If the vessel is unwilling, the gift is not from Him. *"...whoever is of a **willing heart**, let him bring it, as an offering of the Lord;..."* *(Exodus 35:5 NKJV)* *"So let each one **give as he purposes** in his heart, not grudgingly,[18] or of necessity..."* *(2 Corinthians 9:7 NKJV)* It is NOT THE LORD one is feeling if there is a feeling of heaviness and a sense of obligation to give. God said, *"For this is the love of God, that we keep His commandments: and His commandments are not grievous."*[19] *(1 John 5:3 KJ)*

He has no desire to heavily laden our shoulders; the enemy does that. Also man loads himself with his own goals and ambitions. When God gives His good gifts through a vessel, the vessel is given the grace, the freedom, the joy, the zeal and the delight to give. His yoke is easy, His burden is light when coupled in service with Him. If you are feeling enslaved and yoked in giving, find out why. Search your own heart and motive.

The third measure of giving is to give with cheerfulness. *"For God loves a **cheerful**[20] **giver**."* *(2 Corinthians 9:7 NKJV)* Note the word "attractive" in footnote # [20]. Attraction has drawing power. Attraction draws, allures, magnetizes, gravitates, inclines, pulls, etc. So if you feel repelled toward giving and have no cheerfulness at the thought, listen to your heart.

If you are having trouble getting started sharing your gifts, perhaps the following will help you. The Lord quickened to me that all encompassing **Who, What, Why, How, Where and When** list. If you are practiced in the gifts, you may want to see if this seems to fit the way you minister.

When the Lord begins His drawing power to reach out to a certain individual, usually the first group He brings to mind is Who, What and Why. Later the how, where, and when seem to fall into place:

1. **WHO** - The mystery of the Lord's drawing power begins when someone comes into focus. We are with him in an actual physical circumstance or he comes to us within our thoughts. Although we have not been alerted, there is a gift to give, the Lord has begun His process. He has identified the "WHO."

2. **WHAT** - Shortly following who, we discover "WHAT." A problem has emerged and we recognize a need.

3. **WHY** - Usually simultaneously, we understand "WHY" it is needed. At this point, we desire to give to that person's need. This is the time to

pray and rely on the Lord to show How, Where and When the need is to be met.

4. **HOW** - "HOW" is the transportation of the gift. It can be through a spoken, written or visual word, a physical or spiritual touch. Usually, when we receive a gift to impart, we understand the vehicle by which it will travel. However, there are exceptions. Sometimes when a person receives a word of knowledge about someone, he will waver between two thoughts, do I share, or do I pray? Check the three standards in giving: ability, willingness and drawing power. If there is hesitation, a repelling to give forth in person, reluctance, no cheerfulness, no personal desire or choice, or no ability... Then PRAY. If you have a strong desire to share, then share. If you feel drawn to pray, then pray. If nothing is drawing you, put it on the shelf and wait upon the Lord. He will bring the six words to line up in His perfect timing.

5. **WHERE** - The Holy Spirit will bring to mind the environment best situated to give. Obviously, it is not good to give a foot massage while someone is chopping wood! The same is true for any gift shared, there is a wise, tactful and prudent place to give a gift. Most frequently, the Holy Spirit will impart common sense. *("...And let it be, when these signs come to you, that you do as the occasion demands; for God is with you.." I Samuel 10:7 NKJV)* Sometimes extenuating circumstances do require an explicit location. If that is the case, the Holy Spirit will give that supernatural understanding. Most of the time, "WHERE" is common sense.

6. **WHEN** - Timing is the last to line up. I have noticed He prefers to leave the timing to me simply because He wants me to be a cheerful and prompt giver. However, I always ask Him to reveal His perfect timing. If the timing is important He will impart that understanding. On most occasions, I give when all six words have lined up and I realize the opportunity is NOW. I do not falter at timing because my faith tells me He knows exactly how long it will take for me to discover the person, hear his need, why he needs it, then understand where and how. My faith tells me He already has the receiver timed perfectly with my timing to hear and dispatch. Usually the opportunity shows itself. Timing also requires tact, wisdom, and common sense. When in doubt about when to give, use common sense. If still in doubt, WAIT. The holy boldness, faith and courage He desires does not come through doubt. Give Him time to establish you before going forth. Establishing comes through confirmations.

I have noticed there are occasions when He has lined up all six words, with my willing cheerful heart to give, but then given me the guidance to "pray" it, rather than give it. When these occasions happen, they have been a true sacrifice and gift; giving my desire to give back to Him and letting Him do it HIS WAY, and in His timing. People who have a ministry of prayer will frequently have this happen, having the means and opportunity to give, and yet yielding their will to the Lord and allowing Him to do what He wants.

As much as we desire to give, we empty ourselves to His will. This is a "strengthless" place to be, desiring so much to help something be better, and yet completely relying on Him to make it better HIS way. In yielding our own strength we become weak. His full miraculous power is then made available to go forth unhindered by flesh.

— SHARING GIFTS —
52. HE SPEAKS THROUGH HIS SUPER ON OUR NATURAL

The Lord once asked me if I could separate eggs after they were scrambled. I thought that was a strange question until He said, *"You and I are scrambled eggs."* It took me a long time to really understand how it applied. For a very long time, I was stifled in applying His guidance because I was waiting for His supernatural touch. The fact was I'd had plenty of them, but I was still unsure of what was Him and what was me.

Then I realized He didn't want it to be that way - me versus Him. He wants to express Himself <u>through</u> us, with our personalities intact. He has deposited a portion of Himself in each one of us, and He created each of us differently for a reason. He is so big and so multifaceted, it takes a whole universe to even begin to express Who He is and what He wants to say! One day I realized it was His super on my natural. As I stepped out and shared what was on my heart, He was there. He was not only with me but also feeling the same thing I was. We were in the same vessel but I hadn't really swallowed that when it came to applying His guidance to make decisions and share.

I once had a very funny experience swallowing how close He really is. The following is an excerpt from my journal: "I had an interesting thing happen to me last night. I have not given much thought to the fear of the Lord or the fear of angels. In fact I have always felt that I would be loved so much, I wouldn't suffer any fear of the supernatural. But last night I was fast asleep and I turned over and the clock said 11:10. My eyes were so heavy with sleep I couldn't keep them open for more than a couple of seconds at a time. I would keep peeking because I really wanted to see it turn to 11:11.[21] I don't know how many times I did this and every time it still said 11:10. Then finally, in my mind, I started to count back from 10 - 9 - 8 -7 - 6 - 5 - 4 - 3 - 2 -1- blast-off! That is what I said in my thoughts and **exactly** on the word blast-off the clock turned to 11:11.

Terror struck my heart!!!! It was the oddest experience. I had the sudden realization that the Almighty God lived inside my body, and even though I thought I was the one counting, it was **Him** and I hadn't known it. I had a supernatural encounter with God, and it was within me! So incredible, it's hard to even explain. My first thought was, "The Almighty God lives inside of me!" I know that must sound rather stupid because that is what the Holy Spirit teaches us, and we are also taught about the fear of the Lord, but this was experiencing it first hand. It was as close as I could get to Him and still not see Him. (Talk about invasion of privacy!) We have no idea!!!! Boy are we blind. Please, Lord lift the veil and prepare me for You! I had never realized this, but we can't get any closer to Him than His being inside of us. It is like watching our cat Cuddles and John. He will pick her up and she just goes into ecstasy when he scratches her. She pushes her little head as close to him as she can get. She leans into him with all her might. But even in the closest intimacy you can have, it is still not as intimate and private as having Him live inside and recognizing that. WOW. Lord help me to recognize You and draw fellowship from Your abiding Presence constantly!" (end of journal insert)

So how does all this apply to His guidance? This book is displaying the ways the Lord has chosen to speak to me, and some of them are natural as through our personalities, and some of them are supernatural as gifts from Him. He wants to reach out to us and through us with a scramble of both. It's not one or the other, it's both. This is the time when the Lord is drawing very close to the earth, to reach out and collect His final harvest. There is going to be a rain of His supernatural as the world has never seen before. And the way He is going to touch the world is through people. If you are waiting upon Him for guidance, remember to balance both sides. This book is filled with 101+ super and natural ways He can guide you. Always remember the most important concept to applying any of them is quickening and revelation. Without them it is a dead end road.

1 Ministry: {Some translations say service}; Attendance (as a servant), aid, service, minister, office, relief. [1248 Gk Strong's] (Acts 6:1-7)
2 Hospitality: hospitable, fond of guests. From a word meaning to be friendly to one. [5382 Gk Strong's from 5384]
3 Exhortation: Imploration, solace, comfort, consolation, exhortation, entreaty. From a word meaning to invite, call near, invoke, implore, beseech, desire, entreat, etc. [3874 Gk Strong's from 3870] (1 Thessalonians 4:1)
4 Giving: To give over, share, impart. {Also translated contribute}. [3330 GK Strong's]

5   Ruling: To stand before, to preside, practice, maintain, be over, rule. {Also translated aid, superintend, lead, leadership.} [4291 Gk Strong's] (Acts 9:15)
6   Mercy: Compassionate, pity, mercy, tender. [1653 Gk Strong's] (1 Timothy 1:13)
7   Helps: Relief. From a word meaning relief, succor, participate, help, partaker, 5 support. [484 Gk from 482 Strong's] (Ex 4:14-16)
8   Governments: Steer, pilot, direct, govern. {Also translated administration}. [2941 Gk Strong's] (Exodus 18:18-26)
9   Perfecting: Complete furnishing. It's from a word meaning to complete thoroughly, repair, adjust, fit, frame, mend, make perfect, prepare, restore. [2677 Gk Strong's from 2675] (Ephesians 4:12)
10   Apostle: He that is sent, a delegate, a commissioner, ambassador. [652 Gk Strong's] Webster's states a delegate is a "representative, or a person acting for another."
11   Prophet: A foreteller, inspired speaker, poet, prophet. [4396 Gk Strong's]
12   Watchman: To lean forward, to peer into the distance, observe, await, behold, look up, wait for, keep the watch. [6822 Heb Strong's] [Anything he saw coming was announced to the people he stood watch over and protected. The Lord also called His prophets, seers].
13   Hedge: An enclosure, fence, hedge, wall. It is from the same verb, make up the hedge, meaning to wall in or around, close up, fence up, hedge, enclose, make up a wall, mason, repairer. [1447 Heb Strong's from 1443]
14   Standing: The act of abiding, tarrying, enduring, continuing, being employed, remaining, etc. [5975 Heb Strong's] Gap; Break, or breach. [6556 Heb Strong's]
15   Evangelist: One who announces good, declares, brings glad tidings, preaches. [2097 Gk Strong's]
16   Pastor: Shepherd. [750 Gk Strong's] Pastor; To tend a flock, pasture it, to graze, rule, associate with (as a friend), companion, feed, keep, shepherd, etc. [7462 Heb Strong's]
17   Teacher: Instructor. [1320 Gk Strong's] (1 Corinthians 12:28)
18   Grudgingly: With sadness, grief, heaviness, sorrow. [3077 Gk Strong's] Necessity; Constraint, distress, needful, necessary. [318 Gk Strong's]
19   Grievous: weighty, burdensome, grave, heavy. [926 Gk Strong's]
20   Cheerful: To be propitious, merry, hilarious, prompt, willing. It comes from a word meaning attractive, merciful, gracious. [2431 Gk Strong's from / 2436]
21   *11:11 story in #79 in Chapter 7*

CHAPTER 6:
GOD SPEAKS THROUGH THE HOLY SPIRIT

"...your body is the home of the Holy Spirit God gave you, and He that lives within you... So use every part of your body to give glory back to God...For you are God's temple, the home of the living God, and God has said of you, "I will live in them, and walk among them, and I will be their God and they shall be my people." (1 Corinthians 6:19,20 TLB / 2 Corinthians 6:16B TLB)

Tuning in is the key to hearing Him through His Spirit. Tuning in is not a ritualistic form of meditation, although meditation (pondering) upon His Word is great. Rather, tuning in is bringing into focus what is happening. It is a recognition of what is going on instead of just mundanely living life's routine. We are fearfully and wonderfully made, *(Psalm 139:14)* and we house the very God of the universe within. Jesus said, *"The Spirit of Truth, Whom the world cannot receive (welcome, take to its heart), because it does not see Him, nor know and recognize Him. But you know and recognize Him, for He lives with you [constantly] and will be IN you....and My Father will love him, and We will come to him and make Our home (abode, special dwelling place) with him." (John 14:17, 23 AMP)* What a privilege! How He wants to increase our measure of hearing Him!

53. HE SPEAKS THROUGH HIS STILL SMALL VOICE

"My sheep hear My voice and I know them and they follow Me." (John 10:27 NKJV) "But the Lord was not in the wind; and after the wind an earthquake; but the Lord was not in the earthquake: and after the earthquake, a fire; but the Lord was not in the fire: and after the fire, a still small voice...Elijah heard it...And, suddenly a voice came to him, and said, What are you doing Elijah?..." (1 Kings 19:11,12,13 NKJV)

Other than seeing Jesus, there is nothing more precious to a Christian's life than hearing His still small voice. To think that He can live within our hearts is amazing, but to know He also SPEAKS there is wonderful. He lives inside, and no matter how far away eternity is, He will not leave or forsake us. One can be locked up in the darkness of a room and have complete fellowship with Him. What a gracious God we serve!

There are two main ways to hear Him within our thoughts: to our mind, and through our mind. They are not the same. **Hearing His still small voice TO our mind is a totally unbiased, objective experience. Our personality has no involvement in what He says, or when He says it.** An example is being in a room with someone, while having your eyes closed. You do not know if that person will say something, and if he does, you do not know what will be said or when. There is no control over the speaker, there is no involvement in what, when or if he speaks. This way of hearing bypasses the soul or personality, because there is no personal involvement. When the Lord speaks, it is a gift — a gift of approach into your world, your private space.

The other way of hearing the Lord is THROUGH our thoughts. Through our thoughts is subjective, meaning with involvement of our soul or personality. Many have thought they heard the Lord's still small voice, when in reality it was their own thoughts. The Lord does speak to us through our thoughts, also inspires them, but this is not hearing His still small voice. It is easy for Christians who are first hearing Him to fall into error, simply because they have not yet heard His still small voice enough times TO KNOW THAT THEY KNOW they are hearing Him and not their own thoughts. Hearing Him through our thoughts is in Chapter 4, "He Speaks Through Our Personalities."

It is not easy to describe His still small voice because it is without sound. However I will try to explain the way His voice sounds to me! In listening to any kind of thought, I do not hear voice patterns, pitch, timbre, tone or depth within my mind. I merely hear thoughts. His voice "sounds" the same as my thoughts. I can receive emotion from what I hear, and can also figure out by the message how the Lord is feeling sometimes, but still there is no pitch in hearing His still small voice. The only complete distinction in hearing my thoughts vs. His voice is 100 percent unbiased objectivity. I RECOGNIZE what I've just heard is not a part of myself. It was not formulated from my own mind or personality.

I was a Christian for several years before I had the privilege to hear Him in this way. I think some are like me, either not knowing He can speak to us this way, or not recognizing Him when He does speak. His voice is so quiet, sometimes I haven't noticed He has spoken until AFTER He has said something. It is the same as being involved in the deep reverie of your own thoughts, and someone speaks into your world. You don't notice that something has been spoken until after something was said, and you tune in. When this happens you also have to tune in by trying to recall what you just heard.

Many, are like me who have lived in such "noise" they cannot hear the silence of His voice. Noise comes in many fashions and modes. The foundation of all noise is the word DISTRACTION. The Lord says: *"Be still, and know that I am God."[1]* *"Commune with your own heart upon your bed, and be still."[2]*

The easiest way I have heard Him is to be literally at rest, and in silence — in other words, resting in bed. The attitude of being quiet is not to say He is asking us to live monk style lives in silent meditation. However it is true when we live cluttered lives it is very difficult to hear His still small voice during the day when we are first learning.

HE SPEAKS IN 1ST PERSON

When the Lord speaks to me it is in four distinct ways: first, second, third and fourth person! In English grammar, "first person" refers to the speaker as the personality being reflected. Words like "I" are spoken. When the Lord speaks in first person, it is what the Bible calls mouth to mouth, even apparent speech. *"With him will I speak* *mouth to mouth, even apparently, and not in dark speeches..."*³ Moses was the friend of God, and the Lord spoke to him in direct speech.

As a personal example of this kind of speech; one time I was camping and wearily falling into my sleeping bag, I said to the Lord, "Lord I really want to hear You tonight but I also really want to sleep as I'm so tired!" I was used to hearing from Him at night, and that is why I prayed that prayer. But when I prayed it, I was just praying it, not expecting Him to say anything back to me. I heard His still small voice say, *"I AM with you."* When I heard this, it was such a very tender moment and I was deeply touched even though it was such a simple Word for Him to say. I thought about it later as to why such a simple Word would touch me so. I guess it is because what I said to Him was just a passing conversation, but He not only cared enough to listen to what I had to say, but also acknowledged it, even though what I had to say to Him was not exactly an earth-moving statement! He is so big and we are so small, and He really cares how we feel.

Another example was when I was doing dishes and just minding my own business, not really thinking about anything. His still small voice interrupted my quiet space and said, *"I love you."* Talk about a heart melter! So precious! Although I am accustomed to hearing His voice, both of these times were so precious to me. One, because I was not expecting Him to reach out to me. And two, because they had such a profound and comforting touch upon my heart. Only the Lord can bring such simplicity and yet give such a deep sense of life giving Words. When we hear Him in first person, it is a real treasure. Even though I hear His still small voice a lot, I do not hear Him speak to me in first person very often. It is a very personal and intimate comfort when He does.

HE SPEAKS IN 2ND PERSON

Hearing the Lord's still small voice in second person is hearing riddled speech. (King James translates riddled speech as "dark speech.")[4] As opposed to first person in English grammar, second person does not refer to the speaker, (as in using words like I and my) and when I hear Him speak to me in this way, He merely states a riddle. The understanding of His riddles is not an instant process. Riddles need an understanding of allegorical language[5] built through the quickening and revelation of His Spirit.

An example of this kind of speech is: *"Mike, the Statue of Liberty."* (Name changed) I heard Him speak this to me about a friend's husband. He had fallen away from the Lord and was given over to many captivities and decay. When I heard the Lord share this with me, He unveiled the beauty of His Word. The Statue of Liberty is a monument to freedom that had become cracked and decayed. However, under a great amount of work, it was later repaired and restored. He was going to do the same for Mike. What beautiful promises He speaks!

Other examples of riddled speech: one time I was praying for a minister and the Lord said, *"His shoes are too small."* I knew that the Lord wanted to extend his foundations by way of ministry. Another time I was supposed to be in a season of rest, but I was very restless. I heard the Lord ask me, *"Have you ever seen someone wrestle their nightgown?"* It was His tongue in cheek way of saying I was doing anything but rest! Another time, I was earnestly waiting for some specific direction and was hearing nothing. He finally said, *"A set of directions depends on the wind going to the right or to the left."* (Isaiah 30:21) I suddenly realized the reason I wasn't receiving any directions was because He wasn't changing direction!

Some verses using the Hebrew word for riddled speech are under footnote number:[6] Here are various reasons why the Lord chooses to speak riddles:
1. So the hearer will immediately recognize the thought as totally distinct from his own.
2. To give "meat" to chew, to teach the process of discernment and revelation.
3. To train the hearer not to be impulsive in interpretation!
4. To give the hearer confidence in the sovereignty of God. (HE speaks it, and it will happen HIS way.)
5. To give reason for complete reliance upon Him for understanding or interpretation as opposed to the independence that plain speech gives.
6. To train the hearer to WAIT upon Him.
7. To unveil the truth, in the fullness of time.[7] (Not prematurely disclosed.)

HE SPEAKS IN 3RD PERSON

Third person is not about the speaker or the hearer, but about another. When I hear His still small voice in third person, it is what the Bible calls "perceiving men's thoughts."[8] It is important to understand this gift is not horizontal. The relationship of hearing is not an "ability to tune into man." That is the counterfeit. Rather, as I am tuned into the Lord, HE speaks His still small voice of someone else's motives or even feelings. It is HIS voice, but I understand the Lord has revealed the intents and motives of another for His specific purpose.

The story of Ananias and Sapphira in Acts 5 is a scriptural example of Peter perceiving their thoughts and motives, through the Holy Spirit.

When I hear the Lord this way, it does not always reflect only one person. He may speak it as though it refers to one person, but when I begin to apply it, I realize it is about several people or it may be as large as a reference to the body of Christ. When I am identifying seasons, it often comes from these kinds of Words.

An example of this kind of hearing: (and it may sound unusual to you, but it was the Lord) I heard the Lord say, *"How are you? I am very tired."* When I heard this I began praying for all those I could think of, as I realized they were weary and needed a strengthening from the Lord. Later I heard confirmations from several people that said that particular week was very physically exhausting for much of the body of Christ.

HE SPEAKS IN 4TH PERSON

I know there's no such thing as 4th person in English grammar, but I don't know what else to call it! This "4th" person is when I hear His still small voice simultaneously superimposed over another's voice. It happens at the exact same time I hear another speak, and it is only a word, line or sentence. All of a sudden the volume goes up on my actual physical hearing by several decibels on a particular word, line or sentence. It is a physical hearing, but I also hear His inner voice at the same time. I can be in a large crowd, in another room, or outside near groups of people, and all of a sudden the volume goes up on only a portion of some sentence. The 'volume' of my physical hearing is not altered by how loud someone speaks. The volume is affected because I hear two people speak at once - the Lord and the person. Once I realize it is the Lord speaking to me, I take the time to ponder what I just heard, then apply it.

As an example of such, I had been concerned about a misunderstanding I'd had with another person. I had really been praying about it, knowing there was little I could do except pray. I heard the Lord say, *"I'll take care of it."* Then a while later as I was still fussing about it, I overheard a line on the news, where someone said, *"It's behind us now."* At the same time the newscaster said that phrase, I heard His still small voice say the same thing superimposed over it. With His superimposing, it sounded as though the volume on the TV had gone up for just that sentence, although I knew it had not. With this second confirmation, I was finally able to stop fussing and find peace about the situation.

Another time, I was in a Chinese restaurant and I heard a lady several tables away say, *"It's time for a change."* I heard the Lord's voice say the same thing at the same time she said that. My impression of her voice went up several decibels on that phrase, and even though she had been talking before and after that phrase, only that phrase stuck out because the Lord's voice brought emphasis upon it. I understood from this that a change would shortly be coming and to accept it when it came. Shortly after that, I reorganized this book for better flow and order and in the process it was in quite a state of upheaval. I remembered that Word and it gave me confirmation that even though things looked in disarray, the Lord saw this ahead of time and He would help me through it.

HE SPEAKS THROUGH HIS INNER AUDIBLE VOICE

There is another way He speaks to us on the inside that is not so still and not so small. I have heard others refer to it as His inner audible voice. I have heard Him speak this way several times, and it is quite loud, with definite emotion, and it sounds like it is outside the ear, but it really is not. Contrary to His still small voice, His inner audible voice has pitch, timber, emotion and decibels. He also speaks like this in an outward, audible voice and that is when He opens our literal, physical ears which is under another heading in this chapter.

One example that comes to mind is a good one for several reasons. First, it proves that we can hear the Lord even when we are not at rest, not quiet and are not pausing! I was "cosmic bowling" with my son and a group of teens one night. The bowling pins and our clothes glowed in the dark from ultraviolet lights, the strobe lights were flashing, and circling rainbow strobes were filtering through a layer of "fog" over the area. Of course, this was all really neat — except for the blaring stereo speakers directly behind me! My innards were shaking from the sound and I could hardly believe I used to dance to this kind of noise when I was a teen!

As I was getting ready for my turn to bowl, I heard the Lord say very loud, (it's a good thing He did!) on the inside of my thoughts, *"Chosen one."* It was so out of character for where I was that I laughed out loud (not that anyone could have heard me!) I immediately remembered the scripture that says: *"I can never be lost to your Spirit! I can never get away from my God! If I go up to heaven, you are there; it I go down to the place of the dead, you are there."* (Psalm 139: 7-8 TLB) As I thought of that verse, laughingly I said back to Him, "Lord even in here You are with me!"

54. HE SPEAKS THROUGH VISIONS

The Word says in the last days the Holy Spirit will be giving many visions and dreams. "In the last days" God said, "I will pour out my Holy Spirit upon all mankind, and your sons and daughters shall prophesy, and your young men shall see visions, and your old men dream dreams." (Acts 2:17 TLB)

Visions are a special and unique way of hearing from the Lord. Some speak of vision as a general term, as in visualizing a future perspective, or goal. However, the Greek and Hebrew refer to vision[9] as sight.

A Biblical vision is a literal, spiritual and sometimes a physical happening. It's not a product of the mind, imagination or logic. Receiving a vision is a gift from the Lord: an experience of sight, not the imagination. For purposes of definitions there are three types of visions:

1. Pictures on the screen of the mind.
2. Visions of gazing wonder.
3. Being carried away in the Spirit.

HE SPEAKS THROUGH PICTURES

Pictures, in my experience, contain one scene and usually appear in a flash without prior notice. I cannot remember seeing a picture when I was given the time to stop and look. It happens very quickly, and remains just long enough for me to notice and then it vanishes. **There are four types of pictures noted here**:

The strongest and most vivid I see are at night when asleep. Although it is not like the vividness of gazing visions, it is the most vivid of pictures. When it appears, I see, then the Lord alerts me and I understand with my conscious mind what I just saw! I also see the same kind of picture visions when I am at deep rest and communing with Him - with my eyes closed and not asleep.

One fun example happened the night after my husband and I had been playing the game Rummikub.[10] (Pronounced like Rummy-Cube, looks similar to dominoes, plays like Rummy.) That night in bed I saw a flash picture of a Rummikub with the number 222 on it. The Lord went on to say something about me, which I dutifully wrote down in the midst of my slumberous fog before crashing back to sleep. The next morning I looked up the number 222 in my Strong's Exhaustive Concordance. I was tickled to find that the number 222 means Alexandria, which is where my name Sandy comes from. It was a delightful confirmation to what I heard that night.

The second type of picture I see is when I'm awake, but with my eyes closed in worship. It is received like the others, but is more subtle and less vivid. My eyes are closed, therefore I see it on the screen of my mind. It's important to note, when it is flashed on the screen of my mind, in no way is it related to thoughts or imagination. We can have day dreams as humans and some see with their imagination quite clearly. Artists especially have this skill. A picture from the Lord is not involved with our thoughts. It comes suddenly with surprise and is not a part of us or our mind. It is an experience that happens TO us, and not through us. (Through us is our involvement with thoughts of our mind - to us is an uninvolved surprise.)

As an example of this particular kind of picture, I was standing in a service worshipping the Lord with my eyes closed and I saw a very faint, but definite picture of a pair of angel wings standing in front of me. Then I saw the wings enclose me as though in a hug. I was so touched by this I just stood there in awe. It was a simple picture, but I was thrilled. When a friend came back to her seat, I told her the story of how I had always wanted to be hugged by God. And I had just been hugged by God through His angel!

As she heard me share this, she asked a strange question. She said, "Did you see me?" I had no idea what she was talking about. Evidently she was in the corner with a pair of white filmy banner-like flags, moving them back and forth to the music in the same motion I had seen. While she was doing this, she was praying for people and said, "Lord I wish I was an angel so I could fly around and meet people's needs like they do." It was quickened to me that she was unknowingly stating what the Lord had already given her, and that was the authority to loose angels to be dispatched in the meeting in answers to her prayers. I knew she had asked that one be dispatched to me and I told her so. She said, "WOW! I wonder if the Lord would do that for everyone?"

So she got up and stood in the corner again moving her flags. I watched them glide back and forth just like angel wings. As she did this, she prayed over the meeting. Just then, the worship leader knowing nothing of our conversation suddenly changed the words in the song he was singing, then looked over to her corner and sang, "Come on the wings of angels!" I related this to him later, and he didn't even remember doing it. He had been hoping that the Lord was anointing his singing, especially when he sang prophetic words that were not written, so this was a confirmation to him. The whole experience was a wonderful blessing to each of us and it all started by a very faint and simple picture.

Another kind of picture is with the eyes opened. Of all the kinds of pictures I have seen, this is the only one seen through the actual eye. For me, this vision is not vivid. It is very hazy and happens so fast that when I notice it's there, I have enough time to blink my eyes to check out what I am seeing and then it's gone. When I say the word hazy, it is because my eyes are not actively pursuing focus. In fact once my natural eye tries to focus on what it sees, it disappears. The best way to describe it is, it is seen in the Spirit although it is seen through the natural eye.

Like the others it is always a surprise, and if I'm not in a place of reception, it can be missed. Once in church I literally saw an associate pastor as a liberty bell! I was so surprised I blinked and it disappeared. (Right after that he announced his message was going to be on bondage and freedom from captivity. The Lord has such a sense of humor and is so delightful!)

A fourth type of picture is seen on the screen of the mind and can happen with the eyes closed or open. They come in the form of a movie rather than a flash, similar to viewing still slides or a moving movie reel. Coming through the mind, it is like recalling something from memory, but what is recalled is a surprise not yet known. The "movie" floats into the mind, all the while the viewer is fully conscious and aware of his surroundings. The difference between this experience and imagination is that it is a gift: TO, NOT THROUGH the viewer. Yes, what is seen goes through the mind, but it remains with the element of surprise like other visions. It cannot be made-up or forced to happen, because it is a gift.

I have received this fourth type of movie pictures and also heard people speak in them. These experiences are just as though you are seeing and hearing a dream, but you are awake. I call them dream-pictures for lack of a better word. Anna has a good testimony of her movie screen picture visions and I have asked her to share it with you:

"In Home Group, I was drawn to a visitor named Sarah (name changed). As I thought about her, I remembered the beautiful double rainbow I had seen that afternoon. Suddenly I saw a vision of Sarah standing at the very end of a rainbow with the beautiful colors surrounding her. The rainbow and Sarah were very close to me. It was as though the whole world was in that rainbow. I felt enveloped in it as I basked in the glory of it. I asked her, "Does a rainbow mean anything to you?" She was excited and said, "Yes!" I told her I saw her standing at the very end of the rainbow and believed the Lord was wanting to encourage her with the hope of His fulfilling His promises to her. Then she related that she had seen a rainbow in the sky that afternoon while walking with her children and they had all talked about it and what it meant in the Bible.

Later Sarah was lying on the floor after being ministered to, and I saw a movie picture of myself picking up some rose petals on the table and sprinkling them upon her. I was telling her that these were representative of the heavenly pot of gold at the end of the rainbow. They represented the blessings the Lord was going to pour out upon her. Even though I procrastinated, and the meeting changed focus, the movie in my mind would not leave. Finally, I stood up, gathered some rose petals and said, "I felt I was supposed to do this, but I procrastinated." Then I told her the rose petals I was sprinkling upon her represented the heavenly pot of gold at the end of the rainbow and the Lord was going to bless her.

In the following church service, Pastor knew nothing about any of this. He suddenly announced that he wanted us to bless someone financially without our knowing who it was and he took up an offering. Then to my shock he walked over to Sarah and said, "The Lord wants you to know you are very much loved, and this is a representation of it. The offering was taken just for you." Then he prophesied over her. She had just received part of her pot of gold!"

The previous four kinds of picture-visions are similar to hearing the Lord speak TO our mind, vs THROUGH our mind. Seeing a picture through our mind is vulnerable to error and flesh. There is a fine line between imagination and picture visions, however the Lord certainly does inspire our thoughts. But for purposes of this kind of movie picture-vision, the line is best drawn between participation and gift. A gift has no personal subjective participation. There is no alteration of what is seen through the choice of one's will and desire, but it remains a surprise. A gift is WITHOUT KNOWING if, what, where, when, why, it is to be seen. If the above lines up, then it can be relied upon to be untainted by flesh. (This objectivity is only in distinction of our flesh vs the Holy Spirit. The enemy can give objective visions as well, covered in chapter 10.)

The environment for receiving visions from Him is the same as hearing His still small voice: being in a place of reception. Worship, praise, and communion are foundational to being in a place to receive. When we are in that place of relationship with Him, our surroundings fade away. The focus of our thoughts and hearts is turned toward Him, and all else naturally falls aside in giving Him priority. Worship, praise, communion, and relationship are moment by moment decisions of the will. When we choose those moments we are able to receive because we have opened the door to Him.

Because I receive pictures from Him at night, I try to keep a notebook and flashlight by my bed. I have experienced many times seeing a wonderful picture, even pondering it a while before I go back to sleep, but cannot remember it when I awaken. Now my notebook is referred to after many years and my memory is refreshed. Perhaps if you begin to hear the Lord in this manner, you will want to do the same.

HE SPEAKS THROUGH GAZING WONDERS

*"...Peter went up on the housetop to pray, about the sixth hour. Then he became very hungry and wanted to eat; but while they made ready, he **fell into a trance**..."* (Acts 10:9-10 NKJV)

Peter fell into a trance and saw the same vision three times about the Gentiles. *(Acts 10:10-16)* Obviously God wanted to get Peter's attention. Peter had a preconceived opinion about the Gentiles that God wanted changed. It is recorded again in *Acts 11:5-10*. Also Paul had this kind of trance vision while in prayer in *Acts 22:17-21*.

I have noticed several things when the Lord gives me this type of vision. First, even if it is an experience happening TO me, at no time has it gone against my will. At any time I am free to have the vision close down or stop (although it being Him, I don't want Him to stop.) It is not something that takes possession of me and I lose control over my choice or will. In fact the liberty and freedom of my will is such, and the Holy Spirit being so gentle, that at the slightest hesitation He will stop. He desires our absolute childlike faith in a Heavenly Father Who is our Daddy. It is the enemy who binds, hinders, numbs, and chains up our wills. "Gifts" from the enemy are without freedom and liberty.

Secondly, these visions have a lovely common denominator. In some form or another He knocks at my door, and I either hear His voice, recognize His Spirit, or know His Presence. After I recognize Him, I invite Him and receive Him. The recognition and invitation are within my heart. My soul and spirit "leaps" when He is so near, and I either call His Name, or recognize that it is Him. The recognition of the Lord gives great joy, perfect peace, and invokes a strong drawing and longing for Him. It's like His Presence is a giant magnet and I instantly respond to Him.

I have never received Him without my state of spirit, mind, will, and body being completely yielded. It's as though His mere Presence gives me the desire to yield my every fiber to Him to do with as He wills. Always, it is in complete childlike faith in a Father Who is a Perfect Daddy. He knows me and I have no other need. He is EVERYTHING. Yielding to HIM, has always been the focus of every experience in these kinds of visions.

Another detail has to do with the eyes. It is as though the scales are peeled away and I see with absolute gazing clarity. The sight is so real, so vivid, so clear! It is like no sight we see on earth. It makes 20/20 vision seem dull. Emphasis should be on the word "gaze." Webster's defines gaze: "to fix the eyes in a steady and intent look...fixed and prolonged attention...stare." Peter, in Acts 11:6 mentions he fastened his eyes on the sight. That is a characteristic of this kind of vision. It is an absolute fixed focus on what He is showing. The concentration of the eyes is absolute and does not waver, it's like describing a staring contest. Balak mentioned he saw a vision and used the phrase, *"having his eyes opened." (Numbers 24:4 and 16 KJ)*

Visions of gazing wonder are different from picture visions. I cannot remember receiving a picture vision when I had time to stare. They happen too quickly. Wonder visions occur by gazing or staring at the sight for a period of time. Picture visions do not have the extreme clarity of reality. Wonder visions are very clear and the sight is three dimensional as if one is there, but it actually looks more "real" than real life.

The following is a vision of gazing wonder the Lord gave me as quoted from my journal: "When I went to sleep on November 14, 1985, I had a strong yearning for Jesus. As I slept, He came to me and opened my eyes. I saw a huge, gigantic banner unfolding across the sky. It said, "THE LORD JESUS CHRIST." Suddenly I found myself in heaven looking down upon a vast desert. It was dry, brown, flat, and immense. As I gazed upon the lifeless desert, someone was standing above and behind me declaring the scroll of Isaiah 35:

"The wilderness and the solitary place shall be glad for them; and the desert shall rejoice, and blossom as the rose. It shall blossom abundantly, and rejoice even with joy and singing: the glory of Lebanon shall be given unto it, the excellency of Carmel and Sharon, they shall see the glory of the Lord, the excellency of our God. Strengthen ye the weak hands, and confirm the feeble knees. Say to them of a fearful heart, be strong, fear not: behold your God will come with vengeance; He will come and save you. Then the eyes of the blind shall be opened, and the ears of the deaf shall be unstopped. Then shall the lame leap as an hart, and the tongue of the dumb sing: for in the wilderness shall waters break out, and streams in the desert. And the parched ground shall become a pool, and the thirsty land springs of water..." (Isaiah 35 KJ)

After Isaiah 35 had been announced, I heard the Lord say, *"And the desert shall blossom as a rose. It shall happen all at once, and it shall happen suddenly."* Immediately I saw the desert come to life. The sight was astounding and oh so beautiful! Everywhere blossoms emerged: this dry, lifeless region became a spacious garden of color and beauty. Then I came out of the gazing vision. As I woke, I was still in awe of what I'd seen, because it was so beautiful. I knew the Lord was speaking a promise of what He would be doing to our dry desert like lives. He was going to rain His Presence upon us and we would emerge with life and beautiful blossoms."

HE SPEAKS THROUGH CARRYING AWAY

In Ezekiel's vision, he viewed the sights as he was lifted, or carried away, while in the spirit. It is recorded in: Ezekiel 8:3, 11:1 and 43:5.

This is similar to the experience of "flying" in one's dreams at night. It is a state where you feel as light and free as a feather, carried by the wings of angels, all the while gazing at the sight around you. An example of this is a dream where I was sent overseas on an intercession assignment. I was cognizant of an angel carrying me, and all the while we were flying low so I was able to see the ocean underneath me and see the islands coming up. Another time, after I had been taken to see certain things, I was flying towards earth and I could see the earth first as a little ball, then it got bigger and bigger as we approached. I realized I was being carried by an angel, as I could see our shadows.

Paul spoke of himself in 2 Corinthians 12. *"... I will come to visions and revelations of the Lord: I know a man in Christ who fourteen years ago — **whether in the body I do not know, or whether out of the body I do not know**, God knows — such a one **was caught up** to the third heaven. And I know such a man — whether in the body or out of the body I do not know, God knows — how he was caught up into Paradise and heard inexpressible words..." (vs 1-4 NKJV)*. Whether he knew how, Paul at least knew he had been carried away!

VISIONS HAVE A PURPOSE

The following is a list of Biblical references about the purposes of visions:

1. Encouragement, hope, and promise
    (To Abram) *Genesis 15:1-6*
2. Announcement of judgment
    (To Samuel about Eli) *1 Samuel 3:1-18*
3. Reveals secrets and an interpretation of a dream (To Daniel) *Daniel 2:19*
4. Announcement of a servant's calling
    (To Zacharias for John) *Luke 1:22*
5. Announcement of good tidings
    (The women saw a vision of angels announcing Jesus was alive.) *Luke 24:23*
6. Guidance and explicit instructions
    (To Ananias for Saul) *Acts 9:10*
7. Changes an opinion and gives an assignment
    (To Peter about the Gentiles) *Acts 11:5-10*
8. Guidance to change locations
    (For Paul to go to Macedonia) *Acts 16:9*

This section explained three types of visions: pictures, gazing wonders, and being carried away in the Spirit. Remember, visions are completely objective. They happen TO US, not through us. They are and always will be a gift, not something we make happen, seek after or are a part of our imagination.

55. HE SPEAKS THROUGH HOLY SPIRIT DREAMS

Numbers 12:6, 8 in the King James version refers to visions and dreams as *"dark speeches."*[11] Dreams and visions are like puzzles needing to be unraveled to be understood. Dreams are allegories at night that tell a story by giving a sequence of events. There are three kinds of dreams: dreams by the Holy Spirit, dreams of the soul,[12] and enemy dreams.

The pure and perfect gift is a dream from the Holy Spirit. This usually has some mention of the Lord and always glorifies Him, containing His principles and teachings according to the Bible. An example of a pure dream from the Holy Spirit is the following as paraphrased from my journal:

"This was an amazing supernatural dream where I actually experienced the entire thing including the Lord's Presence as it was happening. I was in a large non-charismatic evangelical church worshipping with a full congregation. I was in the balcony and could see everything. There was not a person in the entire place that did not feel and respond to the Presence of God. It was as though He was a giant magnet and drawing out the wild and total praises of His people in this building. There were waves and waves of the Holy Spirit upon the people, and you could hear people's emotional responses and see their subsequent hands raising in unison. I felt His Presence so strong, that He was literally evoking my strong responses.

Then I saw a candlestick standing on the podium, and a shadow slowly passed across it. Suddenly you could hear a pin drop, the people were so quiet. It was an absolute holy hush. I knew it was the glory of God just like Moses' story when he had asked to see His glory. *(Exodus 33:18-23)*

Later in the service, I saw an old friend, who in real life saddened me by breaking off our letter writing because of differences in church doctrine. I leaned over to her and told her we were now talking the same language and were in agreement. I was speaking not just of she and I, but of the whole congregation. As I did this, there were women who had miniature little scissors in their hands, and were busy snipping tiny fragments off the dead, split ends of people's hair. Their tiny scissors were snipping so fast they were a blur. While in the dream, I knew it was an allegory of the Lord cutting away the denomination splits (splitting hairs) and dead works and that these women were angels.

Still in the dream, as I was talking to someone about the awesome meeting, I mentioned that the Lord was also doing the same thing with the Catholics. Someone else mentioned Australia. When I awakened, I heard the Lord say, *"Ecumenical movement. The Spirit is moving. World wide. They're done being spectators."* Then I saw a picture vision of my holding the steering wheel in my car, and the wheel had such a strong pull on it that I just finally let the wheel lead the way! [I literally felt the tug of the wheel, even though this was a picture vision.] Then I heard the Lord say, *"Divine direction."* By this picture, He was saying that we are coming to a time where His leading would be so strong, that it would be difficult to "drive" ourselves away from His Presence, as the tug or force in going our own way would be very tiring. This dream and subsequent Word from Him was an awesome promise of His breaking denominational barriers, where nothing else matters but worshipping Him and responding to His wonderful Presence."

DREAMS HAVE A PURPOSE

The following are scripture references that reveal His desires within dreams:

Genesis 20:3-7: Warning to halt man's purpose, unintentional sin (to Abimelech)
Genesis 28:12-15: Announcement of future promise (to Jacob)
Genesis 31:10: Divine understanding and guidance (for Jacob)
Genesis 31:24: Warning of man's purpose (to Laban for Jacob)
Genesis 37:5-7: Promises for the future (for Joseph)
Genesis 40:5: Foreknowledge of a mystery (about the butler and baker, preparation for Joseph's deliverance)
Genesis 41:1-7: Warning of famine
(to Pharaoh, for Joseph's promotion)
Judges 7:13-14: Encouragement and confirmation (for Gideon's ears)
I Kings 3:5-15: Promise of future blessing (to Solomon)
Daniel chapter 2: Announcement for the future of the kingdom (to Nebuchadnezzar)
Daniel chapter 7: Prophetic revelation (to Daniel for world)
Matthew 1:19,21: Encouragement and confirmation (to Joseph)
Matthew 2:19-21: Exposure of enemy plan and guidance for deliverance (to Joseph)
Matthew 27:19: Confrontation of truth (to Pilate's wife)

When the Lord began giving me dreams, I interpreted them literally. After a long season of going around the track, He revealed to me HIS understanding! Remember, when you receive dreams, they are usually given in allegory form and spoken in HIS spiritual language not your own.

This is not always the case, as I heard one man who functions in the office of a prophet in the body of Christ, say that his personal dreams are almost always literal and happen in real life within a 2-3 day time frame of dreaming the dream. Other dreams that he has for nations and countries are also literal and occur within about a year. However, I consider his gifts the exception. Dreams usually are meat to chew and are not usually immediately understood in every detail, and most often are to be interpreted in allegorical language.

It takes time to ponder and allow the Lord to unfold His revelation. The more complex the allegory, the stronger the meat. Strong meat takes time to discern and understand and should not be impulsively assimilated. If you swallow without chewing, you may end with a stomach ache. I've had a few!

As mentioned before, if you hear from Him in this manner, consider keeping a pen, note pad and flashlight by your bed. Ask the Lord's help to give you the discipline to wake up enough to jot notes down, so that in the morning you can write it out thoroughly. He is merciful to answer your request. If you really want to hear from the Lord, He will help you! Often I thought I would remember and I did not. The sooner the dream is written out thoroughly, the better. I have found that when the Holy Spirit gives dreams, every jot and tittle come to pass and are very important to His message. The details will be important to you and they will probably be referred to after months or even years.

56. HE SPEAKS THROUGH OPENING OUR LITERAL EYES

A close friend of mine was in the bathroom gazing at her apricot towels. Suddenly the word PRESS appeared on the towel. That coupled with other confirmations was the Lord's encouragement this book would be printed.

There are times He literally opens our senses. We encounter the "real" hearing in our flesh. Elisha prayed for the Lord to open his servants literal eyes so he might see the real issue of what was taking place with the angelic hosts. *(2 Kings 6:17)* In daily living, man is not usually gifted to have the eyes to see the angels at work. Elisha obviously knew what it meant to have the Lord actually open his eyes so he might see.

I heard a funny story about a man who was ministering Words to an audience. He said something like, "No I don't know. No I don't know! I tell you I don't know!" It turned out that he had seen an angel standing in the back of the room, pointing to a lady. The minister asked the angel what the lady's name was. Every time he asked, he heard the angel say, "You know." So he consequently said, "No, I don't know." Finally the angel spelled with his finger in the air, Uno. Her name was Uno, pronounced "You know!"

57. HE SPEAKS THROUGH OPENING OUR LITERAL EARS

Job was speaking to the Lord, "I have heard of You by the hearing of the ear, But now my eye sees You." (Job 42:5 NKJV)

In the same manner of literal seeing, it is possible to hear His audible voice, angelic voices, heavenly music, etc. through our literal ears. Anna and a friend were worshipping the Lord while traveling. Afterwards they sat in silence basking in the Lord's Presence. Both of them suddenly heard a heavenly choir. Each thought the other had turned on a cassette tape.

Another time Anna was driving late at night after a storm and as she rounded a blind corner, she heard a voice YELL in her ear, "SLOW DOWN!" She slammed on her brakes and suddenly a huge tree loomed across the road. She had slowed just enough to swerve on to the shoulder and miss it.

The Lord opened my ears and I heard a beautiful trumpet fanfare. When it finished, I saw a vision of the heavens open and heard and saw His rain pour in a mighty gush. He gave that to me in context to a promise of His rains coming. (The pouring out of His Spirit, as in Joel 2.)

58. HE SPEAKS THROUGH OPENING OUR LITERAL SMELL

I know of several who have had their sense of smell opened. They have smelled sweet smelling perfume or flower blossoms while in worship or prayer. I smelled bread baking in an oven when the Lord told me it was the fullness of time for His manna to come forth. I have also smelled sulphur and smoke during a warfare battle with the enemy.

Anna was asleep and was awakened by a wonderful aroma. When it quickly left, she was so disappointed that she asked the Lord if she could smell it again. Ever so gently, as though wafted on a gentle breeze, she smelled it again. This happened many times. Each time she tried to analyze what she was smelling. At first the primary smell seemed to be spicy like carnations, but then again she would smell a rose or a lily, or gardenia. It seemed as though it was the culmination of walking through a fragrant garden.

She did a word search on spice and found the scripture, *"His cheeks [are] as a bed of spices, [as] sweet flowers: his lips [like] lilies, dropping sweet smelling myrrh." (Song of Solomon 5:13 KJ)* She had forgotten this was the description of His face! She realized He had His face next to hers!!

59. HE SPEAKS THROUGH OPENING OUR LITERAL TOUCH

Many experience their sense of touch being opened, especially while operating in the Word of Knowledge in the I Corinthians 12 gifts. They can feel warmth in their body where the Lord is healing someone else. While in prayer and intercession, some feel in their body the wounds of another. I have also heard testimonies where someone who was being healed literally felt His hand touch them. Some have felt angels arms next to theirs during worship.

I was in a meeting where the speaker was calling out Words of Knowledge, and a member in the audience stood up and said, "There's someone here who has a strong pain in their right shoulder! Please come, so I can pray for you, as I have to get rid of this pain!" He knew the pain in his shoulder was not his own, and sure enough a lady came forward. It was quite humorous, since the meeting was being conducted by an out of town guest who was fluent in prophesy and Words of knowledge. He laughed too and the meeting went on while the man in the audience came forward and prayed for the woman.

60. HE SPEAKS THROUGH OPENING OUR LITERAL TASTE

The scripture says, "Taste and see the Lord is good." (Psalm 34:8 KJ) Maybe David knew what that really meant! Ezekiel ate God's Word, the roll. "So I opened my mouth and he caused me to eat that roll...Then did I eat it; and it was in my mouth as honey for sweetness." (Ezekiel 3:2-3 KJ)

61. HE SPEAKS THROUGH BEING TRANSPORTED IN HIS SPIRIT

There is a kind of "renewed" transportation that will be taking place in these last days. It is being transported in the Spirit. John the disciple had an interesting thing happen in his vision: *"And I, John, am the one who heard and saw these things. And when I heard and saw, I fell down to worship at the feet of the angel who showed me these things. And he said to me, "Do not do that; **I am a fellow** servant of yours and **of your brethren** the prophets and of those who heed the words of this book; worship God." (Revelation 22:8-9 NASB)* The man who appeared in his vision was a man, not an angel! Now how did that occur unless he was literally transported in the Spirit?

Another time after Philip finished ministering to the eunuch, the Holy Spirit literally transported him out of the desert and back to town. *"And when they were come up out of the water, <u>the Spirit of the Lord caught away Philip</u>, that the eunuch saw him no more: and he went on his way rejoicing. But <u>Philip was found</u> at Azotus: and passing through he preached in all the cities, till he came to Caesarea."* (Acts 8:26-40 KJ)

I recently heard of a man who was in bed groaning and praying under a painful pancreas attack. Suddenly, a Mexican man from a small village who had been praying to be used by the Lord, appeared at his bedside. The Mexican said, "I have been sent to pray for you!" He was a real man with real skin. He was <u>not</u> an angel!

Anna took two others to an elegant birthday lunch in another town. It ended up that one of them got a nail in her crepe so they all received their meals at no cost. They were very blessed. As they drove to see the view from a nearby mountain, they were praising the Lord and lost track of the time. As she looked at the clock, she saw it was a little after 4:00 with choir practice at 5:00. She said, "Uh oh, looks like we are going to be late for choir practice." They continued to sing on the way home and were having a wonderful time. When they came to a town which should have been 1 hour and 20 minutes away from the top of the mountain, she looked at the clock and it was 4:25 - an hour's jump in time from the mountain top!

I have also heard of testimonies where people have been in two locations at the same time. One was at home in their body, which was in a trance, vision, or just dreaming. And the second was where they were transported to another place to minister. — Only the other place was real, their ministry was real, the people were real, the people remembered the ministry later, and it wasn't just a dream! In these last days people will be transported in their dreams at night to far away lands, and they will minister to other people prepared and waiting for them! Wonderful and incredible and exciting things are going to happen in these last days. God is going to pull out the plugs to bring in His last day harvest! He's going to use every available vessel to reach out and touch a hurting world. All He wants, is our, "Yes Lord, send me!"

62. HE SPEAKS THROUGH FALLING UNDER HIS POWER

"The priests could not stand, to minister by reason of the cloud." "He said unto them, "I AM He", they went backward, and fell to the ground." "And when I saw it, I fell upon my face." "There remained no strength in me...and my face toward the ground." "I fell at his feet as dead..." (2 Chronicles 5:14 KJ, John 18:6 KJ, Ezekiel 1:28 KJ, Daniel 10:8-9 KJ, Revelation 1:17 KJ) *Also Saul fell to the earth when the light shined from heaven. He was*

confronted with the truth of Jesus and the choices he had made in his life." (Acts 9:4)

If you've ever been to meetings where people are being prayed for, you may have seen them fall. Man's physical frame doesn't hold up well under the power of God. (Sometimes the muscles feel like jelly.)

During this experience, when people are under His power, they can be asleep, or even unconscious as though in a trance, or they can be awake. It is a time when the Holy Spirit is personally ministering on deeper levels of the subconscious and spirit. It can be a time of strong deliverance from the enemy, or the person may receive a vision at this time, or hear the Lord speak to them personally. Healing can take place, as well as gifts and anointing imparted from the Holy Spirit.

I have seen people who fell under His power and were never touched by another. I have seen people fall who were touched by the person praying. I have seen them fall softly as though on billows of clouds, I have seen them fall so hard it is as though they were knocked over, and yet they didn't feel a thing. Anna had a precious experience of falling under the power of His Presence, and she has always referred to it as being in the midst of His glory cloud and feeling His intense love.

I have had several experiences, all different. One poor experience happened when I was "prayed" for by an evangelist. I was pushed over, fell on a concrete floor, hurt my tail bone and the back of my head. I had a migraine headache the rest of the day. I wouldn't recommend being prayed for by people who make an effort to push people down! I remember lying on the floor in pain, and certainly didn't hear from the Lord.

And yet I have also been blessed when people reached toward me in prayer and I literally felt something flow through my body, fell under the genuine power of it, and then got right back up again! (However I would not recommend that as He often ministers in the time while you are lying in His Presence.) I also have "fallen" under His power at night when I was already lying down in bed! It's the same experience, only my body was already lying down. (I have always fallen under His power when He has visited me at night during gazing visions.) When His genuine, powerful, Presence has touched me like this, I have always felt that He imparted something within me of Himself.

My recommendation is if you really want to get prayed for but you are afraid of falling, just kneel in the prayer line, or when the person comes to pray for you, ask if you may sit on the floor. There is nothing wrong with that, and if it takes a barrier away from your heart in receiving a wonderful blessing from the Lord, then do it.

Sometimes I see people literally get drunk in the Spirit when they fall under His power. They laugh, they fall, they can not walk and can barely crawl. They can barely sit. It is very funny to watch! The person tries to get up and move but simply can't. This only makes them laugh harder. It is a great time of refreshing to the person. I have no idea why the Lord does this, but it is scriptural! *"For these are not drunken, as ye suppose, seeing it is but the third hour of the day. (Acts 2:15 KJ) And be not drunk with wine, wherein is excess; but be filled with the Spirit;" (Ephesians 5:18 KJ)*

    I heard a testimony of a gal who fell under the power of His Holy Spirit, and her experience portrayed so much, I asked her permission to share it with you. As a background to her story, she had just been rejected by her husband, and was also seriously doubting whether God really loved her. During this time, she had been praying and said to the Lord, "Father I love You" and He responded back by saying, *"No You don't."* She was flabbergasted that she had heard Him at all, let alone by what He said to her. It took her a few days of thinking about it to finally admit that He was right, she did not really love Him. She began to cry out, "Lord show me how to love You. I can't see You, I can't touch You, I can't feel You, I don't know how to love somebody like that!"

    Later a person gave her a Word of Knowledge of having seen a picture-vision of a chain around her neck with a lock and sign stating "Keep out." She knew it was an accurate portrayal of her heart, and that she had put the sign there herself. She wanted Him to love her, but at the same time she was afraid of Him and wanted to keep Him at a distance. She cried and prayed more earnestly, "Lord help me to love You. Help Me to believe You love me!" This all led up to the night she was slain in the power of His Holy Spirit.

    During a series of special meetings, she had been thinking about the Holy Spirit, and questioning some of the things going on in the meetings. She kept saying, "Holy Spirit, if You are there, and You are real, I need to meet You." When she went up for prayer she was slain in His Spirit. While she was lying there, she felt Someone standing on her feet. Wanting to get up and run away, she finally asked, "Why are You standing upon my feet?" *"I'm the Holy Spirit and I'm standing on your feet because I don't want you to get up, I want you to stay here."* During this whole time she kept smelling her favorite candy bar, Three Musketeers, and was really enjoying the smell. She knew that it was His humorous way of saying He was One of the Three in the Three Musketeers, and it was His delectable way of introducing Himself. He was light hearted and humorous with her and yet at the same time serious.

    The next thing she remembered was His taking her to heaven. She remembered briefly passing through a place where there was grass, trees, flowers, a river and golden pathways. She instinctively knew this place would be hers some day for it was very familiar to her. Then He took her to a room and Jesus was there. He put His arms out to her and said, *"Welcome. This is the place that I have prepared for you."* She immediately remembered the scripture that said, *"In My father's house are many mansions and I go to prepare a place for you."* Her room was made of knotty pine, and in the corner was a big feather bed with a fluffy white comforter and a big rocking chair beside the bed. *"He said, this is the place I have prepared for you. Do you remember what I did before I went into My ministry? I worked with My Dad, and he was a carpenter. I built this for you with My own hands."* She was deeply touched because she realized He really did build it with His own hands, and with so much love just especially for her. Then He picked her up and placed her in the bed. He held her face in His hands and kept kissing her face saying how much He loved her. She felt so protected and loved and safe and warm and secure and at peace. He kept touching her face as He sat beside her in the chair. He continued to do this and speak to her as she drifted off to sleep.

After the vision, while she was in worship, she met the Father. Her earthly father had not been a good example and she knew she looked at God with the same eyes. She had always felt that God was either frustrated with her, angry with her or disappointed in her. So it was hard for her to let Him in. Then in worship she saw the angels and a big white heart with streamers falling down touching her face. The Father was there and kept saying to her, *"I love You."* Finally, something broke within her and she said, "I love You Papa!" She never wanted to come out of that place of the Father's heart. It was so precious to her.

She had several confirmations to this vision. Someone said she had been very still and "out" for at least three hours. A lady later ministering from the podium looked straight at her and said, "There really are real houses made of real wood there!" Later, while she also was relating her testimony from the pulpit, she said she knew there were people sitting in the audience who needed to experience the Lord's love. As she spoke this, one young lady's face in particular kept coming into her mind, but she said nothing. After she shared her testimony, the pastor prayed for her and again she was slain in the Spirit. She passed through the same place in heaven as before and into the Lord's welcoming arms in the special place He had prepared for her. While still in the spirit, she saw this same young lady standing below on the golden pathway. Then she heard the pastor call out this one's name. Later she found out that she was prayed for and also fell under the power. This lady also received an awesome experience of the Lord's love.

As another confirmation to her being kissed on the face, five months prior to her experience, I had been listening to a tape where the speaker was sharing how much Jesus loves us as a bridegroom loves His wife and that we should feel loved like a bride. As he said this, I immediately thought to myself, "I'm too ugly to feel loved like that." I winced at thinking that, knowing He had heard, and apologized to the Lord for thinking that, because of course I knew that He loved me. But it came from deep inside my heart and I knew He knew it. That night I heard Him say to me, *"Father's Day. I long for you.* **Shower you with kisses***. I meant that. Ugly. Perverted."* He meant He didn't see me as ugly and the enemy had perverted my ability to truly receive the Father's love.

As a confirmation to my hearing this, a month later I was in bed and my son came to wish me good night. I had been reading past rhema, and it was opened to the page where I had heard the above. My son was playfully looming over me as though he was going to kiss me good night, and then he hesitated and started searching my face to decide just exactly where he was going to plant it. He waited so long (and grinning all the while) I said, "I'm going to be a nervous wreck by the time you kiss me!" Suddenly he showered me with kisses all over my face. I was giggling and then still under an attack of kisses, I remembered the rhema. I said, "Hey did you read that page when you leaned over????" He didn't know what I was talking about so I pointed to the line, "Shower you with kisses." He thought that very funny. I thought it quite an amazing confirmation that the Lord was serious about getting through exactly how He feels.

63. HE SPEAKS THROUGH TREMBLING IN HIS PRESENCE

The Lord reigns; Let the peoples tremble! He dwells between the cherubim; Let the earth be moved! (Psalm 99:1 NKJV) Tremble, O earth, at the presence of the Lord, At the presence of the God of Jacob; (Psalm 114:7 NKJV) Hear the word of the Lord, You who tremble at His word: "Your brethren who hated you, Who cast you out for My name's sake, said, 'Let the Lord be glorified, That we may see your joy.' But they shall be ashamed." (Isaiah 66:5 NKJV)

Along the same lines of falling under His Power, is trembling under His Power. When the manifested power of the Lord shows up, the human body is such a weak vessel, our muscles are not able to handle it. Sometimes His power will rest upon one's hand and the hand will tremble. Sometimes the legs will shake and tremble, sometimes the whole body. I have seen people who look like they are being plugged into the light socket of God's electricity, and they shake all over. Sometimes others who touch those who tremble receive a touch from the Lord, just like electricity is passed from one to another! Through trembling, the Lord speaks to us of how awesome He is.

One time years ago, Anna and I were attending a conference on spiritual gifts. When the time came for body ministry, Anna's hand started to tremble and I was awestruck looking at it. The Lord's Presence was really upon her. Then she heard the Lord's inner <u>audible</u> voice say, *"Touch them on the forehead."* So she stepped out of her chair and starting touching people on the forehead. They all fell under the power of the Holy Spirit, in their chairs and on the floor. It was pretty amazing since we had never experienced this degree of ministry before.

There was one particular lady who was being ministered to by a group of Pastors and as Anna walked by she stretched her hand through the circle and touched the lady's forehead. The lady went down - POW! The pastors were so surprised that they all looked around trying to find who touched her! Anna was so shy she kept on moving and they never knew. I was hysterically laughing watching the whole thing in the background because I knew how shy she was by watching the expressions on her face. The next day they announced from the pulpit that there was a lady there the day before who was touching people on the forehead, and they wanted to find her because they had a testimony of a gal saying, "God touched me! I felt electricity go though me and I'm healed!" Anna shrunk down in her chair, and a few minutes later we exited out the back door! I'm sure the Lord got a good laugh out of the whole experience, as He told her that He had "kissed" her in front of her brethren! She being shy, responded like any Christian girl would, being kissed in public by her Beloved for the first time!

64. HE SPEAKS THROUGH ANGELS

Paul said, "Do not neglect to show hospitality to strangers, for by this some have entertained angels without knowing it." (Hebrews 13:2 NASB)
"Are they not all ministering spirits sent forth to minister for those who will inherit salvation?" (Hebrews 1:14 NKJV)

"And he went out, and followed him; and did not know that what was done by the angel was real but thought he was seeing a vision. When they were past the first and the second guard posts, they came to the iron gate that leads to the city; which opened to them of its own accord: and they went out, and went down one street; and immediately the angel departed from him." (Acts 12:9,10 NKJV)

Angels play an important role in our life, for they serve us as a gift from God. One of the reasons they do not make a habit of openly declaring themselves is because they are created to glorify Jesus and to serve, not to publish their own identity and find followers.

In this day and time there is much renewed interest in angels. Unfortunately, the new age movement has also incorporated this. So beware when you listen to angel stories. Be on guard for any enticing story that would encourage a long time relationship with a guardian angel or even a friendship. The Bible says the enemy can be camouflaged as an angel of light, and the new age movement encourages having spirit guides who can appear in the form of an angel. They say each person should get in touch with these beings and have a relationship with them.

The difference is subtle, for angels are active in our lives, and they do love and encourage us, and sometimes talk to us, as the Bible says. I have read many stories of people who were delivered by angels, and I believe in times of intense long term trauma, an angel can have a temporary relationship with that person. However, the Lord wants us to seek Him and have a relationship with Him. He doesn't want our faith displaced towards angels being our source, HE wants to be our source.

I personally believe that angels are dispatched with assignment, at the moment we pray. *(Psalm 103:20)* I also believe an intercessor's faith can actually strengthen the angel's ability to fight through enemy territory as well as dispatch immediate help to people in need. However the angels do not want the glory for this, as they are here to serve the Heavenly Father and us who are heirs of salvation. Stories about angels can be very encouraging, just keep your priorities straight and love our Father more for sending them to help us. *(Colossians 2:18)*

I had a funny experience having to do with angels. The Lord was trying to teach me that angels are my helpers, and they are dispatched with assignment the moment I pray. They are actually waiting for us to understand our authority, so they can get busy and do what they do best. Often we have the resources available to help many people, but they are not dispatched via the angels because we do not pray.

Anyway, I had been thinking about angels, and wondering about my guardian angel. Because I hear so much from the Lord at night, I often get enemy opposition. So I have learned to take authority over such until I hear Him clearly. One night I was wondering what giant, husky, warring angel the Lord had posted beside me and feeling kind of cradled by the thought. Then bam, I heard the enemy, so I rebuked it in Jesus Name, then prayed the blood of Jesus over our door posts and then asked for a nice giant warring angel to stand guard.

I heard the enemy say, "I think they want us to leave!" As I heard that, I realized the enemy was talking about the angel standing guard as well as myself and I was encouraged. Then I saw a picture vision of the face of a very pretty girl angel. Her smile was so loving and precious and it was kind of a tongue in cheek smile. I saw her eyes literally twinkle, and then she winked at me! I was so astonished and then immediately I thought, *"THIS is my husky, giant, warring angel?????"* My faith went to about zero. Then I remembered the subtle ploy of trusting in angels, instead of the Lord, and also the authority He's given me. It was very funny and I instinctively knew that the reason she winked was to say, "I guess we showed them!"

I learned something that day. Number one, I was a chauvinist! Number two, the Lord wanted my faith in Him and in the authority He's given me, not my faith in the angel standing guard. Number three, my authority must be more than I thought, or else with so much opposition, I would certainly need a nice, burly angel to protect me - at least one with a sword! [Sorry Lord, I just had to put that in!] The whole thing was very funny to me and we all had a good laugh.

HE SPEAKS THROUGH GIFTS OF THE SPIRIT

"But the manifestation of the Spirit is given to every man to profit withal. For to one is given by the Spirit the WORD OF WISDOM; to another the WORD OF KNOWLEDGE by the same Spirit; To another FAITH by the same Spirit; to another GIFTS OF HEALING by the same Spirit; To another the WORKING OF MIRACLES; to another PROPHECY; to another DISCERNING OF SPIRITS; to another divers kinds of TONGUES; to another the INTERPRETATION OF TONGUES..." (1 Corinthians 12:8-10 KJ)

65. HE SPEAKS THROUGH THE WORD OF WISDOM[13]

The word of wisdom is the supernatural gift, imparting insight to hone in on a core issue. It clears away the clutter by giving understanding and revealing the true nature of things.

Frequently the word of wisdom is evident in a problem solving situation, such as when the Pharisees posed a problem as to whether it was lawful to pay taxes to Caesar. Jesus honed in on the issue by presenting the picture of Caesar's face on the coin and saying, *"...render therefore unto Caesar the things which are Caesar's; and unto God, the things that are God's." (Matthew 22:21 KJ)*

I heard a line from a sermon that was quickened to my ears as a word of wisdom. The pastor gave an example of an Indian in a service who gave the following response to a message: "Heavy wind, loud thunder, but no rain." I thought the Word spoke well of promoting miracle ministries where people's hearts become expectant, then disappointed. Such heavy promotion also subtly alters priorities to exalt the supernatural experience over a relationship with the Lord.

66. HE SPEAKS THROUGH THE WORD OF KNOWLEDGE [14]

The word of knowledge is the supernatural imparting of facts not previously known to the giver.

Purposes for this gift are to:
1. Give warning - *(2 Kings 6:9)*
2. Confront - *(Acts 10:15)*
3. Exhort - *(Acts 9:17)*
4. Uncover sin - *(2 Samuel 12:7)*
5. Disclose man's thoughts - *(Acts 5:4)*
6. Identify healing - *(John 4:50)*
7. Reveal God's thoughts - *(Acts 9:16)*
8. Perceive what is missing - *(1 Samuel 10:22)*
9. Ignite faith - *(John 4:39)*
10. Give encouragement - *(John 1:48,49)*

In the previous list, I used some Old Testament scriptures as examples of the Holy Spirit's gifts because God has never changed. It was the same Holy Spirit back then, as it is now after Pentecost. The only difference is the Holy Spirit came upon the prophets, priests, etc., and did not dwell within them.

There are five ways the word of knowledge is received: through sight, hearing, knowing, the senses and the spoken word.

1. **Through sight**:
One receives sight through pictures, visions and dreams. In a public setting a word of knowledge through sight will usually come through a picture. A particular picture not mentioned in the vision section, is seeing a word written. I have seen the writing of words by God's finger, my hand, a computer, scriptures in the Bible, etc. Seeing a picture of the written word is a common word of knowledge, through sight. *(Daniel 5:5)* Anna saw the word, "FAITHFUL" written in bright letters across the forehead of a man while she was ministering to him. He said that he had been told that by others which also confirmed and blessed her.

2. **Through hearing**:
The Lord will often speak necessary facts to the one ministering. He can speak to our thoughts, through our thoughts, or in an audible voice. *(Acts 9:7)* The same is true with hearing angels speak.

3. **Through knowing**:
Sometimes the word of knowledge just happens by an inward knowing. When this occurs, the giver knows he has received revelation

from the Lord. *(Matthew 9:4)* One time I was sitting near a gal in a conference, and we were sharing the chair between us for our Bibles and note pads. As she wrote something down, then placed her paper on the chair, it started to fall off the chair. As I reached out to grab the paper, the allegory was quickened to me that the devourer was trying to steal her Word. I knew in my heart this was true even though I had never met her.

I asked the Lord if this was so and if I should share it. Then as she stood up, her notebook fell to the floor. This was my confirmation that I really understood. So I prayed for an opportunity to share with her, and after the meeting was over I asked her if she had been given a Word from the Lord some time in her past, where she deemed it valuable enough to write down, but since then was doubting it. She looked absolutely astonished and said, "Yes, I recently almost burned it," and she had come to the conference asking the Lord for a special Word from Him about it! I told her that the enemy had dispatched a spirit that was attempting to devour that Word and that she needed to protect it.

I explained how when the Lord gives us Words, they often come in seed form. We must keep them as in Mark 4, and through the keeping process, they will bear fruit. Sometimes, in the keeping, we must stand just like the seed does and bear up under the cold windy times, the dry hot times and still hold onto that Word. In time, the Word He gives us will bring forth fruit with patience. After I shared this, I prayed for her and rebuked the devouring spirit. I asked the Lord to send her confirmation and encouragement to keep that Word in her heart and not let go of it. She was deeply blessed. To this day, I do not know the Word she had been given, but I know the enemy wanted to steal it.

4. **Through senses**:

The word of knowledge can be received by the Lord opening the senses of the one ministering. A feeling of warmth or pain may come in his own body where the Holy Spirit wants to touch and heal in another. Sometimes the Lord will open the other senses as He sees fit. (Seeing, hearing, smelling and tasting.) *(2 Samuel 5:24)* I have a friend whose hands sometimes get very hot when she prays for people. It is a sign of the healing power of the Lord upon those she touches.

I was once listening to a lady's testimony about losing her husband and how the Lord fills that void. At the same time, I was suddenly hit by a deep sense of loneliness while sitting by a precious friend. It was so intense that I began crying and the tears just flowed. I knew I was feeling her pain and continued to cry as I put my hand on her knee. I told her the Lord felt her pain, and these were His tears for her. He knew and He understood. We cried together and she was comforted that the

Lord knew and understood her deep pain of loneliness. She mentioned several weeks later that she had not forgotten that and that it was such a comfort to her during her difficult times.

Another time, I was driving in the car to see a lady, and my heart suddenly started to race and my breath became short. It was so out of character for me, and I said to myself, "This is fear I'm feeling!" I was perfectly happy that day, and certainly not thinking anything fearful. I rebuked the spirit of fear and anxiety in Jesus' name, and I immediately felt better. When I arrived at my destination, the lady volunteered she had been suffering panic attacks and had one that morning prior to my arrival. I knew that was exactly what I had felt and that my overcoming that spirit actually delivered her into peace.

5. **Through the spoken word**:
The word of knowledge can also be spoken through the one ministering, without his foreknowledge. The word simply pops out, and after he speaks it he realizes it is a gift from the Lord. *(Luke 1:42)*

I had an interesting training from the Lord in learning to recognize the word of knowledge. Although I'd probably had thousands of pictures, and even more in hearing, I had little practice in those *knowing* times where I actually recognized it as the word of knowledge. Then one day as I opened the mail box to place my mail inside, I noticed another letter inside. I knew something was wrong with the letter before I turned it over. *(Word through knowing.)* So I picked it up and saw that it was from my son, intending it to be mailed. As I looked at it, I still had the nagging feeling that something was wrong. I carefully looked to see that he had addressed it properly, then said, "Oh well, it will come back if something is wrong." *(Word through speaking.)*

That day after the mailman had left our mail, he also left that letter in the box, not mailed. Then the Lord opened my eyes and I could clearly see that there was no stamp! Now I thought it rather unusual that He blinded my eyes as I went through such scrutiny over the letter, knowing in my spirit something was wrong, even before I ever looked at the front of the letter. Then I realized He was teaching me that the inner knowing was the Holy Spirit, and it was a word of knowledge. I realized I'd had that feeling many times before and never realized it was the gift of the word of knowledge functioning in every day situations.

67. HE SPEAKS THROUGH THE GIFT OF FAITH[15]

There are different kinds of faith recorded in the Bible. The one recorded in 1 Corinthians 12 is miracle faith. It's believing for a specific circumstance based on Who God is. It is a sudden surge of assurance God will move and perform His Word.

The gift of faith was manifested in Elijah's life when confronting the prophets of Baal. He challenged them to have their false god answer by fire. They did their incantations to no avail. Then Elijah had 12 barrels of water poured on his altar.

He prayed, *"Hear me, O Lord, hear me, that this people may know that You are the Lord God, and that You have turned their hearts back to You again. Then the fire of the Lord fell and consumed the burnt sacrifice, and the wood and the stones and the dust, and it licked up the water that was in the trench." (1 Kings 18:37-38 NKJV)*

As an example of the gift of faith, I was in the Doctor's office with a friend who had just undergone laser surgery for glaucoma. When the nurse took her eye pressure, the reading was worse than before the surgery, and I knew in my heart that it was a lie of the enemy. After the nurse left, my voice rose up firmly and said that it was a lie, and that I did not accept that reading! I rebuked the enemy and told him he could not steal from us in Jesus' Name. When the Doctor came in, he rechecked the pressure. It was much better and he apologized for the error. I do not know if the nurse read it wrong, or if she read it correctly and that the pressure was a "gift" from the enemy, and then after my faith rose against it, the pressure came down. Either way, I truly experienced a gift of faith that was not my normal mode of operation. I knew, without a doubt, that the enemy was trying to steal something, and I simply was not going to accept it. The faith in my heart was a gift and was a strong and firm force against opposition.

[Faith is the creative element that dispatches forces with assignment in the unseen world.]

68. HE SPEAKS THROUGH GIFTS OF HEALING[16]

Gifts of healing are divinely imparted to mend and make well. Healing can take place as an immediate event, or through a process. Gifts of healing have authority over the enemy to release the shackles of infirmity. This brings deliverance to the captive.

An example of immediate healing was: *"And the whole multitude sought to touch him: for there went virtue out of him, and healed them all." (Luke 6:19 KJ)* An example of a progressive healing was when Jesus led the blind man out of town, made mud and placed it on his eyes. When Jesus asked if he saw anything, he replied, *"I see men as trees, walking. After that he put his hands again upon his eyes, and made him look up: and he was restored, and saw every man clearly." (Mark 8:24,25 KJ)*

Lucy (name changed) had a friend who was very ill at the hospital. She had suffered heart problems for years and was on heavy medication for it. After anointing her friend's feet with her chap-stick, (I'm sure the Lord chuckled at that!) she held onto them like she did another man's the week before. [That man's heart had been shocked many times and he was on a respirator. After thinking about praying for him, she had awakened one morning with a picture of her holding onto his feet and praying. As it turned out, when she and four others filed into the intensive care room, the only place for her was at his feet. He was miraculously healed of heart problems while they prayed.]

This experience with the man's healing, gave her tremendous faith to pray for her friend that day. After the chap-stick anointing ☺ and as she prayed in tongues her friend received great heat and tingling through her arms and chest. They both had waves and waves of goose bumps and physically felt the Lord's Presence with great joy. They were anything but religious, laughing uproariously, and wondering what would happen if a real pastor walked in and saw them. They knew she was healed but she had promised to have an Angiogram done with a catheter going into her heart, and she decided to go ahead with it. Lucy had absolutely no peace about the test and pleaded with the Lord about it. As it turned out, her friend seriously convulsed during the test. However, the good news about the Angiogram was that they found a healed heart. Later, when she went to the Dr. for her checkup, she told him the Lord had healed her heart and he said, "I don't know who healed your heart, but you came out the winner!"

69. HE SPEAKS THROUGH WORKING OF MIRACLES[17]

Miracles are a display of God's "super," over our natural. They are often manifested in both creative healing and power over the natural forces of this world. The account of Elisha and the floating ax is an example of a miracle: "...but as one of them was chopping, his axhead fell into the river. "Oh sir," he cried, "it was borrowed!" "Where did it fall?" the prophet asked. The youth showed him the place, and Elisha cut a stick, and threw it into the water; and the axhead rose to the surface and floated!" (2 Kings 6:5-6 TLB)

In the last days we are going to witness many miracles. People will walk on water and air. They will walk through violent mobs and be unharmed. Some will minister in a crowd and then disappear to some other place. Others will be sent to multiply food. You name it, we'll probably see it. *"Most assuredly, I say to you, he who believes in Me, the works that I do he will do also; and greater works than these he will do, because I go to My Father." (John 14:12 NKJV)*

As in the above paragraph on supernatural miracles, we tend to forget that miracles are a display of "God's super over our natural", and think less of miracles occurring in our every day lives. However, they are none the less outstanding. I have asked a friend to share the story of the "miracle well." "The Lord awakened me many mornings in a row with His inward audible voice saying, *"Drill a well."* I didn't think I had the money to do this, but was reminded that I had exactly $4,000.00 in a Life Insurance Policy which I could cash. One morning I saw a picture-vision of a hand pump, an electric pump, an elevated 500 gallon holding tank, hot water pipes attached to my wood stove, and where the well was to be drilled. So, I decided to go ahead.

My first question to the well drillers was, "How much will it cost?" They really thought that was funny. "We won't know until we drill it, because we don't know how deep we are going to have to go." I gulped and told them to go ahead. I was nervously counting each time the drill went down — they had said it was ten dollars each time! Bang! - 10 dollars, Bang! - 20 dollars, Bang! - 30 dollars. Finally I gave up and quit counting. ☹

Suddenly, they came to the door and said, "Hey, we have your well drilled. You've got 12 gallons a minute." No sooner had they said it than I heard the Lord say, *"Tell them to keep drilling!"* I didn't even have time to think about it, it just popped out of my mouth, "Keep drilling." They looked at me as though they thought I was losing it! I quickly closed the door and really told the Lord what I thought! He replied, *"You will have 25 gallons a minute."* I was nervous. I paced back and forth, counting the drill bangs and then the thought floated into my mind, *"Tell them to make a test."* I watched water pouring out of the hole and said, "Please make a test." And they did. "You can't imagine how much water you have!" I said, "Yes I do, it's 25 gallons a minute!" [Later when I had the water tested for minerals, they said it was one of the most perfectly balanced waters they had tested.]

I told the drillers the whole story about the Lord awakening me and everything that had led up to it. They put in the hand pump, and the pressure tank, and the 500 gallon pressure tank with the necessary plumbing, so that I could have gravity flow into the house from the holding tank. When I got the bill it was $4134.91. I called them and told them that they had put something in that I didn't need and to remove it because I only had $4,000.00. An hour later they called me and said, "We think we have a way around the $134.91. If we can bring people out to see your system, we'll chalk it up to advertising." Miracles still happen in every day life.

70. HE SPEAKS THROUGH PROPHECY[18]

Prophecy is the inspired speaking forth of the mind of God.

When hearing the Lord through the gift of prophecy, give Him time to confirm His Words in other ways. His confirmations will safeguard against false prophecy. There are some standards by which prophecy should comply:

Prophecy will:
1. Be in one accord with the scriptures.
   (2 Timothy 3:16)
2. Glorify Jesus, God's Son. *(1 John 4:1-3)*
3. Edify, not tear down. Build the body toward wholeness, not bring division or strife. *(Ephesians 4:12)*
4. Love the sinner, hate sin. *(John 8:3-11)*
5. Convict, but not condemn. *(John 3:17)*
6. Present the Lord as a solution, if it declares a problem. *(Ephesians 3:20,21)*
7. **Be non-controlling**. *(2 Timothy 2:24)*
8. Be valid through the proof of time. *(Deuteronomy 18:21,22)*
9. Be tested. *(1 Corinthians 14:29)*
10. Be a sign to the unbelievers. *(1 Corinthians 14: 24,25)*
11. Exhort. Gives invitation and entreaty. *(1 Corinthians 14:3)*
12. Comfort. It consoles and encourages. *(1 Corinthians 14:3)*
13. Be given in proportion to the speaker's faith. *(Romans 12:6)*

Even the best of prophesy can be misdirected because of human input. I have known people who have heard the Lord's Word, and yet not conveyed His heart and intent through prophesy. Usually this happens, because although they have actually heard the Lord's Word about certain issues, they take it another step and <u>attempt to interpret how the Lord is feeling.</u> For the most part, these prophesies are in error because they interpret God to be some angry force that is wrathfully spanking His kids. I am sure anyone who has ever heard prophesy has come across this at one time or another! The best way to prophesy is to stay within the scripture: *"But he who prophesies speaks edification and exhortation and comfort to men." (1 Corinthians 14:3 NKJV)*

Edification means to build up, to promote another's growth. Exhortation means to console, encourage and comfort. Comfort also means to calm. *[#3619, 3874, and 3889 Strong's Exhaustive Concordance, Greek.]* The best example I have ever heard of prophesying was when a man was called out of an audience and told, "It's not over, until it's over." He was told even though he thought he had retired and life would be down hill from there on, the Lord had plans for him and he had yet his best to offer others and to God. It was a very consoling and encouraging message to someone who thought he was too old and outdated. The message was so encouraging that his wife who sat next to him cried joyful tears.

The highest standard for all prophesy is love. Those who prophesy are called to encourage the bride of Christ, and will be held accountable as to how they treat His bride. No matter what the message, any harsh prophesy short of love is abuse.

71. HE SPEAKS THROUGH DISCERNING OF SPIRITS[19]

The gift of discerning of spirits is the ability to discriminate spirits. There are four types of spirits: man's spirit, God's Spirit, angelic spirits and evil spirits.

1. Samuel went through the process of discerning the spirit of man, in choosing David to be king. God told him not to look on the outward appearance, when going through the selection process. He discerned the brothers who stood before him, refusing each as the choice to be king over Israel. God allowed Samuel to go through this process until David stood before him. The Lord then spoke and said, *"This is he." (1 Samuel 16:6-13)*

2. Eli discerned God's Spirit was talking to the boy Samuel, when Samuel could not. *(1 Samuel 3:1-9)*

3. Hebrews 13:1 says, *"Do not forget to entertain strangers, for by so doing some have unwittingly entertained angels." (NKJV)* The Lord's angels are not always obvious in their appearance. Sometimes we need to discern that they are angels! The scripture also says that the enemy can be disguised as an angel of light, therefore we must discern whether the angel serves the Lord or the enemy. *(2 Corinthians 11:14)*

4. Paul opposed the evil spirit that was actually saying something good: *"These men are the servants of the Most High God, who proclaim to us the way of salvation."* Paul discerned the spirit to be one of divination, and rebuked it. *(Acts 16:16-18 NKJV)*

Some Greek definitions for discerning have negative

connotations: dispute, oppose, hesitate, contend, differ, doubt, be partial, stagger, waver. These words also happen to describe the process the receiver of discernment goes through. The enemy is a liar and deceiver. He tries to camouflage his works by attempting to look good. When the receiver of discernment is confronted with something that appears good on the outside, but isn't, it becomes a stumbling block to his spirit. His flesh sees and hears that it is good, but his spirit is disputing, opposing, hesitating, contending, differing, doubting, staggering, and wavering against the outward appearance.[20]

I had an occurrence when I heard a spirit say to me that there would be a break through in a meeting that I was attending that day. It was a good message, and even said something about the Lord. But my spirit hesitated even though it was a good message and then suddenly I knew that this was a religious spirit. I rebuked it in Jesus' Name, and it gave me all kinds of clack, being very angry because the Lord had made it manifest. It was a lesson that not all things heard are the Lord's voice, even though they sound like His voice. Christians need discernment, especially when it comes to the supernatural.

72. HE SPEAKS THROUGH TONGUES[21]

The gift of tongues is speaking in a language that is unlearned. The purpose of tongues:

1 To communicate with God. *(1 Corinthians 14:2)*
2. To build up or edify and confirm the speaker. *(14:4)*
3. A sign to unbelievers. *(14:22)*
4. To pray and sing. *(14:15)*
5. To bless and give thanks. *(14:16,17)*
6. Supplication (praying) for the saints. *(Ephesians 6:18)*
7. To build faith. *(Jude 1:20)*

There is much misunderstanding and fear concerning speaking in tongues. Some think it is an emotional experience overpowering the senses, taking control over the will and speaking faculties. But it is no different than people just opening their mouth to speak. When people talk, they speak in all different tones, decibels, emotions, etc., but people do not speak without CHOOSING TO. Speaking in tongues is merely the choice of speaking, but it happens to be in another language. Speaking in tongues is a rational choice of the will to communicate with the Lord in a language that transcends our understanding. It enables us to pray according to His will without our flesh rebelling. The tones, decibels, responsive emotions, etc. are the subjective choice of the speaker. They can be inspired by the Holy Spirit but it is still the person's choice to participate.

The objective experience (uninvolved gift to the speaker) of speaking in tongues happens not in how it is said, but what is said. Usually when the Holy Spirit first gives this ability to a person, little syllables come to mind. The language is formed by these syllables coming together to form words as the person speaks them. However, when the speaker speaks with fluency, there is no pre-thought to the mind and the Holy Spirit simply gifts the language as the person speaks. Sometimes, when one first receives this gift, he is only given a few syllables to start, and not a complete language. The language will grow in time.

There is much controversy over speaking in tongues and to be honest, I am not settled on any of it, nor does it matter to me, because in spite of it all I speak in tongues. When people receive the gift of speaking in tongues, not everyone receives in the same way. For myself, I went to kids camp in my teens and was prayed over to receive what they called the "Baptism of the Holy Spirit" *(Acts 1:5)* I was supposed to feel the Holy Spirit come upon me, then speak in tongues. I felt nothing when they prayed. I was expecting some bolt of lightening to come down from the sky and hit me in a whoosh of the Holy Spirit. But they simply prayed, and I simply thanked Jesus like they told me to do. End of sentence.

However, an hour later as I laid in my bunk bed, little foreign sounding syllables popped into my mind. So I spoke them with my head under the pillow. It was one sentence. My counselor told me that could happen, and to be faithful to practice my new language and it would grow. So that is what I did. I spoke my one sentence faithfully for about a year. (To this day, I still remember that sentence, of which I will tell you about later.) Then one day I was driving to school singing a popular love song along with the radio, and the second verse was sung in French. So I started singing my own pretend "French" to the words. By the end of the song, I had a complete and wonderful language, only I didn't know it! However, every time I sang that song I would sing it in my "pretend language" even when they were singing in English. It was so beautiful I didn't want to sing it in English. Then one day I started singing other popular love songs of the day the same way. Then the realization hit me, I was doing what the Bible called "singing in the Spirit"! *(1 Corinthians 14:15)* "Wow! Is this finally the expansion of my new language?" So I stopped singing and just spoke it. Sure enough, there was a full blown language!

Now, not everyone will struggle as hard as I did. The reason it took me so long was because of doctrinal currents against me. I was told speaking in tongues was of the devil and that the occult speaks in tongues. It didn't seem to connect with me that Paul in the Bible spoke in tongues all the time. *(1 Corinthians 14:18)* The only reason I had the courage to receive it, was because of the loving counsel of a dear lady who shined with the love of God. I felt that if she could love me like that, and she spoke in tongues, then she certainly wasn't of the devil. Simply put, I knew the devil couldn't love and she was no devil.

Since that time long ago, now that I am fluent in the spiritual gifts, I have come to realize that the devil can not create. Only God can create. The devil only mimics, only copies the real thing. So of course the occult speaks in tongues, that's because God created the real speaking in tongues!

The controversy continues, but I am not into doctrinal issues. I can remember sitting in a Bible class, where the teacher had written four large sections of all the verses and scriptures that different denominations believed about one particular doctrinal issue. Then on section number five, he said, "And here is what we believe." I sat there confounded, because I couldn't see the difference between making this one more right than the others. Each mode of doctrine was using the same Bible, pulling out its own scriptures to defend its own stand. I shook my head and learned a lesson bigger than the classroom that day. Who's to say who is right? That day I decided to forget doctrines, I just wanted God.

So what do I believe about speaking in tongues? It is an enduement of power *(Acts 1:8)* that gives a person a greater ability and strength to live life the way the Lord intended it. Do I believe that in order to receive this greater power you have to speak in tongues as an evidence? In the places where the enduement of the Holy Spirit is recorded in the Bible, most of them say they spoke in tongues. However there are places it doesn't mention tongues. *(Acts 4:31, Acts 8:15-18)* That doesn't mean tongues were not present, it just doesn't mention tongues. So do I believe in order to be endued with His Holy Spirit you have to speak in tongues? I have no idea! When I was prayed for, I was told I had received, but I didn't feel different or speak in tongues. But an hour later I spoke one sentence. That was the measure of my ability to receive at that time. I don't know any more than that.

I received a couple of wonderful confirmations about speaking in tongues. One time I was praying in tongues and in English over people I'd met on the Internet and I saw a picture-vision of a flat bed truck driven by 2 angels. On the flat bed truck were a whole bunch of packages, each wrapped and looking exactly like the size of bricks. The Lord told me I was dispatching supplies. So I asked Him what those bricks were. He said, *"Each individual prayer."* Then a few days later I listened to a tape where a man was given a vision that every time he spoke in tongues, he saw packages the size of bricks come down from heaven that were deposited inside of him. When they were deposited, he felt a strengthening of his inner man. He was praying supplies for himself.

Remember that one little sentence I mentioned when I first

received tongues? When I shared it with Anna, who also had been indoctrinated against tongues, she said it sounded like Spanish. So she looked it up in her Spanish dictionary. She was so surprised at the meaning, she also received the Baptism of the Spirit.

Twenty-five years after that, having completely forgotten its meaning, Anna happened to ask me if I still remembered my one little sentence. I spoke what I remembered and she again looked up the words in her old Spanish dictionary, and this is what she found; my sentence was translated, "Door of a port hole released. They eat with Daddy." This was my commission from the beginning. I didn't know I was repeating a request thousands upon thousands of times. I was bombarding heaven and didn't even know it! I believe part of that fulfillment is the completion of this book. It is a good lesson in the importance of tongues.

73. HE SPEAKS THROUGH INTERPRETATION OF TONGUES[22]

The gift of interpretation of tongues gives understanding to an unknown language. This understanding is not necessarily a word for word translation. Interpretation also edifies those who hear. (14:5) *One who speaks in an unknown tongue should pray that he also may interpret.* (14:13)

The scripture says tongues is the language of men as well as angels. I have heard testimonies of people who have spoken in an unlearned language and those in the audience have recognized the language. A friend told me a story where a preacher in a foreign country just started speaking in tongues from the platform. Many wonderful conversions took place because even though he was just speaking in tongues to the Lord, they understood what he said.

At other times, the language may be one of angels and no one would recognize it unless through an interpretation. *(1 Corinthians 13:1)*

1   Psalm 46:10 KJ
2   Psalm 4:4 KJ
3   Numbers 12:8 KJ
4   Dark Speech: puzzle, riddle, proverb, hard question. It is from a word meaning to untie a knot. [2420 Heb Strong's from / 2330 Heb]
5   Chapter 9, Understanding What God Speaks
6   Daniel 8:23, Proverbs 1:6, I Kings 10:1, Judges 14:14
7   I Corinthians 2:6-8, Ephesians 3:9-10
8   Luke 5:22, Acts 5:3
9   Vision; gaze, look, behold, see, sight, and view. [2375/2377 Heb Strong's and 3706/3705 Gk Strong's]
10   Rummikub® - A game made by Pressman® Toy Corp.
11   Dark Speech; puzzle, trick, riddle, proverb, hard question. It is from a word meaning to untie a knot. [2420 Heb Strong's from / 2330 Heb Strong's]
12   Chapter 4, He Speaks Through Our Personalities
13   Word; something said. [3056 Gk Strong's] Wisdom; wisdom, wise, clear. [4678 Gk Strong's] (Acts 6:10)
14   Knowledge; Knowing, knowledge, science. From; to know, be aware, perceive, be sure, understand. [1108 Gk Strong's - From 1097 Gk Strong's] Strong's]
15   Faith; Persuasion, credence, conviction, reliance upon, constancy, truth, assurance, belief, faith, fidelity. [4102 Gk Strong's] (Acts 9:40)
16   Healing; A cure, healing. From 2390 Gk Strong's - to cure, make whole. [2386 Gk Strong's] (Luke 10:9)
17   Miracles; Force, miraculous power, ability, abundance, meaning, might, miracle, power, strength, violence, mighty work. [1411 Gk Strong's] (Acts 19:11)
18   Prophecy; Prophecy, prediction. From the word prophet, foreteller, inspired speaker, poet. [4394 Gk Strong's] (Acts 11:28)
19   Discerning of Spirits; Judicial estimation, discern, disputation. From to separate thoroughly, withdraw, oppose, discriminate, decide, hesitate, contend, differ, doubt, judge, be partial, stagger, waver. [1253 Gk Strong's from 1252 Gk Strong's]
20   1253 Gk Strong's: Judicial estimation, discerning, disputation.
21   Tongues; Tongue, an unaquired language. (Acts 2:4, Mark 16:17) [1100 Gk

	Strong's]
22	*Interpretation of Tongues; Translation, interpretation. [2058 Gk Strong's]* *(I Corinthians 14:26-27)*
19	*Discerning of Spirits; Judicial estimation, discern, disputation. From to separate thoroughly, withdraw, oppose, discriminate, decide, hesitate, contend, differ, doubt, judge, be partial, stagger, waver. [1253 Gk Strong's from 1252 Gk Strong's]*
20	*1253 Gk Strong's: Judicial estimation, discerning, disputation.*
21	*Tongues; Tongue, an unaquired language. (Acts 2:4, Mark 16:17) [1100 Gk Strong's]*
22	*Interpretation of Tongues; Translation, interpretation. [2058 Gk Strong's]* *(I Corinthians 14:26-27)*

CHAPTER 7:
HE SPEAKS IN AND OUT OF TIME

74. HE SPEAKS WHEN WE GIVE HIM TIME

When building communication with the Lord, it is important to give God time and resist impulsiveness and assumption after hearing Him.

I have a solitary game on my computer that is possible to win every time if played correctly. All the cards are visible, and laid in vertical piles. Winning the game is based on choices of moving cards around from one stack to another. A card may have an opening to move on top of another pile, but timing is everything. You have to look ahead to see the ramifications of moving at that time. It might be better to move another card pile first.

One day as I was playing the game above, the concept was quickened to me that this is how the Lord works His will on earth: TIMING IS EVERYTHING. People making choices, in a series of waiting and moving, just like the cards. Each time people move when and where they are supposed to (either by actions or reactions), their lives get more organized and line up for future "breakthroughs." This could not happen without first being willing to wait on the Lord for His timing.

In practical terms, just because there is an opportunity, doesn't mean we are supposed to take it — and just because we see a place to move, does not mean we are supposed to move there at that time. Movement can be achieved by people's actual physical decisions, thus producing physical, spiritual and emotional ramifications. Or movement can be internal decisions no one else knows about, yet having great significance. All movement requires a decision. And all decisions have ramifications. In other words, cause and effect. **Therefore, it is vital to**

wait for Him to line things up through HIS time.

There needs to be a balance between waiting and moving. He doesn't want to raise children who are afraid of their own shadow, afraid to move. He also doesn't want robots or wooden puppets for children. We don't need God's guidance to brush our teeth. Likewise, some spiritual movement is practical. We can live our Christian life expecting God to use us, to touch others as we live among them. When the Lord was trying to convince me of this during a particular season, He gave me the following inspired Word (excerpt from my devotional book, *Words to Ponder*):

Blended —
We are one. You and I. You will begin to recognize this as I confirm your way. I pour Myself into you and blended we reach out together. Did you think I wanted puppets for sons? - Yes, willing and movable vessels. Yet not wooden. It is YOU I desire, ALL of you. I gave you a personality unique as your fingerprint. No one can match your mold. Together, we blend and touch others.

I do not want to strip you as you seek to do My will. As you empty yourself and wait, you forget I MADE you human. I could have made you an angel but I made you a living person and send you to other living persons. Together we will move. Words are lifeless without My Spirit. You speak it, I quicken it. I go before you and prepare hearts. We will work together.

The opposite of waiting is impulsive hearing. Impulsive hearing is reaching out and grabbing a Word and running away with it without thought or consideration. It is quick action without wisdom of how or when His Word is to be applied. *"Discretion will preserve you; understanding will keep you."* (Proverbs 2:11 NKJV)

When the Lord intends to speak an entire paragraph, but only speaks a bit at a time, it is because He wants a series of reactions and actions from us as a result of hearing His Word. It's as though He has a long range plan in saying something, and He knows if He said it all at once we would not be prepared to receive it. Therefore, He gives one bit at a time, until He reaches His goal of the entire paragraph! When we pounce on a Word from Him, and do not give Him time to clarify it or tie it down with reference points, then we miss His intent.

Similar to impulsiveness is assumption - the temptation of jumping to conclusions, either before He is finished speaking, or before understanding takes place. It is so easy to jump ahead of God. Sometimes this can get us in a pickle.

One day my son John and I were walking in the mall together. I was walking too slow for him and he would get ahead, then stop and wait for me to catch up. This happened several times. "Mom, you gotta remind me every now and then that you're my Mom, because since you walk so slow, I tend to get ahead and then walk next to someone I think is my Mom!" This was a private joke in reference to another experience that happened earlier in the summer. We were at Fred Meyer and while I was waiting in line at the cashier, I saw John walk up to a lady in the next line over. He cut in and stood right behind her. He was standing so close to her, I realized he must think I was that lady! I started laughing and laughing. Finally he looked up through the candy shelves between us, straight into my laughing face. He looked horrified! Then he quickly ran over to me. I looked at the lady and she also thought the whole thing was quite amusing. (John didn't think it was funny at all!)

The same thing can happen with hearing the Lord. We get in a hurry and assume something is Him and it isn't. Also mistakes can be avoided, if we do not assume we understand. He may speak on several occasions, for several weeks, and perhaps years before giving His "punchline." If conclusions are drawn too early, it may cut Him off from all He is wanting to say. Bring what is heard back to Him and let Him clarify it, confirm it, making His Word a nail in a sure strong place. *"I will fasten him as a nail in a sure place."* (Isaiah 22:23 KJ) This takes time. Wait for Him.

His Words, no matter what form they come in, are exactly like the parable of the sower and the seed. *(Mark 4)* When He speaks His Words they are received as a seed, then they must be kept with patience. The "kept" part is a long growing process. The wind, the rain, the storms, the sun, the heat, the dry time: keeping His Word will enable us to go through them all. His Word must be confirmed and planted like an anchor, where nothing coming against it will cause it to drift from its anchored mooring. Being confirmed and planted takes time. Give God time.

75. HE SPEAKS WHEN WE WAIT FOR CONFIRMATION

"In the mouth of two or three witnesses shall every word be established."[1]

Seeking the Lord through confirmation is a very important and exciting concept. In fact it is so important, that when I first wrote this book, I had it in chapter one as a foundation principal. And even though it is a very vital link in our relationship with the Lord, especially in following His guidance, I took it out because the premise of chapter one is that no matter what Word is spoken, and no matter what source the Lord uses, the three principals of quickening, revelation and discernment must <u>always</u> be present. This is not so for the confirmation principle, as there are times when waiting for a confirmation, that it could cause the right moment for giving to be lost. Examples of such are in meetings when there are words of knowledge, healing, wisdom, exhortation, etc.

Outside of the above example, learning to wait upon Him for confirmation is indispensable in our relationship with Him. The idea of seeking Him for confirmation comes from the scripture, *"In the mouth of two or three witnesses shall every word be established." (II Corinthians 13:1 KJ)* When we are seeking God's guidance, or questioning whether we heard the Lord, we need to verify that He has spoken and that we understood what He said. This is a Biblical concept and He wants to make us strong and stable in our hearing His Words.

His Words will become like a hook, a nail, or an anchor on a boat. If something comes against us to rob us of that Word, ("hath God said?"[2]) then we can run back and check that nail. **Yes, His Word is secure and strong, bearing up against the weight because it has been confirmed**, clarified and established. It is safe. Enough time has been given for Him to make His Word sure. It is settled, strong and stable. If a storm comes against us, we can come back to that place and know His Word is solid. **Confirming and establishing is HIS business. He wants that. Your part is to give Him time to do so.**

He can bring confirmations to us in any form. The 101+ Ways God Speaks is a list of confirmations. If we receive something He has said to us, and it isn't enough for us to stand firm, then He will come again. He is very patient with our needing to be made firm in His Word. He will speak the Word to us as often as HE knows we need it for it to become that anchor. The emphasis is on the He knows, because being confirmed is a very cozy place to be; our human nature likes to stay there! There comes a time when HE says it's time to move on and GROW. The confirmations stop (in relation to that particular Word) because He knows what He has given is exactly enough to last through the obstacles that will come against it.

I have a delightful

There are three concepts to remember when receiving confirmations of His Words:

1. **What you hear must be in one accord with the Bible. (2 Timothy 3:16,17)**

2. **What you hear must be quickened by His Holy Spirit and give life. (John 6:63)**

3. **When in doubt, don't move. The Bible says "Whatsoever is not of faith, is sin." (Romans 14:23 KJ)**

story which spans a thirteen year period concerning the Lord's timing, sprinkled with His confirmations, all having to do with the launching of this book. The Lord had previously given me a "writing" promise of my launching out on the wings of faith. Being given a picture-vision of a space shuttle, I knew it had something to do with that promise. Then later when we purchased a computer and turned it on for the first time, there was a beautiful scene of a space shuttle on the screen! I was tickled at the confirmation.

One day, feeling I had waited forever for His promises to come to pass, I was watching my son play a computer game; the scene was inside a space shuttle. There would be a few paragraphs of text, then a menu would pop up saying, "Do you want to wait or continue?" He had a choice to click on one of the boxes. He clicked on "Wait." Recognizing the allegory of the connection between the space shuttle and the word "Wait," I certainly was interested in the outcome of this! To my dismay, this same process of text, with the same question must have repeated seven times! Each time he clicked "Wait." I became frustrated watching, and asked him, "What are you waiting for!" [It was more of an exclamation than a question!] He simply replied, "For the countdown to start."

Boy did that get me. It was another confirmation from the Lord: *"Yes, you will launch out, but no matter how frustrated you are - it will be in My timing!"* I got the point and was tickled at His humorous way of confirming me once again. Years later, when it WAS time, He certainly reconfirmed His point, as you will see with the following confirmations.

As a background to this story, I had previously placed a little note in my Bible that was a prayer request to the Lord. I asked that when it was time for the book to go forth, <u>He would send me at least three out of the ordinary confirmations that it was time</u>. That little note stayed in my Bible over the years. Then suddenly it was time and His series of confirmations came.

I visited a church and my eyes glanced at the banner on the wall. It said, "Now is the time." It was so quickened to me that I recorded it in my journal. A short while later I attended a conference at the same church, and the guest speaker looked up at a wall banner and read out loud, "Now is the time." He said that was an interesting confirmation, because earlier that morning he had heard the Lord say those exact words. Then I took my little niece to church there. During the service, she drew a picture of that banner hanging on the wall, and wrote, "Now is the time." I just shook my head and grinned.

During the same week she drew that picture, I received another set of three out of the ordinary confirmations all in one day. I was listening to a tape and the speaker broke his train of thought and said out of the blue, "Oh by the way, there are some of you out there who have been waiting upon the Lord for the right time to be launched into ministry." Then he yelled very loud, "THE TIME IS NOW!" Then he yelled a second time, "THE TIME IS NOW!" I was covered in goose bumps, and the Lord thoroughly had my attention. Then the man paused a long quiet pause and literally bellowed a third time, "**NOW! CONSIDER YOURSELF TOLD!!!**" I was really laughing and very blessed by this as I knew these were very special love gifts from the Lord specifically answering my prayer requests of long ago.

The <u>same day</u> I received a letter in the mail from a friend. As she was sitting in her chair, having just finished reading a draft of my manuscript, the Lord literally opened her sense of smell and she smelled the herb Thyme. [This is pronounced TIME.] She sent me this as a Word that the Lord was saying IT WAS TIME, along with the allegory of the different uses of thyme as a herb. That night I went to bed early and cuddled up in my blankets and pillows and pulled out a notebook of past rhema. I turned with anointed hands to a page and my eyes bugged out. On that particular day's entry I had written about cleaning out our camping trailer, getting it ready to sell, and I had found an old, yellowed, crinkled hand written note by Anna. Before I read it, I knew it was something she had heard His still small voice say to her in the middle of the night, many years ago when we were camping. On the note was one sentence: "Now is the time!" (Her note is a perfect testimony of how the Lord's Word never gets lost, but bears fruit in the exact time and season of His purpose.)

During the <u>same</u> two week period that I received all these "NOW IS THE TIME" Words, a magazine came in the mail. On the front cover was a full page picture of a space shuttle. The headline read, "Launching into 1997."

The final two weeks prior to sending the book to the printer, He sent me four more confirmations. A friend, not knowing my decision to go ahead and print the book by July 1997, told me, "The Lord has a Word for you. He says, 'Now is the time!'" She did not know the above story and I did not tell her as we were in a meeting. I just smiled, thinking I can hardly wait for her to read this!

A week later, I was in the midst of cleaning off my desk and came across the original note I had in my Bible. I started to throw it away and just couldn't do it. I read it once again: "If it is <u>not</u> time for the book, I ask that <u>when</u> it is, I will have three obvious, out of the ordinary confirmations, following Your still small voice to me. In Jesus Name. (signed) Sandy." Thinking about the fact it had been in my Bible for thirteen years, I said, "He's answered this, I guess I don't need it anymore." It was a reluctant, kind of sad thought as I stood over the garbage can. It was like letting go of an old companion. — Not the piece of paper, but what it stood for - the joy of seeing the Lord bring His promises and confirmations to pass.

I thought, "I have really been blessed by all His confirmations to me. But I'm just not ready to give this note up yet. Maybe He will bring me one more!" I felt kind of guilty thinking that when I had been given plenty. But you have to understand that thirteen years is a very, very long time to wait. And the child in me just wanted one more - not for the lust of a sign but for the joy of relationship. What I didn't realize when I was thinking these thoughts, was that He <u>heard</u> me. It look Him about eight hours to answer that thought.

The next morning I was creating some flyers for the back of the book. I decided to search for a graphic in one of my graphic books.[3] I opened the book to the section I wanted and my eyes fell on the following three graphics, in the order in which you see them here. Note, I did not look for the graphics, my eyes just fell on them, one, two, three. By the third one I was hysterically laughing!

After I was through laughing, (or so I thought) I glanced again at the "Plan Ahead" graphic. I suddenly noticed the calendar was the month of July. I was so tickled! July was my hopeful book launching date. He had previously given me rhema that I interpreted to be that month. However, for the most part, they were Words needing interpretation because they were not plain speech. I needed confirmation that I had interpreted them correctly, and here it was right on the page!

All these confirmations were so precious to me. And even more delightful is my truly receiving His love behind them. Do you see that it is the same wonderful God, regardless of how long it takes for Him to answer our prayers and desires? Do you see His love behind all these wonderful and precious out of the ordinary confirmations? All those years I had turned to the note in my Bible expecting God to answer it and He certainly did not disappoint me. He chose some very out of the ordinary ways!

CONFIRMATION IS IMPORTANT

1. When the timing in giving a gift is vital to it being received.
2. When we are moving on issues of faith, having no circumstances to support the move.

3. When we do not understand what God is saying or why He is saying it.
4. When we are sifted or being tested.
5. When we are fearful and not sure.
6. When others do not agree.
7. When we are not yet established.
8. When we are wavering.
9. When He has spoken a promise.
10. When we wait for His promise to come to pass.
11. When we are seeking His guidance whether to wait or to move.
12. When we are standing in the gap for others. If we make a mistake it may have bad ramifications for them.

76. HE SPEAKS IN SEASONS IN OUR LIVES

"To every thing there is a season, and a time to every purpose under the heaven." (Ecclesiastes 3:1 KJ) "The eyes of all look expectantly to You, And You give them their food in due season.." (Psalm 145:15 NKJV) "...a word spoken in due season, how good is it! (Proverbs 15:23 KJ) "And let us not be weary in well doing: for in due season we shall reap, if we faint not." (Galatians 6:9 KJ)

To understand God's time table, is to understand His calendar. Few, if any, know that! We need to understand that He carries out His plans in seasons. We are synchronized with His timing whether we know it or not. When trying to understand what is going on, it helps to plug into the knowledge of what season it is.

I have witnessed seasons of slumber, resurrection, promotion, repentance, cleansing, praying, worship, sifting, wavering, vision, promise, movement, warfare, standing, waiting, retraining habits, weakness, faith, expectation, etc. That list and many others are like months within a year. They don't have the same time frame as our months, but they are equivalent to durations of time within a larger clock.

His larger clock works within seasons of winter, spring, summer and fall. I stood through a very long season He specifically called "winter." That winter lasted 3½ years. I was very happy to see it end. (Believe me, winter does end, and spring does come.) To identify a specific season, it helps to understand the following section on unity.

77. HE SPEAKS THROUGH THE SYNCHRONIZING OF GOD'S PEOPLE

"Till we all come in the unity[4] of the faith, and of the knowledge of the Son of

God, unto a perfect man, unto the measure of the stature of the fullness of Christ."
(Ephesians 4:13 KJ)

"Behold, how good and how pleasant it is for brethren to dwell together in unity!"[5] (Psalm 133:1 KJ)

When we want to understand His season, it helps to be plugged into communication with other Christians, then we can discover patterns we have in common. These patterns can be literal, as in literal circumstances, or spiritual, as in symbolic stories within our lives. When God moves, He moves on behalf of the individual and the group. In belonging to the body of Christ, we are merged into the gears of His large time clock.

He gave me a vision once of a mass of gears. As one gear moved, it moved another, and another. As I viewed the individual gears, they moved in little circles, touching other gears moving in similar circles. Each small gear was joined within a huge structure of gears which joined into giant gears, moving more slowly. All these gears turned into people and their arms were linked in a circle. As one person moved, it began the process and they all moved in synchronization. Then I saw the connection of gears turn into a replica of His clock. As He merges us within its gears, His overall clock moves <u>very</u> slowly. Synchronizing a group of people like this would be practically impossible in the flesh. Only the Holy Spirit can do this incredible task.

The Lord often uses the unity of His people to confirm us with His Words. They are like the above gears providing places in which to link and become grounded. One time, when John and I went on a bike ride and I tried to stand up on my three speed bike, my gears popped out of place and the pedals slipped. I found if I put my thumb on the gear thing, (sorry, female word) I could press down a little and it would be OK. But the allegory shouted at me because they were gears. (I was really into gears because of the above gear vision the Lord had given me.) I kept thinking, "Lord, I have nothing to push against, they keep slipping."

When I came home, I collapsed in front of the TV to see what my husband was watching. It was a science documentary about physics and the universe, of which I barely understood. However, I watched because it had a reoccurring picture of gears moving in a clock! Of course, each gear was a different size, and as one moved, another did, and so on. "Lord what are You trying to tell me? What is the allegory of my gears slipping?" I noticed the biggest gear had a pendulum kind of bar that had two pointers, one on each end. When the bar swung one way, the pointer would connect with the big gear, and push or move it forward one space. Then when the pendulum moved back, the pointer on the other end would catch another gear on another side. I said, "That's what I need to get me moving!" — An anchor, a hook, a lever that would hold me in place... in other words HIS WORD CONFIRMED and driven in a sure strong place. It was a matter of timing. The reason my "gears" were slipping is that I still needed confirming, all within His timing of fulfilling His promises. He was telling me that if my ability to launch out and move was unstable, then I needed to wait for more confirmation until I had a secure foundation.

If you seek to plug into understanding God's season, as related to the unity of patterns of believers around you, it is vital you experience His quickening and revelation power. Without them, your knowledge will be empty and you will become a false prophet unto yourself, following signs. When the Holy Spirit quickens your desired understanding, it is like a pool of water on a hot day. Soak it up and find refreshment. Call others to join you. They need understanding too!

78. HE SPEAKS IN CIRCLING THROUGH TIME

"Oh Lord, You have examined my heart and know everything about me. You know when I sit or stand. When far away you know my every thought. You chart the path ahead of me, and tell me where to stop and rest. Every moment, you know where I am. You know what I am going to say before I even say it. You both precede[6] and follow[6] me, and place your hand of blessing on my head." (Psalm 139:1-5 TLB)

Educators have studied and analyzed how people learn. There are various learning theories and one is the spiral method. It is similar to a spiraling funnel of information circling outward. Many textbooks are built upon this theory. In the early childhood years, issues are introduced. As each year passes, more and more information is built around those original ideas.

Think of an isolated dot of information. Consider the perspective of that dot. Looking at a dot of information, it is a dot. There is no reference point, no common denominator, nothing to connect. Now draw a continuous circle starting at the dot, making the circle larger and larger, around itself. When the first circle of information passes around the dot, it now has some sort of reference point of understanding. Another circle and its reference grows. Has the dot changed? No the original dot has not changed. More than likely, its original perspective has.

Why does God speak this general way more often than an outline format, or one, two, three? Although organized, outlines are ideas segmented, separated, and connected by sections. A spiral can join numerous ideas, weaving them into one continuous flow. However a spiral can take one concept, build upon it, join it with another and another, then focus on any concept it chooses yet still link directly with other concepts.

An example is how this book is written around the word "quickening." The message and importance of the Holy Spirit's quickening is mentioned many times. Does the first "definition dot" on quickening change? No, but eventually the perspective of its importance does.

When God speaks in circles, it also gives us a chance to breathe when information crowds our "dot." He moves in and touches, moves out and gives us room. - Circling around the issue, expanding, clarifying, providing reference points, adding a new perspective. Sometimes, it takes years for the Lord to circle issues in our life if we are not willing vessels to listen to what He is saying. Sometimes, He continuously circles around issues for weeks or even seasons, trying to get past our inability to comprehend. It is important not to jump on a dot of information with a mad dash. If we wait, undoubtedly He will circle again with more input.

The Bible gives examples of how God spoke in circles. The stories, covenants and histories repeat themselves throughout the text. Consider the study of the Old Testament feasts. The original dot of Passover was introduced by killing a lamb and placing its blood on the lintel of the door. This protected the Jewish people on the night the death angel slew Egypt's first born. *(Exodus 12:7)* In the next circle, God told them to celebrate this remembrance as a feast. *(Exodus 12:17)* They circled that feast until Jesus came. He became the Passover lamb and was sacrificed for our sins and became our protection from eternal separation from God. *"For indeed Christ, our Passover, was sacrificed for us." (1 Corinthians 5:7 NKJV)* All the feasts are introduced, and have been in the process of circling outward to their prophetic fulfillment.

Much of the Old Testament introduces Jesus. The New Testament circles that information through Jesus' life. We join that circle and live Jesus' life in us in like manner. The next generation will join us. The circle grows and God continues to reveal Himself. One day we will see Him face to face and know Him as we are known.

It is said that something has to be repeated seven times before it is permanently etched in our brain. Repetition is important in establishing facts. Stories, covenants and history were repeated many times in the Bible by the Lord restating issues to the people. In this same manner, I have noticed the Lord repeats His Words to me, each time perhaps with a slightly different angle, each time circling the issue until I finally "get it." Then, when I finally figure out His perspective, He repeats it just to confirm that I understood, then He repeats it again to sink it deeper!

The way I keep His Words to me is to record them on the computer. Through an easy search method I can keep them in remembrance and understand at a deeper level what He is talking about, other than just that moment in time. *"But that on the good ground are they, which in an honest and good heart, having heard the word, keep it, and bring forth fruit with patience." (Luke 8:15 KJ)*

For instance, He may speak concerning the Word, *"graduation."* In context to that Word, He may share some concepts about graduation and what that means on a spiritual level. Then, perhaps a few more months pass, and the term graduation is once again introduced (via all the various means of hearing Him in this book) and it connects with the last time I heard Him speak to me about graduation. I know it is some time in the future and I am to prepare for this. Several years later, He continues to bring up the concept which I have faithfully recorded in the computer. Only this time He says the time is imminent! Now I do a search on the word graduation or graduate, etc., and find all the times He has spoken to me about graduation. Throughout those circles, He weaves His perspectives on what graduation means, and it becomes clearer and clearer, then suddenly He is saying *now* is His time for graduation.

79. HE SPEAKS TIMELESS WORDS

The wonder of His Words, stories and etc. is that His Word is eternal. At the moment of quickening, it gives instant life to our hearts. Yet, next time He may quicken the same story and it will have another application for another set of circumstances. His Words always grow WITH us. That is because it is HIM speaking.

It amazes me how so many people can walk away from a sermon, each fed and met at their point of need. If you ask what the need was, each will say something different. Only God can take one Word and quicken it so many ways. His Word HAS to be eternal to reach us all!

As mentioned before, I belong to a small group where each of us keep a daily journal of things the Lord is speaking into our lives. When we compare days, often we will find that He will talk to us about similar issues within the same time period. What amazes me, is that His Words are so flexible to cover so many applications. Someone else in the group may have heard something prophetic for the future, but when I read it, it can be applied to the natural circumstance of what I just went through. One person may hear a Word and it has a total different application for each of us, not only spiritually but physically. Other times I may read something a year later and realize I am going through the same thing, and His Word is quickened for an entirely new set of circumstances.

When our cats Cally and Cuddles shared the same pillow, I often rubbed both of them with one hand at the same time. I grinned and thought of how big God is and how He touches us in the same way. They purred and sometimes they'd realize I was loving the other cat, and sometimes they were oblivious, thinking they were the only ones in the world. Take notice when another person shares what God is speaking into his own life at the moment. It may have a larger application. If you stop and think about it, it may touch your own life as well!

80. HE SPEAKS THROUGH NUMBERS AND CLOCKS

"Therefore, be on the alert— for you do not know when the master of the house is coming, whether in the evening, at midnight, at cockcrowing, or in the morning— lest he come suddenly and find you asleep. "And what I say to you I say to all, 'Be on the alert!'" (Mark 13:35-37 NASB)

The Lord often mentions timing when He speaks of seasons, years, months, days, hours, minutes and even seconds. When the Lord quickens numbers, sometimes they represent a period of time. Once I saw an abacus, my fingers dividing four equal rows of seven buttons each. I understood that to be exactly four weeks to the very day. The detail was precise and I marked it in my journal calendar.

I have a pastor friend who had a most interesting experience with numbers. It all started the year before when he prayed, "Lord, please come and pour out Your Spirit upon us. Do anything You want, I just want to know that it is You and not some deception of the enemy." About the same time he noticed every time he looked at a digital clock the time would consistently be 11:11 (AM and PM). This continued for several weeks.

Then one morning when he was rushing to get ready for an appointment, he looked at the clock - 11:11. He said, "Lord?" Immediately he had a sense it was a scripture, but determined not to look, lest he select the one that suited him. At the end of the day, as he rolled into bed he glanced at the clock to see what time it was. You guessed it — 11:11. The next morning, again 11:11. "Lord, *which* scripture?" Finally He heard the Lord say, *"Luke!"* This was the verse: *"If a son asks for bread from any father among you, will he give him a stone? Or if he asks for a fish, will he give him a serpent instead of a fish?" (Luke 11:11)* At last he understood.

The Lord was answering his prayer by saying He had given him a written guarantee that if he asked God for something he would not get a counterfeit. That night as he went to bed he again glanced at the clock - 11:11 PM. The next day he shared this with his leaders and after the meeting an elder's wife walked into her bedroom and glanced at their clock. It was 11:11.

That Saturday he prepared a message that would end with the 11:11 message and when he went to bed that night he looked at the clock — again it said 11:11. Smiling, he went to sleep. Sunday, he preached the message and glanced one time at the back wall of the church. It was 11:13 which was significant to him because the Lord had said He wanted to pour out His Holy Spirit that morning. Luke 11:13 says, *"If you then, being evil, know how to give good gifts to your children, how much more will your heavenly Father give the Holy Spirit to those who ask Him!"* That night when he went to bed the clock said 11:13! From this, he was absolutely convinced they had received the move of the Lord which was the outpouring of His Holy Spirit!

The story doesn't end there. After I had heard about the 11:11 message, we had a fun confirmation to the above story. John said, "Hey look!!! Our clock says 11:11!!!" I started laughing, and said, "I gotta write this down!" John, knowing nothing about 11:11 asked me, "Why? Is that another parable?" (I am always noticing allegorical parables, and he knows that.) I said, "Yes." He wasn't satisfied with that answer and was curious. So I told him the long story about 11:11's. When I finished he couldn't run fast enough to look up Luke 11:11.

Shortly after that, he and I started noticing 7:11's. It became so frequent we were both wondering what it meant, just like Pastor. We saw 7:11 in our bedrooms, on the TV, on the microwave, on his wrist, in the car, on the computer. 7:11's were popping up everywhere. John was reading the Bible through for the first time, and the first day he read the New Testament his eye immediately jumped to 7:11. He could hardly believe his eyes! *"If you then, being evil, know how to give good gifts to your children, how much more will your Father who is in heaven give good things to those who ask Him!"* (Matthew 7:11)

After that, the Lord started using 11:11 and 7:11 to confirm things He was sharing. One in particular was that He was promising the body of Christ an entire season of 11:11's! YES LORD! Then one night I had a dream that many people's journals were sprinkled with 11:11 on lots of pages. When I woke up from the dream I heard the Lord say, *"11:11."* Immediately following, I glanced at my clock — it said 11:11.

Then an amazing thing happened. One night in the car John started counting 10, 9, 8, etc. I looked at the digital clock and it said 7:10. I realized what he was doing, so I started at 19, 18, 17. etc. After doing my countdown very methodically and in perfect rhythm, when I got to 4, I slowed and said, "fooouuurrr, thhhhrrreee..." and then it turned to 7:11. If I had not stalled out the 4 and 3 it would have been absolutely perfect on the dot! From that day on, I understood that we were in a season of "countdown" towards 11:11-7:11. And of course, the Lord confirmed that understanding with more you-know-whats.

Right before I added this 11:11 story to this section, I was going through my journal to find more stories or examples that I could add to the book. When I searched, I was happy to find 26 more tidbits. As I sat in my car at a stop light, I thanked the Lord for giving me so many and then I was reminded that part of my promise was that I was going to be a food gatherer for the body of Christ. I realized that was what I was doing, collecting stories for hungry people. I was feeling kind of silly, and somewhat jokingly I said, "OK Lord, I'm supposed to gather food, so let's gather some!" As soon as I said "some," I glanced up through the windshield. There looming directly above me was a 7-11 grocery market sign. (He had the last Word on that one! ☺)

Between digital clocks, car odometers, wrist watches, video camera timers, VCR's, computers, microwaves, score boards, exercise bike timers, signs and broken calculators — for all the trouble the Lord has gone through, all I can say is <u>THIS SEASON IS REALLY GOING TO BE GOOD!</u>

Other than the Lord quickening clocks and numbers to cross reference with scriptures, there is another way the Lord quickens numbers to me. Often when I see a vision or hear Him, I will glance at the clock and note the time. This is an instinctive thing prompted by the Holy Spirit though a glance of my eyes. The clock time is quickened to me and so I record it with the vision or Word. Later I look up the clock time in the Greek and Hebrew numbers from the Strong's Concordance. This is often a wonderful confirming addition to His Word.

The following happens to be a literal example: I saw a vision of 19:42 on the face of a digital clock. The 42 seconds were flashing. Then I heard the Lord say, "Cloud. I AM with you. Follow Me." The Strongs number 1942 in the Hebrew meant 'calamity' and in the Greek, it meant a 'covering or veil'. I understood the Lord was telling me He would cover me or protect me from calamity by the cloud of His Presence. Since I also saw the number 42 flashing, I looked it up separately. In the Hebrew it meant 'my father is delight' and in the Greek it meant 'holiness'. The Lord was affirming that He is holy and my delight, and He had indeed spoken this Word of promised protection.

1   Matt 18:16, II Corinthians 13:1, 1 Tim 5:19. The various meaning of confirmation (Acts 14:22) are: confirm; to support further, reestablish, confirm, strengthen. From to set fast, to confirm, fix, establish, steadfastly set. [1991 Gk from 4741 Gk Strong's] Some English synonyms of confirm are to authenticate, verify, proof, further, ratify, sanction, endorse, assent, approve.
2   Genesis 3:1
3   Graphics from Zedcor, Inc. DeskGallery Collection © 1996. Used by permission.
4   Unity; unity, unanimity, agreement. [1775 Gk Strong's].

5   Unity; union, unitedness, together, altogether, all together, alike. [3162 Heb Strong's]
6   Precede and follow (TLB) = Beset (KJ); to bind, besiege, confine, cramp, secure, to shut in, to shut up, enclose, put up in bags. [6696 Heb Strong's]

CHAPTER 8:
HE SPEAKS IN A FAVORABLE CLIMATE

The Lord is wanting to spend quality time with you, hear what you have to say to Him, and respond. This happens through creating the right environment for you to talk to each other. It is helpful to understand He most often speaks in an environment conducive to His Presence and there are things we can do in our lives to nurture a place that is compatible. These are not necessarily requirements for hearing the Lord, as He reaches out and speaks to anyone who will listen, any time, any place. Rather, these are recorded here for those who want to hear Him to the greatest extent possible, on a continuing basis.

81. HE SPEAKS WHEN WE HAVE FAITH

Two people who do NOT have a common language begin to communicate. The tribesman with guttural mumbles asks the white hunter a question. Hesitating and scratching his head, the hunter responds with a shrug.

These two are not communicating. So instead, the tribesman speaks a word or sentence by drawing a picture, using sign language and pointing to the surrounding environment, while the hunter listens and applies. In the process they form common reference points and begin to understand general ideas. **This is not a word for word translation.**

There is a foundation of faith that must exist between the two communicating. — A faith that says, "I believe that you just spoke to me, and I believe I can come to understand what you said." **For true communication to exist in the listening process, there needs to be a certain measure of faith that goes beyond the language of the mind and penetrates the heart with belief.**

The Bible states these facts about faith:
1.   **Faith comes by hearing Him speak.** *"So then faith comes by hearing, and hearing by the word of God." (Romans 10:17 NKJV)*
2.   **We each have a portion:** *"...God has allotted to each a measure of faith." (Romans 12:3B)*

3. **Our faith can grow:** *"...Lord, increase our faith." (Luke 17:5 KJ)*
4. **It describes faith:** *"Now faith is the substance of things hoped for, the evidence of things not seen." (Hebrews 11:1 KJ)* The Living Bible says, *"What is faith? It is the confident assurance that something we want is going to happen. It is the certainty that what we hope for is waiting for us, even though we cannot see it up ahead." (TLB)*
5. **The Greek definition for faith**[1] (also belief) is translated: {persuasion, credence, conviction, reliance, constancy, truth, assurance, belief, faith, fidelity.}
6. **We cannot please Him without faith.** *"...without faith it is impossible to please Him, for he who comes to God must believe that He is..." (Hebrews 11:6 NKJV)*
7. **To do anything without faith is sin.** *"...for whatever is not from faith is sin." (Romans 14:23B NKJV)*

As the Lord speaks to you, and you find "Words" together, faith grows and blossoms. The Bible says Jesus is *"...the author and finisher of our faith..." (Hebrews 12:2 KJ)* He not only is the source of our faith, but also the completer.

Sometimes the particular Words the Lord speaks to me ***go through a faith process*** of sifting, wavering and quickening before they become planted and firmly established into a strong, bold faith:

1. "SIFTED faith" - The Words of the Lord are turning in circles without a secure, stable, home. I KNOW I have heard the Lord - I just don't know how it applies. This is faith with no sense of balance, security, or establishment.[2] It is like a small screw in a big hole, turning round and round never becoming set or secure.

2. "WAVERING faith" - I know the general place the Word applies, but don't understand what He means. This swings back and forth between different opinions. The wobbly screw needs to be deeper in the hole to be in a sure, strong, place. This happens with time and confirmation concerning what is believed.[3]

3. "QUICKENED faith" is like a screw sunk into the right place. The Lord speaks a Word and I discover a place it fits. When the quickening comes it has finished its turning, finally finding its proper placement, its niche.[4]

4. "**BOLD faith**" is when I know that I know. Having complete confidence on the inside, I know and understand what the Lord is saying. This is complete faith without doubts and with absolute assurance.[5]

When we have grown to the place of complete faith, we come into what the Bible calls Sabbath rest.[6] It is a place where we no longer struggle with an issue in life. We hear the Lord's perspective on a matter, rest, and believe Him. We cease from our own restless pursuits and trust Him. Sabbath rest is perfect belief in His Words to us.

One of my favorite examples of what I believe is someone entering sabbath rest is Smith Wigglesworth.[7] He was an anointed preacher in the early 1900's who led thousands to salvation and healing. He was very close to the Lord, in fact testified of seeing Him. In the process, he overcame enemy opposition. One particular night the devil stood in his room, and when Wigglesworth saw him, he said, "Oh, it's only you" and turned over and went back to sleep. That's what I call sabbath rest! He knew his opponent, understood his own authority over such, and simply rested in that truth by literally going back to sleep! That's **bold** faith.

82. HE SPEAKS WHEN WE ABIDE IN JESUS

Sin caused an eternal separation between mankind and the heavenly Father. He loved the people of the world so very much that He sent His son Jesus Christ to earth, to live among them and then die on the cross for their sins. Those who believe that Jesus was God's Son, and died for their sins will have the gift of eternal life.[8] That means that if we tell the Father our sins and ask Him to forgive us, He will accept us because Jesus paid the price.

Not only did Jesus die, but He overcame death, raised from the grave, visited many who were mourning His death, then visually returned to heaven in the clouds. He told us that even though He had to leave this earth, He would not leave us without comfort. He would send us the gift of His ever abiding Presence through the Holy Spirit - His very essence. That's quite a gift! *"...I will ask the Father and he will give you another Comforter, and he will never leave you. He is the Holy Spirit, the Spirit who leads into all truth. The world at large cannot receive him, for it isn't looking for him and doesn't recognize him. But you do, for he lives with you now and some day shall be IN you. No, I will not abandon you or leave you as orphans in the storm - I will come to you."* (John 14:16-18 TLB)

In the Old Testament, the Holy Spirit visited and came upon individuals, but since the day of Pentecost, (the fulfillment of an Old Testament feast) we can have His Spirit dwelling <u>within</u> us. Now, we can have a much greater intimacy available to us in hearing God than they ever experienced. *"For I tell you that many prophets and kings have desired to see what you see, and have not seen it, and to hear what you hear, and have not heard it." (Luke 10:24 NKJV)*

The question arises does God speak to people who do not believe in Jesus Christ as their Savior? The answer is yes, God speaks to everyone at any time in any place in every means. God speaks always. Whether we hear or understand Him is another matter. It is very difficult to hear what He is saying when we do not have the Presence of His Holy Spirit within us to help make the connection. Remember, quickening is a requirement of hearing Him speak, and quickening can not happen apart from the Holy Spirit. When you pray for those who do not know Jesus, pray that the Holy Spirit will visit them and draw them to the Lord. Jesus said, *"No one can come to Me unless the Father who sent Me draws him." (John 6:44 NKJV)*

Jesus spoke a key concept when He spoke about abiding in Him. Notice how many times the following scripture mentions the word abide: *"**Abide** in Me, and I in you. As the branch cannot bear fruit of itself, unless it **abides** in the vine, neither can you, unless you **abide** in Me. I am the vine, you are the branches. He who **abides** in Me, and I in him, bears much fruit; for without Me you can do nothing. If anyone does not **abide** in Me, he is cast out as a branch and is withered; and they gather them and throw them into the fire, and they are burned. If you **abide** in Me, and My words **abide** in you, you will ask what you desire, and it shall be done for you. By this My Father is glorified, that you bear much fruit; so you will be My disciples. As the Father loved Me, I also have loved you; **abide** in My love. If you keep My commandments, you will **abide** in My love, just as I have kept My Father's commandments and **abide** in His love. These things I have spoken to you, that My joy may **remain** in you, and that your joy may be full. (John 15:4-11 NKJV)*

The Greek word for abide is translated: abide, remain, dwell, continue, tarry, endure. It means to continue to be present, to be held or kept, to last and not to perish, to endure, to survive and live in a condition of waiting.[9] If you were to substitute each word in this translation for the word abide in the above verse, it gives you an added understanding of what it means to abide in Jesus. To me, it means to hang on tight to Jesus and His Words, to not give up (and thus to survive), and to wait for Him no matter what! Those words are hang on, tenacious words depicting a deep abiding trust and reliance upon Him. He said if we abide in Him, His joy will "remain" in us. Guess what the word "remain" means? It is the same Greek word as "abide." Therefore, if we hang on to Jesus' Words, His joy will hang onto us!

To those who believe in His Name, Jesus left us a checkbook

with His signature on it. That means He delegated His authority to us. And we can use that authority against all forms of darkness. *"And I will give you the keys of the kingdom of heaven, and whatever you bind on earth will be bound in heaven, and whatever you loose on earth will be loosed in heaven." (Matthew 16:19 NKJV)* We have been given the power in Jesus' Name to bind the forces of darkness, and loose ourselves or others from its grip. This authority is available to anyone who believes in the Name of Jesus. The devil hates the Name of Jesus! He shrinks from the very thought. The Bible says to resist the devil and he will flee from you. *(James 4:7)*

In relation to hearing more from the Lord, He wants us to use this authority against the devouring enemy who would seek to steal our daily hearing. If you want to hear more from the Lord, in the Name of Jesus, bind the devourer on a continuing basis, and loose the Words of God to come to yourself. Also loose your own ears to hear and your heart to understand what He says, in Jesus' Name. This really works.

When I wrote the first draft of this book in 1984, I was accustomed to hearing from the Lord on a continuing basis, and then I began to get interference from the enemy. At that time I was reminded of the verses when Daniel prayed to hear from God to receive understanding. An angel was sent to him the day he prayed, but it took twenty one days for the angel to fight through opposing forces.[10] If it took the angel that long to get through, shouldn't we remain consistent to pray and use the authority He has given us?

It helps to loose the angels to do their work, when we join with them, and we need to use our authority against the opposition who would delay God's Words from getting through. When I began taking consistent authority over the enemy, from stealing my daily portion of Words from God, I began to hear more and more. The key to this is not only believing in the Mighty Name of Jesus to loose what is bound or delayed, but also to not give up.

83. HE SPEAKS WHEN WE LET HIM LEAD

I have a pastor friend who saw a wet spaghetti noodle and a large hand come down and push it across some glass. The noodle only piled up instead of moving forward. Then he heard the Lord say, *"My people are like wet noodles, you just can't push them. You have to draw them."* Then he saw the same hand take hold of the noodle and pull it. The noodle became straight again.

God uses our personalities to lead us. When it comes to our making a decision, He initiates it, draws us, gets our attention, then says, "It's yours, you decide!" The Lord is not a controller. He does not force us to do something we do not want to do. He leaves the decision of whether we will follow, up to us. He wants our personalities, our own heart, to want what He wants. That's why He draws us, He does not want to push or control us into doing what's right.

84. HE SPEAKS WHEN WE YIELD

I received an insight about God's *multiplication* factor while looking at some scriptures. The Bible says, *"For whom He foreknew, He also predestined to be conformed to the image of His Son, that He might be the firstborn among many brethren." (Romans 8:29 NKJV)* That means that our destination is to become like Jesus. And Jesus' destination before His resurrection was death to His own will by yielding His life to the Father's will.

Jesus said the only way a plant lives forever is to continue to produce fruit. The way it produces fruit is for the grown plant to die after harvest, and allow its seeds to be planted back into the ground. The single seed, and thus the plant, is multiplied many times over. He said, *"Most assuredly, I say to you, unless a grain of wheat falls into the ground and dies, it remains alone; but if it dies, it produces much grain. He who loves his life will lose it, and he who hates his life in this world will keep it for eternal life. If anyone serves Me, let him follow Me; and where I am, there My servant will be also. If anyone serves Me, him My Father will honor." (John 12:24-26 NKJV) "Then He said to them all, "If anyone desires to come after Me, let him deny himself, and take up his cross daily, and follow Me. For whoever desires to save his life will lose it, but whoever loses his life for My sake will save it." (Luke 9:23-24 NKJV)* This kind of death to self is a decision to yield our own personal desire over a circumstance and say, "Lord, if this is Your will, then I accept that You know best." *"Not my will, but thine be done."*[11]

This is a painful place to be, but it has glorious rewards of a multiplied life. Jesus chose to yield His own will and lay His life down as a *righteous* seed for the sake of multiplying that seed to all who would believe on Him. His death multiplied righteousness for an entire world. The Bible says that only the Father brings forth the multiplied life: *"I planted, Apollos watered, but God gave the increase. So then neither he who plants is anything, nor he who waters, but God who gives the increase. Now he who plants and he who waters are one, and each one will receive his own reward according to his own labor. For we are God's fellow workers; you are God's field." (1 Corinthians 3:6-9 NASB)*

The Father chose that Jesus' physical death would be increased beyond the grave, by bearing the fruit of eternal salvation for anyone who would partake of that fruit. Like Jesus, when we go through death to self, the Father chooses what fruit our yieldedness will produce. Every person is different, therefore every person will have a different harvest of the fruit of their decisions.

Not everyone who is a Christian will go through death to self-will. The fact is, we can be as close to God as we want to be. *"And He was saying to them, take care what you listen to. By your standard of measure it shall be measured to you."* (Mark 4:24 NASB) *"Draw near to God, and He will draw near to you."* (James 4:8 NASB) Because we have a choice, death to self will not be chosen by everyone. But those who want God above everything else are willing to follow Jesus Christ even to the cross. As a result, those people will hear God on earth, in the greatest measure available to mankind.

85. HE SPEAKS WHEN WE ARE AT REST
Stillness of the heart is essential in hearing from Him. "Be still, and know that I am God." (Psalm 46:10 KJ)

I remember reading about a man who walked every day to commune with the Lord. As his gate closed behind him he learned to deliberately leave the cares of this world behind. He mentioned how it took time to let it all go and then be absolutely quiet in His Presence. He understood the struggles and wars that came against hearing the Lord.

Most of the time, the place within the heart needs to be very quiet when one is receiving something from the Lord. The struggles of the emotions, mind and body are to be put to naught while His Presence melts the cares of this world. The paces and forces of today's world can rob one from being in that place of reception. Fear, anxiety, pain, tiredness, worry, tension, distractions, etc. are all enemies of that quiet and peaceful place.

Noise and stillness dwell within the heart. They are the places within us that determine our level of distraction or our level of quietness. Most can identify thought distractions by closing their eyes and thinking about the Lord. They soon discover their thoughts have wandered far away. The content of those thoughts is the "noise" in our life. Stillness is a place of complete rest in Him, garrisoned by His peace. There are no conflicts or struggles in being still before Him.

One time I had a battle while the Lord was teaching me this concept. I was earnestly desiring Him and seeking Him in fellowship. But every few minutes my mind wandered off to something else. I would catch myself and apologize to Him, and come back only to wander away again. It was during this process I received a picture-vision. Someone was trying to call me and kept getting a busy signal! Then I heard the

Lord say, *"Distracting spirits."* I understood they were forces sent to oppose my hearing. I rebuked them in Jesus Name, and my mind was finally able to rest in quiet communion. He allowed the battle, wanting to teach me more about overcoming the enemy and his ploys.

By abiding in His Presence, we can actually be doing or thinking something else and still hear His quickened Words in all forms. The heart can find a place of such subjection and quietness that it has rest and control over all other places of activity and opposition. *"There remains therefore a rest, for the people of God. For he who has entered His rest, has himself also ceased from his own works, as God did from His. Let us therefore be diligent to enter into that rest..."* (Hebrews 4:9-11 NKJV)

There is a balance in learning how to be quiet in His Presence. He is not necessarily asking us to live monk style lives, where we withdraw from people and stay buried in a prayer closet twenty four hours a day. However, when I was first learning how to hear His still small voice, (described in chapter 6) I needed to withdraw from outer distractions like noise, therefore the best environment for me <u>was</u> a quiet separated place.

I once witnessed a funny example of the opposite of this in visiting a church service where everyone was very demonstratively worshipping the Lord and having a wonderful time placing their whole selves into it! I happened to glance at the guest speaker in the front row. He was sitting straight up in his chair, with his eyes closed, outwardly doing nothing. The worship lasted a good hour, and so did he. It struck me as quite humorous. I knew exactly what he was doing! He <u>really</u> wanted to hear the Lord, since he was the guest speaker! He had grown to a place where he could hear the Lord no matter what was going on around him.

HE SPEAKS WHEN WE PAUSE

"...a woman named Martha welcomed them into her home. Her sister sat on the floor, listening to Jesus as he talked. But Martha was the jittery type, and was worrying over the big dinner she was preparing... But the Lord said to her, Martha, dear friend you are so upset over all these details! There is really only one thing worth being concerned about. Mary has discovered it — and I won't take it away from her!" (Luke 10:38-42 TLB)

In the early days of my journey, He began to train me to stop before Him. I can vividly remember being thoroughly engrossed in getting the dishes done, getting out of the kitchen and on with life. I was completely goal oriented and set on getting them done quickly. While standing at the sink, in the midst of water and food splats, I would hear this little Voice say, *"Come sit at My feet."* That was the last thing I wanted to do. He had touched an idol:[12] ambition, goals, and MY time.

My philosophy in life was, "Hurry up and work so I can hurry up and enjoy living." This situation was a little complex because I did enjoy sitting at His feet! The way I pursued that philosophy was another matter. Was I willing to pursue Him, in HIS TIMING, and in HIS WAY? At first the tug-of-war went back and forth. Of course, when I heard Him say this, it was only when I was in a dead-heat to get my goal accomplished. Or it might be when I had only one more thing to do. He pursued the issue until I was so yielded it didn't matter if I ever did the dishes!

It was not until later I realized the second lesson He was teaching me. After that inner war ended over ownership of my time, I realized He was also retraining my basic philosophy: hurry up and work, so I can hurry up and have fun. Through a process of learning to be still like Mary at Jesus feet, I have now discovered the better way —sitting at His feet <u>while</u> doing the dishes! I finally understood His point was not only setting a time away from life to be with Him, but learning to be with Him as I lived my day. I found that the joy in life is having a <u>relationship with Him in the process</u>.

Hearing Him is a stopping place in all of living; stopping what we are doing, whether spirit, mind and soul, or body, to recognize HIM. We live in the rush-rush of a busy world. It is so easy for our personalities to get caught up in the race. We can be educated in all the places to pause and hear Him, but forget to do so. When we ask for help, the Holy Spirit will retrain our daily habits to include stopping places to hear Him, for He is our Teacher.[13]

Even though we remember to pause and include Him in what we are doing, it doesn't mean He will speak. <u>Only His Presence is the quickening power that speaks life within our pauses</u>. However, if we take the time to pause because we desire Him, He may very well answer. Whether He has anything He wants to say, He loves our fellowship and wants to respond to us. It takes two to have a relationship: one who speaks, and one who listens.

One day on errands, I caught the tail end of a sermon on the radio. He was asking, "How much time do you spend alone with God every week? — Not with someone praying, or things like that, but just honest intimate one on One?" He talked about how we can't expect the Lord to be intimate with us, if we do not give Him time. When I arrived home our cat Cuddles saw me coming. (We called her that because she loved to be loved!) She jumped up on the little table outside, expectantly waiting for me to come love her. (I trained her to know that she would get a lot more loving if she jumped up to my level!) So there she was with perky little ears just waiting on the table. After I gave her attention,

I went inside and around back to the patio door. She ran as fast as she could and jumped on the patio table! I laughed and loved her some more. Then I put water in her dish and emptied the garbage. When I came back, she was sitting up militant style facing directly towards me, ears up and at attention very expectantly waiting for me to pass her way again! It was so precious. I could see the allegory plain as day; you can't help but love someone and give them extra attention when they are just sitting there waiting for you! I thought of the sermon and how we need to spend time alone with Him. Lord, make us available to Your quickened touch, just like Cuddles!

86. HE SPEAKS WHEN WE PONDER HIS WORDS

"Let the words of my mouth and the meditation of my heart be acceptable in Your sight, O Lord, my strength and my Redeemer. (Psalm 19:14 NKJV)"

The word meditation means to ponder, imagine and study. It is like a cow chewing her cud. In the digestion process, she brings the food back up and re-chews. We meditate when we bring His Words back to memory and ponder — rethinking their application, reconsidering, questioning. I have noticed many times, during a quiet moment as I remember His Words, that His Holy Spirit is very close and enlightens things I have not seen before. *(Revelation)* He also brings other things to memory that I didn't know applied and suddenly I realize they also fit. *(Quickening)*

To ponder His Words, we only need a quiet pause, not a "guru" concept of a place of meditation. One time while I was bowling, I was thinking about (or meditating upon) waiting on the Lord for the right timing for the book to go forth. I saw an unusual thing happen to my ball and when it happened I immediately recognized the allegory and what He was saying. The ball was caught in the pit, turning circles and spinning over and over. It was supposed to roll towards the spout and travel back to the chute where the bowler picks up the ball. I watched other balls come back, but not mine, it was still spinning its shocking pink halo around and around. I remembered the Hebrew meaning of the word "wait" in the scripture, *"But those who **wait** on the LORD Shall renew their strength; They shall mount up with wings like eagles, They shall run and not be weary, They shall walk and not faint. (Isaiah 40:31 NKJV)"* The word wait means to bind together by twisting.[14]

As I was still pondering the allegory of waiting upon the Lord for His right timing, my ball finally went into the spout, traveled back to me, and then did the same thing right at the chute. Instead of popping out and rolling into the tray, it began to spin and spin, as a 2nd confirmation

that I understood that He was speaking to me an allegory. I finally had to reach in the chute and bump the ball a few times to get it to pop out. As I pondered His past Words to me about waiting upon Him for His timing, I realized He was saying:
1) I had watched other people go forth while I was still circling.
2) My waiting had been twice as long as I thought it would be but it was almost time for the book to be published.
3) When the time came, it would require my reach, oomph, and participation to get it out of the chute!

87. HE SPEAKS WHEN WE FOLLOW OUR CONSCIENCE

Paul said our conscience bears witness that we have the law of God written on our heart. "For it is not merely hearing the Law {read} that makes one righteous before God, but it is the doers of the Law who will be held guiltless and acquitted and justified. When Gentiles who have not {the divine} Law do instinctively what the Law requires, they are a law to themselves, since they do not have the Law. They show that the essential requirements of the Law are written in their hearts and are operating there; with which their conscience[15] (sense of right and wrong) also bears witness; and their {moral} decisions - their arguments of reason, their condemning or approving thoughts - will accuse or perhaps defend and excuse {them}." (Romans 2:13-15 AMP)

      One day at a fast food restaurant there was a cup of coffee on our tray untouched. My husband asked me if I ordered it. I thought he had. I realized someone else must have ordered and paid for it, and it was placed on the wrong tray. I felt I should return it.

      This all took place within the few seconds it took to think the thought and identify truth. I promptly took the cup back and thought nothing else about it. That night I saw a vision of that coffee cup. Then I saw what looked like the ten commandments etched in stone, pulsating like a heart beat. *(See above scripture)* The Lord was telling me He was well pleased that I had followed my conscience.

      It was a simple thing for Him to be pleased about but He was training me to identify my conscience, and be prompt to obey it. I had lived my Christian life, never really thinking much about my conscience. I had followed it (most of the time!) as a child, but I never placed a label on what it was or what it felt like, or acknowledged it as an important part of hearing God. The Lord took me through a season of learning to identify His heart call within my conscience.

      When we break the law He has placed upon our heart, our thoughts accuse or excuse, and our conscience bears witness that He has written His law upon our hearts. In other words our thoughts either charge us with some offense, or give a plea of defense when our behavior is accused. When our action (or reaction) is placed on trial our thoughts begin to accuse us.

Once during this "conscience" season I bought a potted plant with the saucer. Running through the rain in the parking lot, I wondered if the saucer came with the plant. It was clear in color, different from the pot. I didn't remember being charged for it. When I got to the car, I took out the receipt and there was no extra charge for the saucer.

I struggled with my thoughts. I didn't mind paying the money, I just didn't want to brave the rain and the crowds. I wished I had realized the situation at the check stand. I could not live with the doubt on my conscience so I went back into the store. The lady said it came with the plant and I owed her nothing.

I came home that day with a clear conscience to enjoy my plant with freedom of heart. Paul said, *"And herein do I exercise myself, to have always a conscience void of offense toward God, and toward men." (Acts 24:16 KJ)* The Lord arranged an entire season of opportunities to help me identify that my conscience was perceiving truth, and that my thoughts were testifying to this as well.

Months later, I received an extra pop on our tray and took it back. The woman at the counter said, "Oh that's where it was! I knew I had poured it." I smiled as I returned to my seat, remembering that season. I wondered if I was being tested, but then realized it was a confirmation. There was no wrestling, struggling, or tug-of-war with my thoughts and conscience. Somewhere in my walk with Him I had overcome. If the thought came that I was not lining up with truth I simply altered my course. There was no war inside because I was yielded to following my conscience.

I trained my son to identify his conscience. From a very early age, when he would tell me he had spilled the milk, or had tracked dirt onto the rug, I would thank him for telling me the truth. Because it was an accident, and he didn't try to cover it up, I was not upset. Even before he could pronounce the word conscience, I took the time to help him identify his feelings. I would ask him if he remembered how badly he just felt because he goofed, explaining that feeling was his conscience. And when he told me about his problem, it made his conscience feel much better, not only for being forgiven, but also for his confession. *(Jeremiah 3:13)* He would smile and go his merry way.

Later in life when he approaches greater issues he will have been trained to identify his conscience, and enjoy the good feeling it brings to obey it. ***As an adult we can become more sensitive to our conscience if we take the time to STOP, PONDER, LISTEN to the struggles going on inside.***

When we follow our conscience, we are saying, "Yes God, I want to please You and follow You. I want to hear more from You." Remember the verse that this book is based upon says, *"Take heed what you hear. With the same measure you use, it will be measured to you; and to you who hear, more will be given.* <u>For whoever has, to him more will be given</u>; *but whoever does not have, even what he has will be taken away from him." (Mark 4:24-25 NKJV)* That means that we ourselves measure the amount we hear the Lord. If we want to hear Him more, we need to be accountable with what He has given us, and He will increase our portion of hearing Him.

88. HE SPEAKS WHEN WE DO NOT STRIVE

"...But indeed O man, who art you to reply against God? Will the thing that is formed say to him who formed it, "Why have you made me like this? Does not the potter have power over the clay...¹⁶ Woe to him who strives with his Maker... Shall the clay say to Him who forms it, What are you making?...¹⁷ The Lord spoke to Job: "Shall he that contends with the Almighty instruct him? He that reproves God, let him answer it."¹⁸ One classic phrase quoted so often from Job: Job said "Though he slay me, yet will I trust in him: ***but I will maintain mine own ways before him."***¹⁹

I read a testimony of a gal who received visions and talked to the Lord face to face. The way she came into His Presence was through worship. I *really* wanted to talk to Him face to face! I thought if she can

> *Job said: "But I will maintain mine own ways before him."*
> **The word maintain in Job 13:15: reprove, to be right, argue, decide, justify, defend, rebuke, etc. (3198 Heb Strong's)**

do it, so can I. So I tried. And I tried again. Nothing. I tried harder. Still nothing. Then I launched a campaign and decided to stay up all night if I had to, worshipping Him and seeking Him. I was very tired, and still I kept on. Finally exhaustion set in, I gave up and went to bed. That night I received a vision. This is what I saw! A vision of me trying to jump to heaven. The Lord said nothing to coincide with the vision. He didn't have to. I figured it out all by myself. Heaven's too far to jump.

Do you remember the example in Chapter One, when I heard Him for the first time? Since it was such an eventful milestone in my life, in analyzing it later, I thought that the hoarse voice and the exhaustion made a difference. After all, what else could it be, since He had never spoken to me before? In truth, I wasn't striving with Him at all, I was just thoroughly caught up in Him, and enjoying His Presence for hours. Without my noticing, I became tired and lost my voice.

However, if I'd had a purpose in the worship, song and prayer, in which I went on and on, and on and on, (you know what I mean) for a specific reason, how do you think it would make Him feel? Think how you'd feel if someone wanted something from you, and wouldn't let up until you said yes! That is striving. There is a place for persistence. But it is not meant to be with the attitude of **butting our heads against Him.** [A Pastor friend said something cute in a sermon: the difference between a sheep and a goat is that the goat is always saying, "but, but, but."]

Demanding Him to give answers and guidance is an example of striving. Our attitude needs to be humble, yielded and willing when we approach Him. The lust for knowledge is a wrong motive for seeking answers from Him. It is commonly manifested by pushiness - a push and drive to zealously gain answers. He desires us to pursue Him, but not for the wrong motive. We do not have the rights, arguments, decisions, or justifications to demand God to answer. In seeking His guidance, we cannot demand understanding, we can merely ask. When we strive with God for any reason, we EXPECT Him to act a certain way, and do not give Him room to be Himself. May we yield our wills and let go of our striving. If we love Him, we will yield and give Him space to make His own choices.

Job is a perfect example of striving with God. In standing against his enemies, he insisted on maintaining his belief system. He insisted he was right, argued, decided, justified, and defended his stand. Yet even though Job's belief system was accurate about Him, when the trial was over God rebuked Job for maintaining his own way before Him. *(Job 13:15)* What does that mean? Job's belief system did not allow God to have freedom of choice. God said He was God, and could do anything. Job did not understand why he was being tried when he knew his belief system was accurate. Job's downfall was his expectations of God - he did not give God room to be Himself and freely choose His own will.

In having a relationship with Him, we need to be willing to let God be God, and choose the way He desires His Word to be applied. This is especially true in waiting for His promises. We strive against God when we inaccurately hold His promise — for instance, having a written note of promise from someone, going before him and demanding he perform, because he gave us the note. I have seen many who have continued to strive against God about His Word and how it should apply in their lives. I have watched them go around the same track for years, simply because they refused to release their will to His plan.

The way we can hear more from the Lord and have a living joyful relationship with Him is to let go of our striving expectations and let Him be God.

89. HE SPEAKS WHEN WE LIMIT FLEECES

Using a fleece is a comforting way to please the soul and personality, but it is not recommended as a pattern of relationship with the Lord. Most people use fleeces by stating a certain need for guidance: "Lord, if You do such n' such, then I know I'm supposed to do such n' such." Notice the if-then clause. This clause suggests making a contract with God on YOUR TERMS. When a person lays a fleece before the Lord, he is putting God into a position to answer according to his way, not God's. It is controlling the limits of circumstances and asking God to fit that mold.

There are those who lust for signs. (The Pharisees wanted signs, rather than Jesus. They did not see *HE WAS the sign*.) People who look for signs are also vulnerable to falling into a snare. They are ones who lay fleeces before the Lord on a <u>continuing</u> basis. One satanic realm of influence is the lust for signs.

God knows the heart, and may answer a fleece, as recorded in Gideon's plight. Notice the awe and respect of Gideon's heart in approaching God in this manner. Placing the fleece before the Lord was with great caution as unto the fear and respect of the Lord: *"And Gideon said unto God, Let not thine anger be hot against me, and I will speak but this once: let me prove, I pray thee, but this once with the fleece, let it now be dry only upon the fleece and upon all the ground let there be dew." (Judges 6:39-40 KJ)*

The fleece was a request to God, and God answered as His gift. This was not without consequences. God wanted Gideon's army cut down to 300 men. It was not that God was angry so Gideon had to make up for the use of the fleece by cutting his army; but that the fleece and answer were very much like a contract. Gideon suggested a contract on Gideon's terms. God answered. Then God gave Gideon God's terms: 300 men.

The scriptures suggest God is reasonable, listens to the will of man, and is willing to be flexible and work with him. He is our Good Father. However, we should not test Him to see how far He is willing to bend. This whole concept is something to be approached with reverence, respect and awe. He's not Someone to bargain with in the market place. Those who use fleeces on a regular basis are asking for trouble.

Fleeces suggests a flexible part of God's nature, but when we draw the line of flexibility it is best WE BE THE FLEXIBLE ONE.

If one has the wrong motive: a lust for signs, lust for knowledge, demanding (striving with) or testing and proving Him, one day the Lord will thresh out that leaven in the heart through a sifting process.

There is one other reason God would cut this weed out. There are people who have been accustomed to using fleeces with a pure desire to find out His will. He knows the heart, and perhaps will even answer for a season on their terms. Yet there will come a day when He wants them to grow and come out of this type of relationship with Him. Fleeces put God in a box, He is not cheerfully willing to stay there for very long! There are many of ways to hear from Him without putting Him in a box. He desires to bring His own up and out, seeking Him on His territory.

90. HE SPEAKS WHEN WE PRAY

"And when He had sent the multitudes away, He went up on the mountain by Himself to pray. Now when evening came, He was alone there." (Matthew 14:23 KJ)

There are different kinds of prayer which can be likened to a teacher having different teaching styles. One style is similar to a salesman who talks AT the students. There's a lecture with no pause for questions or response. It's the same with prayer; this kind of prayer may be quite fluent and say a lot, but there isn't a lot of pausing when the Lord can get a Word in edgewise. This is a one-way communication when the person talks and the Lord listens. The person is not to blame for this behavior, as it probably hasn't dawned on him that the Lord MIGHT want to say something back!

Another kind of prayer is like a teacher who talks WITH the students. Instead of standing at the blackboard, the teacher is out among the students perhaps sharing a bit, then pausing for the students to ask questions and give a response. It's a two way process of communication and learning. And that process can be fun. It's the same way with talking to the Lord, He also wants to participate and give a response.

There are also different times to pray. In the above scripture, Jesus withdrew from the crowds so that He could have fellowship with the Father. Quiet time alone in prayer is a wonderful and strengthening place to be.

Most often, I pray outside that quiet time. If I have something on my mind, I don't wait for the "prayer closet" opportunity to say it. My prayers are more like a conversation with Him. It doesn't matter where I am, I just say it. (I mostly pray in my mind, because I'm not that much of a natural talker.) Often when I say something to Him, He will say some small Word or phrase back to me that can open up an entire scope of

His answer. The Lord is an expert at saying powerful and simple punch lines that open all kinds of cross references and common denominators to my mind.

For instance I was feeling badly over a person who very rarely expressed emotion. One time I was hoping for a smile or something in the way of excitement at a certain piece of news I had to share. Again at little response, I immediately said, "Lord it sure would help if You could help her become a little more emotional!" Then I heard Him say, *"Layers."* Immediately I remembered a little saying I had written in high school, *"Like the layers of an onion are the barriers of frightened hearts."* I knew this person well and understood her daily pain. I immediately recanted and said, "Lord, forget it, she needs these layers so that she doesn't hurt as bad!" I knew that if the Lord opened her emotions, then the painful circumstances she was in would cause her to suffer even more greatly. (Now don't get me wrong, often the Lord wants to work through the layers in our hearts so that we will become more honest and sensitive to Him and others. But in this case, I understood to do so at this time would be too overwhelming.) In response to my prayer, His one little Word, "layers" opened up an entire scope and told me <u>His</u> answer to what I had been wishing. That Word gave me much understanding that I would have missed if I hadn't just bounced what I thought off the Lord. In other words, I "prayed" about it. He really does speak when we pray, we just have to pray more and listen more.

91. HE SPEAKS WHEN WE WORSHIP

The Lord dwells in the praises of His people. *(Psalm 22:3)* When we enter worship, there is an intimacy and precious touch as the Lord speaks straight into our heart and melts all our barriers. In His Presence, He pierces our soul with His love and it can touch our life like nothing else. Nothing can separate us from His love once we know it.

Those who are longing for Him with open arms are finding more of Him than ever before. They are enjoying freedoms in worship they didn't know existed. Their "religious boxes" of how to do things properly are falling away and they are expressing their love for Him without restraints. They are worshipping Him with their whole spirit, soul and body.

He's not looking for a people who *play* church, He's looking for a people who *are* His church. There's a difference. His church is His bride, and <u>that bride loves Him passionately</u>. The last day church is going to get excited about God. It's going to pour out, run out, love out and gush out all over the world. There will be only one priority of this last day bride: To love God with her whole heart, mind and soul, and to love others the same way. The Lord will be speaking to His bride by raining the intimacy of His refreshing Presence on those who give Him adoring worship. And He will also be speaking to the world through His passionate bride as her love for Him bubbles over. Look out world!

There is a power available at a group level of worship that is not as available on an individual level. Jesus said, *"For where two or three are gathered together in My name, there am I in the midst of them." (Matthew 18:20 KJ)* There is a synergistic effect that takes place at a group level. If you think about the fact that each person whose name is written in the book of life has a guardian angel, and when two or more gather in His name, their angels also gather.[20] And when two or more gather, there is more faith and more power than just one. Then add the fact that each person who has accepted Jesus as their personal Savior has the Holy Spirit living in their heart, and then add the fact that God's Presence via His Holy Spirit is also present in the meeting. — What a combination of power!

The Bible also says that one will chase a thousand, and two will put ten thousand to flight. *(Deuteronomy 32:30)* You get a gathering of people together in one room worshipping the name of Jesus, and the devil can't stand it. He's out of there in a hurry. More freedom and refreshing is available, simply because the devil isn't around to hinder it! The Lord draws near, rains His Presence and things happen! Dramatic healing, deliverance, anointing and freedom take place.

Because the Lord rains His Presence both in private worship and in group worship, there needs to be a <u>balance</u> between both, for He is not wanting to reach out to us in just one way or the other. There seems to be a difference of opinion between some Mary and Martha people.[21] The Mary's sit at the Lord's feet in quiet prayer and meditation worshipping Him more on a personal level. The Martha's are out mingling and worshipping the Lord in gatherings. In reality, we need both to have a strengthened and nourished life.

The problem is that we tend to do what we feel comfortable with and tend to do what works. If we are used to being a Mary, quietly sitting at His feet, then it may be difficult to come into His Presence in group worship where there is so much distraction. The Mary feels left out even when she participates. One the other side, the Martha who actively seeks the Lord through meetings, tends to feel the Lord is far away when she is away from a corporate gathering. Do you see this dichotomy? If you tend to be one or the other, then be open to the Lord wanting to reach you in the opposite way. He wants to touch every area of your life through every available means of worship and intimacy.

92. HE SPEAKS WHEN WE MAKE HOLY CHOICES

In the Old Testament, the temple was built in three sections. The outer court was where the common activities took place. The inner court was the place of service to the Lord. And the most Holy Place was the innermost place where the Lord spoke to the priest. It was an awesome area to enter. He needed to go through cleansing rites and make sure his life was in order before entering. It is said that he wore a rope around his belt, so that those on the outside could pull him out if needed, for fear of going in themselves. He also wore bells on his robe and those outside could hear that he was still alive and moving around.

We have been cleansed by the blood of Jesus Christ, and we are made holy not by our own righteousness, but because of His. However, when we live an unholy life, it is not a favorable environment for His Presence to dwell. Jesus ate with the unholy people, and loved them. And thus we too should reach out to all. However, enjoying the pleasures of carnality in the same way the world does, leads to a life conducive to inviting evil spirits instead of the Holy Spirit. If you want to hear more from the Lord, then take note of your life style. Today, fellowship with television carnality grieves the Holy Spirit and constricts His freedom in your life, especially in hearing Him in greater portions.

93. HE SPEAKS WHEN WE SEEK COUNSEL

"Where no counsel is, the people fall: but in the multitude of counsellors there is safety." (Proverbs 11:14 KJ)

Have you ever met those who talk incessantly about themselves, never asking how you are? They are talkers and not listeners. Rarely asking for counsel or advice, their independence and self absorption becomes their worst downfall.

The Lord wants us to stand on our own two feet and learn to make decisions. However, there are certain major decisions we should never make without the counsel of at least two responsible, godly, people who know us and whom we trust. Why? Because inevitably, we are blind and not able to see our weaknesses but in most instances, they will be able to ***see our needs and yet still look at the facts***.

The major decisions needing counsel are marriage, changing locations in jobs, life after high school graduation, financial investments, etc.

The second reason why counsel is so important, is for the safety of those we love. *"Where no counsel is, the people fall: but in the multitude of counsellors there is safety." (Proverbs 11:14 KJ)* These major decisions most often directly affect those closest to us, and if we make the wrong decision, they suffer with us. There is a penalty for making wrong decisions and it may or may not have anything to do with justice, or the Lord's rebuke. The greater the decision, the greater the ramifications. Often these outcomes have lasting effects that have lifetime results. Think it through, pray it through, counsel it through, wait it through. Again, give God time. Leave no step out when seeking His guidance.

94. HE SPEAKS WHEN WE FAST

" So He said to them, "This kind can come out by nothing but prayer and fasting." (Mark 9:29 NKJV)

Fasting[22] can break the chains of darkness and help place one's heart in a position to discern properly including God's guidance. There are many motives why a Christian chooses to fast. The most common incorrect ones have to do with 1.) justification and 2.) manipulation. Man carries subconscious guilt and tries to purge and purify himself through fasting as a means to "obtain God." Perhaps some do this unknowingly because their faith level is directly tied to "feeling clean" and accepted by God. This of course is not a proper motive for fasting, but even in our wrong understanding God honors our desire for Himself. We are accepted only because of Jesus Christ, and Who He is, not because of who we try to be.

In the need for guidance and answers, some have a subconscious drive to fast in order to manipulate. They use fasting as a subtle way to persuade God to give them answers. This does not please Him, but in His infinite mercy He may still answer because He knows our desire and need for His guidance.

Of course fasting is an acceptable means for discerning His guidance and hearing from Him. *(Acts 13:2)* But **the Lord chose fasting to prepare man's heart to hear and receive, not to prepare or sway God.**

The following is a breakdown of the pattern of the Isaiah 58 fast. It can be divided into three descriptions: 1. Its format 2. Its promises 3. Its result.

THE FORMAT OF GOD'S FAST
(ISAIAH 58)

"Is this not the fast that I have chosen: To loose the bonds of wickedness, To undo the heavy burdens, To let the oppressed go free, And that you break every yoke?" (Isaiah 58:6 NKJV)

1. **SHARE YOUR SUSTENANCE WITH THE NEEDY (verse 7)**
Literal
   a. Divide your bread with the hungry
   b. Bring the homeless poor into your house
   c. When you see the naked, to cover him
   d. Don't hide yourself from your own flesh

Spiritual
   a. Share God's Words with those in famine
   b. Pray for the captive to come home
   c. Forgive and cover your brother's sin
   d. Pray for your family

2. TAKE AWAY OPPRESSIVE HEAVINESS (verse 9B)
Literal
   a. Remove the yoke from your midst
   b. Remove the pointing of the finger
   c. Remove speaking wickedness

Spiritual
   a. Don't oppress others - not only in deed, but in thought and expectations
   b. Do not criticize or judge your brother's walk
   c. Pray and think kind words

3. SPEND YOUR OWN ENERGY FOR THE NEEDY (verse 10 NASB)
Literal
   a. Give yourself to the hungry
   b. Satisfy the desire of the afflicted

Spiritual
   a. Lay aside your own goals for those hungry for God
   b. Give hope to those in torment

THE PROMISES OF GOD'S FAST

1. **LOOSE THE DARKNESS (verse 8 and 10B)**
   Physical, spiritual or emotional deliverance from darkness:
   a. Your light will break out like the dawn
   b. Your light will rise in the darkness
   c. Your gloom will become like midday

2. **QUICK HEALING (verse 8 NASB)**
   Healing for body, mind, soul, emotions, spirit:
   a. Your recovery will speedily spring forth

3. **YOUR RELATIONSHIP WITH HIM WILL GUIDE YOU (verse 8B, 11, 9)**
   He will answer your plea for understanding:
   a. Your righteousness will go before you
   b. The glory of the Lord will be your rear guard
   c. You will call, and the Lord will answer
   d. You will cry, and He will say, Here am I

4. **QUENCH THIRST AND STRENGTH (verse 11)**
   In trying times, He will give physical and spiritual strength and refreshment:
   a. He will satisfy your desire in scorched places
   b. And give strength to your bones
   c. You will be like a watered garden
   d. Like a spring of water whose waters do not fail

5. **RESTORATION OF THE FALLEN (verse 12 NASB)**
   You will repair other's brokenness:
   a. Those from among you will rebuild the ruins
   b. You will rise up the age-old foundations
   c. You will be called the repairer of the breach
   d. The restorer of the streets in which to dwell

THE RESULT AND PURPOSE OF THE FAST IS:

1. **DELIVERANCE (verse 6 NASB)**
   Break satan's chains that immobilize, restrict, and restrain us from freedom:
   a. Loosen the bonds of wickedness
   b. Undo the bands of the yoke
   c. Let the oppressed go free
   d. Break every yoke

    In today's culture there can be many indulgences. One can have an appetite for that morning cup of coffee, for that TV show, for the closest parking place, for reading the newspaper, being the first in line, or for sleeping in. There are many places of indulgence of the flesh that can be yielded in relation to a fast. The strength of the yielding is totally reliant upon the passion an individual has for whatever is forgone.
    I describe fasting as a type of purging, cleansing, or emptying

oneself of the pampering things that are not supernaturally imparted by God. It is letting go of the "physical" in earnest desire of the "spiritual." The desire for the spiritual, meaning the voluntary choice of God's spiritual answer or provision over mankind's answer or provision.

The most important key to fasting before the Lord is the heart. A fast is **not** intended to:

1. Manipulate God into responding *"Why have we fasted and Thou dost not see? Why have we humbled ourselves and Thou dost not notice?" (Isaiah 58:3 NASB)*

2. Enter into a tug o'war, battling wills with Him...*they ask Me for just decisions... (cont) vs 2 NASB*

3. Provide justification of oneself through cleansing *"...as {if they were} a nation that has done righteousness, And has not forsaken the ordinance of their God" (vs 2 NASB)*

Rather, the proper response of the heart is the voluntary emptying, pouring out, abasing, humbling of self, IN THE INSIDE, before the Presence of Almighty God. It is letting go of the sustenance of self, yielding to Him. With or without the physical characteristics of a fast, the Lord hearkens to the heart.

When the heart is right before the Lord, one will not oppress others, and seek self satisfaction, as recorded in Isaiah 58:3. When the true humility before the Lord comes from the heart, it will show on the outside. For instance, how we live and treat others.

In summary, the promises of the fast the Lord chooses in Isaiah 58 are to disperse darkness, quicken healing, provide guidance, quench thirst, restore strength and

---

GOD'S FAST
SHARE WHAT YOU HAVE
•
BE KIND
•
GIVE OF YOURSELF

GOD'S PROMISES
HE WILL BRING YOU LIGHT
•
HE WILL PROVIDE YOUR RECOVERY
•
HE WILL PROVIDE YOU ANSWERS
•
HE WILL GIVE YOU STRENGTH
•
HE WILL REBUILD YOUR RUINS

restore that which has fallen. Results are often deliverance for the fasting one, or for whom he is fasting.

The concepts in this chapter are some of the things we can personally do to hear more from the Lord. Few people, if any, will comply one hundred percent to any of them. God is a very loving and merciful God. And He understands our weakness. Regardless of our shortcomings, He wants so deeply to reach us on our own personal level. So do not let guilt or condemnation disqualify you from seeking the Lord to hear more from Him! He loves you exactly the way you are and wants to have fellowship with you. The deeper you crave His fellowship the deeper and more accountable your life will become. The Christian walk is a growing, maturing process from infancy to adulthood. We can't learn to walk until we learn to stand. And believe me, God is there cheering us every step of the way.

1. Faith: [4102 Gk Strong's]
2. Luke 22:31,32
3. James 1:6
4. Psalm 119:50
5. Acts 4:31
6. Hebrews 11
7. Noted from the book, "Smith Wigglesworth: The Secret of His Power © 1982 by Albert Hibbert.
8. John 3:13-17
9. Abide: [3306 Gk Strong's]
10. (Daniel 10:12-13)
11. Luke 22:42
12. An idol in the Old Testament was something erected in their lives in which they deemed so valuable that they gave it worship. In the New Testament, an idol is not necessarily given an outward worship, rather it's an inward desire that conflicts with having fellowship with the Lord.
13. I John 2:27
14. [# 6960 Hebrew] in Strong's Exhaustive Concordance
15. Conscience: co-perception. From a word meaning to see completely, understand, become aware. [4893 Gk Strong's from 4894 Gk Strong's] Bears witness: testifies jointly, by corroborating evidence. [4828 Gk Strong's]
16. Romans 9:20-21
17. Isaiah 45:9
18. Job 40:1-2
19. The word maintain in Job 13:15 = Reprove: to be right, argue, decide, justify, defend, rebuke, etc. [3198 Heb Strong's]
20. Heb 1:14
21. Mary and Martha story: Luke 10:38-42
22. Fasting: abstinence. [3521 Gk Strong's]

CHAPTER 9:
UNDERSTANDING AND APPLYING

WHAT GOD SPEAKS
(INTERPRETATION)

95. HE SPEAKS THROUGH COMMON REFERENCE POINTS

I found the following humorous entries on the Internet. I thought they were too cute to pass by. To understand them, is to understand what the Lord goes through in communicating with us!

- "My youngest son once thought that God was a turtle. (God is eternal)"

- "After Sunday School, my friend asked her five year old daughter what she did in class that day. Susie replied, "We gave Jesus a bath!" Susie's mother asked, "What do you mean - you gave Jesus a bath?" Susie replied, "Our teacher said, "Warsh up the Lord.""

- "My five year old is learning the song that teaches the books of the Bible. "Matthew, Mark, Luke and John, Axe the Opposums.""

- "We remind our kids each year that Easter is a remembrance of Jesus' death on the cross and His raising from the grave. My five year old with big eyes asked this year, "How many times does Jesus have to die?""

- "My five year old son and I like to listen to Steve Green, a Christian music artist, while driving in the car. One of his songs has a rousing chorus of "Jesus Christ is Lord." My son, obviously moved by the music, joined in with his own rousing version, "Jesus Christ is bored!!""

- "My grandmother said that when she was a little child, after church she would look around the altar for the hole. I asked her what she meant and she replied, "You know, the pastor talked about 'The Father, the Son, in the hole he goes.' She never could figure out what He was doing in that hole."

When I read these, I thought what perfect examples they are of what it is like to learn a new language. New words are understood by connecting common reference points of things we already understand. And sometimes like these children, when we learn a new spiritual language, our reference points are not exactly what the Lord intended! He must chuckle at some of the things we think He is saying!

In learning a new language, a common reference point is something we already know. When we hear something new, our minds search for a point of reference in which to categorize the new word. For example, a child already knows the shade of red in his old crayon box. This shade is his reference point. In his new box he needs to identify and sort more shades of red. Learning a new language is just like sorting new crayons together with older similar colors.

What the children above did not have, was a solid reference point in which to understand words like, "eternal, worship, Acts, Apostles, keeping in remembrance, Lord and Holy Ghost." These new words were not connected with common reference points in their every day vocabulary and thus their precious minds heard the closest reference point they could find!

I know a gal who was praying over her husband and saw a picture-vision of a bellows. She didn't know what a bellows was and had no common reference point to understand the picture. Later she saw a bellows on someone's fireplace hearth, and remembering her vision, she asked what it was. When she found out that it blew air onto embers to flame up a fire, she knew the Lord was saying He would be blowing upon her husband, stirring and rekindling his life back into passion with the Lord.

96. HE SPEAKS THROUGH PUZZLING TOGETHER MYSTERY WORDS

One only has to read the Bible to know God speaks in mysteries. Do we ever really know what He means? The answer is "Yes, but only through the quickening power of His Holy Spirit."

If there is one main point to this book, it is the importance of His quickening power. All words are empty and dead without it.

When He wants His mystery to unfold, He begins the revelation process, a piece at a time. His mysteries are like big puzzles, with pieces scattered throughout the Bible. Some pieces are linked in context, others are separated through time, then reaffirmed by another writer. It's no wonder Bible scholars spend their whole lives dedicated to unraveling its wealth.

Each piece is a part of the general puzzle, and when the Lord sheds light on it by revelation, that piece is quickened. "Oh, that's where it belongs!" That piece finds its niche, its place. It joins the others awaiting more to come. The unfolding of His mysteries is a gradual process linked with revelation and quickening.

Knowledge cannot be ignored in understanding His mysteries.

Practicing scholarly rules is appropriate. Understanding the original language is helpful. Recognizing He speaks in the Old Testament as types and examples is beneficial, as well as studying the culture, laws and celebrations. These and others will give the puzzle the right color. Yet, the actual mysteries are not openly published, they await His quickening and revelation for those who will listen.

His mysterious Words also come in forms other than the Bible: dreams, visions, life's allegories, parabolic stories and more. What they have in common is allegorical language, interpreted one symbol at a time. These symbols join to tell the story: HIS story, as it applies to our lives.

Interpreting His mysteries is a challenge. When in doubt about a mystery Word, try this rule: In most cases, His Words to us are not meant to be applied literally in the physical but applied to our spiritual lives.

What is a mystery Word? It is a Word that is not necessarily in your every day vocabulary. It's a way of speaking that you don't speak yourself. An example of this is when the Lord said to me, *"Have you ever seen someone wrestle their nightgown?"* He did not mean this literally as in physically struggling with their pajamas. [Notice it *can* be interpreted that way] The season He had placed me in, He had previously called REST. This mystery Word was His way of saying I was not complying!

In my early days of hearing Him I had a difficult time understanding He wanted to talk to me spiritually, not literally. One time He told me He wanted me to prepare an ark for winter. Now if I had known then what I know now, I would have immediately realized the word "ark" is not in my every day vocabulary! Therefore, it was a mystery Word, and should have been applied spiritually. But no, not me. I heard a story about how the ants store up for winter, and a few other tidbits. So I proceeded to fill our trailer with any survival gear and food I could stuff in. I had about thirty buckets filled with salt, grains and the like. I had camping gear and survival gear. Maps, you name it, the trailer was absolutely *stuffed*. That winter came and we parked the trailer in our empty lot behind our house. As the rains came, so did the mud. One day I noticed our tires were almost flat because the trailer was so ladened. I thought, boy if I need this trailer now, it would never leave shore - it would sink in the mud before it was launched!

Winter came and went, and I finally got the point. I gave all the food buckets to the local homeless kitchen! Spiritually, winter did come. And all the Words and promises the Lord had spoken to me, became my survival during a very long, cold season. I had prepared an ark, one that carried me through a tough time. His Words to me became a refuge and a safe place.

Another lesson in interpreting His mystery Words: I have noticed mystery Words almost always have two contrasting interpretations. Not only can they be interpreted spiritually and physically, but they can be interpreted from the Lord's point of view or from the enemy's. For instance, the Lord tells you He's going to pull the feathers out of your nest and teach you to fly. Now this can be very disconcerting, depending upon which view you have! One: "Oh no, something terrible is going to happen and my place of security is going to be dismantled and I'm going to be thrown out!" (enemy interpretation) Two: "Oh wow, the Lord is going to move me to a better place where I can soar on the wind of His Holy Spirit, and have a great time seeing the sights!" (Lord's interpretation)

The stronger the mystery Word, the more noticeable the two contrasting interpretations become. This happens when you hear riddles, or what the Bible calls dark speech. I went through a whole season of hearing riddles. Each and every time they could be interpreted from a negative point of view, or positive. It was a real time of standing in faith for me and overcoming my personal weaknesses.

97. HE SPEAKS THROUGH APPLYING DETAILS

This is similar to the beauty of a painting. The artist places the smallest strokes on the canvas. Without the minute details the expressions of his painting would not be complete. When learning to interpret symbols in our lives with the Lord, the small gifts are equally important. He places the jots and tittles there with care. They are easy to ignore simply because they are "small" gifts. The interpretation will be more complete with the small details included.

I am reminded of the dreams Joseph interpreted for the king. Joseph noticed a pattern repeated twice. He said, *"And for that the dream was doubled unto Pharaoh twice; it is because the thing is established by God, and God will shortly bring it to pass." (Genesis 41:32 KJ)* This small detail was important to Joseph's ears. Joseph also understood the seven ears of corn to be seven years.[1] His ears were quickened that the number seven was an important detail.

Some jots and tittles are described by adjectives. What size? Is it small, large, skinny, fat? What shape? Is it round, square, rectangular, oblong? To what degree? What kind of health is it in? Colors also can have symbolic meaning.

98. HE SPEAKS THROUGH PUZZLING TOGETHER ACCUMULATED KNOWLEDGE

The Lord brought a picture to my mind of a beautiful snow-white bird. Not having any understanding, I waited upon Him for days without any insight. Finally, I went to the library. Not even knowing its name, I found it in a picture dictionary of birds. Amazing facts were quickened to me, pinpointing exactly where I was in circumstances with the Lord.

I would not have received the blessing, if I had not pursued the available means to understand. I felt nothing spiritual about my getting in the car and driving to the library. However the Word says, *"For as many as are led by the Spirit of God, they are the sons of God."*[2] I was not aware at the time of being led by the Holy Spirit to go to the library. It was only later in my PONDERING that the Holy Spirit quickened that scripture to me.

It takes two to have a relationship, and the two need to have the same language. Developing a language requires gathering knowledge. We can use Websters, Ungers, Strong's, and whatever else is available to seek understanding. It's simply a matter of using our mind.

The greater our knowledge of that subject, the greater the possibilities for understanding more of what He is saying. For example, when the Lord told me to consider the butterfly: I first thought of the fact it transforms itself through various stages. I connected that with the idea that I would do the same. But later, as my knowledge of those stages increased, so did my understanding of what the Lord was doing in my life.

99. HE SPEAKS THROUGH BALANCING KNOWLEDGE WITH QUICKENING

There is a difference between having an interpretative language of the mind and having an interpretative language of the Spirit. Yet, they can join in balance to communicate exactly what the Holy Spirit is saying. Learning a spiritual language of interpretation does happen with the intellect. He says, *"Come let us reason together."*[3] He enjoys that kind of relationship with us. However, many go no farther, they know the Lord <u>only</u> with their minds. The Lord uses our knowledge to communicate with us, yet the joy of relationship comes from deep within the heart.

The balance of developing a language of the heart and not just of the mind, is to develop it WITH HIM through the unfolding process of quickening and revelation. Quickening makes something heard relevant and fits a need. Revelation is the fact the Lord has been there, and only now have you just realized it!

In learning the language of interpretation, it is essential to place quickening as the priority, with knowledge following behind. With knowledge first, one is vulnerable to missing the mark because one can read into life what the Lord is not saying.[4] It is possible for one to become so adept at applying the language of interpretation, that one sees every detail of life as a word from the Lord. Only details QUICKENED by the Holy Spirit bring life. Joseph said, *"Do not interpretations come from God?"*[5] If we acquire all the language vocabulary of definitions, and He has not spoken, we prophesy falsely, hearing out of the imaginations of our own souls.[6] We cannot separate His Presence of quickening (and revelation) from the knowledge of a language.

100. HE SPEAKS THROUGH BUILDING DEFINITIONS

For two to have a relationship, they need to communicate in a common language. Learning a language can be a funny experience. Have you traveled to a foreign country, tried to ask a simple question, and the other person turns red, looking all embarrassed? You don't know what you said, but you know you said it!

Much of learning a language of interpretation is a matter of definition. No one knew what the letters "w-o-r-d" were, until someone gave "WORD" a meaning. "Word" became a symbol for a form of expression. Our written language is made up of symbols, which we call letters, and then labeled with definitions we call vocabulary. The same is true in developing a spiritual language.

The Lord builds our spiritual language by symbols or concepts quickened to us by scripture, life circumstances, our family in Christ, creation allegories, visions, dreams, etc. He uses any part of life to teach us definitions. *("If any man have ears to hear, let him hear...take care what you listen to. By your standard of measure it shall be measured unto you." Mark 4:23,24 NASB)* Have you ever been in the same set of circumstances, for the umpteenth time in a row, and finally say, "I wonder if God is trying to tell me something?" When His Word first penetrates our hearts, it does so as an idea or symbol of communication. Then He can speak to us again with that same "word" and we will understand. It becomes easier to hear Him when our vocabulary has grown, for there are more "words" with which to communicate. Definitions applied to these symbols or concepts are built one step at a time, line upon line. Each building block gives meaning and thus adds a word to our vocabulary.

The process of developing a language becomes another means of fellowship WITH HIM, when we do it with His help. By taking time to ponder and search our heart before Him for understanding, we give the Holy Spirit an opportunity to target certain areas. This brings us to that wonderful place of discovery. Finding new definitions can become delightful rather than just a mundane pursuit of the mind.

Discovering definitions is a part of revelation. Not only can revelation happen in recognizing that He spoke, but also revelation happens in recognizing WHAT He spoke. Rather than establishing definitions as an intellectual pursuit, with the Lord's help the Holy Spirit gives the joy of discovery. It becomes a process of hide and seek. He hides the definition from disclosure, (to our understanding) while we search with His help for the meaning. At the precise moment of revelation, the Holy Spirit zeros in on the perfect insight, and that "OH!" pops forth. **Discovering definitions can be a real joy when companioned with revelation and His quickening power.**

FINDING DEFINITIONS

When we have discovered a "symbol," we are to ponder before the Lord to find out its *purpose and function*. When we discover a symbol's function or purpose, we usually will discover its definition. For example, the purpose for hair is a covering. *(1 Co. 11:15)* The Bible also says a woman's hair is her glory. So the spiritual definition of hair could be the covering of God's glory. Or consider the word "stand." Its function is to be upright, in an active position, not at rest. The spiritual definition of standing could be the active place within our faith, expending energy to remain upright. Anything can have a spiritual definition. **Always remember the knowledge will be empty if it's not Him speaking.**

Definitions can be what the Lord gave someone else, or they can be what He has given you. Either way, the definition must become your own to have meaning. Sometimes when you have the foundation of someone else's vocabulary to build upon and are launching out and discovering new definitions of your own, you will come across two opposing definitions: your own, and someone else's. If so, consider the other, but use your own. When He speaks to you, it is personally and as it applies to your own life.

When you practice pondering language definitions with His help, you will gain two values: the habit of looking to Him for help in understanding and the security of knowing that He is the One Who helped you develop it. (That particular security is important when He begins to build upon it.)

The following allegory, is an example of definitions being quickened in my life: **The definition:** Anything that moves and carries people is the definition of my spiritual relationship with Him. He carries me, therefore the definition of any kind of transportation is my relationship with Him. It doesn't matter what it is, auto, bus, skiing, skateboard, boat, street car, etc. The allegory: I am driving my car down a two-way street. I look out the side window, cross over the yellow line and go through a yellow warning light. The yellow line depicts my conscience. I stay on the right side of it to travel safely. The peering out the window is the direction of my focus. The yellow warning is the sign the Lord places in my path to yield, to give right of way.

The pondering: An example of this would mean nothing, unless it is quickened. The Holy Spirit nudges me and I notice it might have a spiritual connotation. I ponder that moment to see if I have my thoughts and intents focused on where He is bringing me. I search to see if I have crossed my conscience in my thoughts, I pause to remember if He has brought other signs to warn me to yield.

If it is true, it will only take a moment for the Holy Spirit to do His work. All He needs is an open door. We open the door by being willing and yielding, pondering and searching our hearts before Him. The Holy Spirit is quick to bring circumstances, thoughts, etc. to mind if they apply. He will bring them like little puzzle pieces one at a time into view, and then fit them into place.

The quickening: The allegory is quickened that I am not looking in the direction He has called me; my thoughts have crossed my conscience and entered the danger zone. He has placed warnings in front of me to slow down and yield my will.

Another example of definitions forming allegories: food is His rhema (living Word). The kitchen is the place in the servant's life where His food is being organized and prepared. The kitchen can be a cluttered disaster, with little room to prepare His food; or it can be neatly organized, with a place for everything, and in order. (Sitting at His feet, reading and pondering without heart distractions, etc.)

One might be a super fast cook, sloppy and anxious to get it on the table, or slow and methodical, and very meticulous. Those who partake of the food, might attack it with great vigor, chewing little, swallowing quantities, and the food might be assimilated and digested quickly; or one might be a very picky eater, eating only certain items very slowly, with digestion taking its time. The allegory could be hilariously true how we approach our lives with the sustenance of His Living Word. However the allegory would be missed, without definition.

The definition of anything carrying people as a symbol of relationship with Him was a symbol in the beginning of my new vocabulary. Today, years later, I do not need the Holy Spirit to quicken afresh the meaning of that symbol. It is simply knowledge I have acquired, a foundation word without the thrill of discovery. It is just a word we have together as a common understanding. It has become knowledge.

The quickening power of the Holy Spirit no longer quickens the WORD automobile, He quickens the CONCEPT. An example could be someone cleaning the dirt off the windows of his car. The quickening moment is when he realizes he is in a season in his relationship with the Lord when he can't see clearly where he is going. It is quickened to him the Lord is going to help clear the vision problem.

> Remember, if you choose a word on this list, it must be QUICKENED to your own personal set of circumstances, or QUICKENED upon the Lord's personal Word to you.

LIST OF DEFINITIONS

When I first wrote this book in 1984, I included this list. Later I felt it was so boring no one would read it, so I erased it. Now, more than a decade later, people are beginning to have dreams and visions and many have no idea what they mean! I began helping others interpret their dreams and realized much of what I was interpreting was based on a language the Lord had already taught me. I wondered again if I should share some of my own language list for others who are on the same road — as what I would interpret seemed to fit their need. Then a gal came to me and said I know what your next book is going to be about! She said I would be writing about how to interpret what the Lord speaks. I told her that was very interesting, as Chapter 9 was my smallest chapter, and I was in the process of questioning whether I should put the list back in the book.

I considered that having a list of what someone else had quickened to them, may take away the personal joy of discovery — and it *is* a joy to build an interpretative language when you recognize His Presence in the process. However, I also realized that if someone has never had an interpretive language before, they may need examples to start. So, after balancing it all, I have inserted this list back into the chapter. The list is certainly not complete, and my language has grown since I wrote it. But it is a sample.

Let me remind you that if you already have a "word" on this list and it has a different definition, keep your own definition. When the Lord talks to us, it is what is quickened to our own ears and our own experience. I have a friend who believes cars are a symbol of his ministry. However, in my past, the Lord and I had already developed that a car (or any transportation) was my symbol of a relationship with Him, (He carries us - His burden is light and easy.) If there is a conflict, keep your own faith. What matters is that you and the Lord have a connection with which to communicate.

Agates - Treasures from Him. *"And I will make thy windows of agates..."* *(Isaiah 54:12 KJ)*

Alphabet - learning the ABC's of a new language.

Aqueduct - God's vessel used to pour forth His Spirit. Also His corporate body joined together to touch the needy.

Arrow - He will make us a polished shaft. *(Isaiah 49:2)* (Piercer, arrow, thunderbolt, speaks. 2671 Heb Strong's) We will be sent in the last day ministry to gather the final harvest.

Baby oil - the anointing of the Lord. See syrup.

Baby-sitting - to care for a child of the Lord. To bring them up and nurture them. See foster parent.

Bass Clef - the foundation or root of something, as in music. See foundation.

Bathroom - a private place of cleansing and preparation in our relationship with the Lord.

Battery - a reservoir of portioned power of the Lord. Portion of enduement. *(1 Corinthians 12)*

Beaver hitting tail - an announcement or warning. See trumpet.

Bedroom - a place of quiet or rest, also of preparation. Being still and waiting upon Him. Also a place of sleep, where one is not awakened to the Lord's work in his/her life.

Bee - an enemy threat. *(Psalm 118:12)*

Binoculars - future sight or perspective. See telescope.

Birthday (or anything related to one) - the birthing of one of God's promises.

Bleachers - to watch

Bread - manna from Him. *(Exodus 16:4)*

Breakfast - the beginning meal after a fast. When one spiritually wakes, this is the first meal served by the Lord. It is breaking of a fast or famine of hearing.

Bridge - forming a bridge, or standing in the gap on behalf of a breach for another. *(Ezekiel 22:30)*

Bugs - enemy pest or irritations.

Bulldozer - created to push obstacles away from the path.

Bullets - see battery.

Busy signal - (on the phone) stop talking, and be available to listen to the Lord.

Cactus hedge - *"With favour will thou compass him as with a shield." (Psalm 5:12 KJ)* [Shield, a large shield as it is guarded by prickliness. 6793 Heb Strong's]

Cage, empty - deliverance. *"Our soul is escaped as a bird out of the snare of the fowlers; the snare is broken and we are escaped." (Psalm 124:7 KJ)*

Calendar - His time, season. *(Ecclesiastes 3:1)*

Camping - pioneering, blazing a new territory. Also means not on the well established path. Also means a temporary home.

Carrots - food (rhema) grown underground, not made manifest until harvested.

Cash register - counting the cost, paying the price. *(Luke 14:28)*

Chimes in the wind - the gentle wooing and call of His Presence. *(Song of Solomon 1:4)*

Climbing stairs - going uphill, against the current, in pursuit of Him. *"Who shall ascend the hill of the Lord?" (Psalm 24:3 KJ)*

Clothing - an enduement or power. (Luke 24:49 endue: to sink into a garment, to invest with clothing, array, clothe, put on. #1746 GK Strong's)

Cold - a place without the warmth of the Lord's comfort. Usually territory occupied by the enemy.

Color Blue - The priest color of the priest's robe. The Entrance into His holy place, intimacy and revelation. (Ex28:31)

Color Red - The color of blood. Sacrifice of Jesus for us and our sacrifice for Him. (Hebrews 9:22, Galatians 2:20)

Color Gold - To be pure, refined, tried as gold. (Malachi 3:3)

Color Amber - The glory of the Lord. (Ekekiel 1:4, 1:27-28)

Color Silver - Redemption (Leviticus 27:6)

Color Purple - Royalty, the color of ruling and reigning, kingship. (Mark 15:17,18)

Color White - The color of the bride and dove, to be pure and holy, without spot. (Isaiah 1:18, Daniel 12:10)

Color Green - the color of new beginnings, prosperity, new growth (Jeremiah 17:8, Psalms 23:2, Song of Solomon 1:16)

Connecting dots - unity in the Lord. See puzzle pieces.

Corn on the cob - complete, fully stuffed and ripe promise of God. *(Mark 4)*

Coupons (or tickets) - already paid for, and/or to redeem.

Cracking a bull whip - cleansing the temple. *(John 2:15)*

Cup - each individual Christian has his own cup to receive and swallow of the Father's will. Each cup is different. *(John 18:11)*

Curtains - a veil that either separates or encloses our relationship with the Lord. The tabernacle (our relationship with the Lord) was made from curtains.

Dance - an outward expression of what the Holy Spirit is saying on the inside. *(2 Samuel 6:14)*

Dining room - a place where one partakes of His sustenance and refreshment.

Ducks, feeding - giving God's meek ones bread from heaven.

Dynamite - power. See battery.

E - the letter "E" on an eye chart. Symbol of one's focus and direction.

Ears - ability to hear Him.

Entrance hall - the place where one waits upon the Lord to enter a destination.

Exercising - the process of using one's will to resist weakness of flesh. *(1 Corinthians 9:27)*

Fan - an agricultural season of winnowing. To blow the chaff from the wheat. *"Whose fan is in his hand and he will thoroughly purge his floor, and gather his wheat into the garner; but he will burn up the chaff with unquenchable fire." (Matthew 3:12 KJ)*

Fenced property - one's divided lot or portion of influence and/or spiritual inheritance.

Fire - the process of purification *"...who shall stand when HE appeareth? for he is like a refiner's fire..." (Malachi 3:2-3 KJ)*

Firecrackers - power. See battery.

Firemen - an army of the Lord raised and given tools expressly for the purpose of putting out enemy fires.

Fireworks - celebration, victory.

Floods of water - enemy engulfment *"...I am come into deep waters where the floods overflow me..." (Psalm 69:2 KJ)*

Foster parent - Numbers 20:12 believe = [buildup or support, foster as a parent or nurse, render faithful. (539 Heb)] To support with an arm, to carry a child. One who carries or cares for a child, guarding and bringing them up. (Gesenius)

Foundation - the lowest place of His dwelling. Much of the "fruit" of its purpose is not outwardly seen. It is the base from which all else grows and springs. A place created to support and bear much weight.

Gears - unity, see puzzle pieces.

Glasses - sight, perspective. See telescope.

Graduation - celebration of a long season of schooling completed. Announcement of readiness to move into a new realm of public influence, and/or promotion in training.

Gum - chewing, but not swallowing what the Lord is wanting to say.

Gun - a weapon against the enemy. See trigger.
Hair - the glory, and covering of the Lord. See clothing. Long hair or clothing represents fullness of growth and/or glorious covering. *(1 Corinthians 11:15)*
Hallway - a place of passing through, without rest, forward progression.
Head on collision - two wills ramming against one another.
Honey - immersed anointing. See syrup.
Horse and plow - a season of breaking up of fallow ground. Making the hard places in one's life, soft and yielded. *"...break up your fallow ground: for it is time to seek the Lord, till he come and rain righteousness upon you." (Hosea 10:12 KJ)*
Horn - {a horn, flask, cornet, elephant tooth, mountain peak, ray of light 7161 Heb}.
Hosing off - cleansing. See soap, also *Ephesians 5:26, 27.*
Icy - territory that is slippery needing to go slowly and with caution.
Jamboree - a joyous gathering where each member participates with creative instinct.
Javelin - sharpened instrument of the Lord. See arrow.
Indian chief headdress - a place of authority.
Keys - the authority we have in the kingdom to halt satan in his tracks. *"...the keys of the kingdom...whatsoever thou shalt bind...whatsoever though shalt loose..." (Matthew 16:19 KJ)*
Kitchen - the place of preparation of manna. Being at Jesus feet, cooking His living Word within our heart.
Life jacket - protection from enemy onslaught in learning to swim through the circumstances with one's head above the water. *"...he shall be holden up: for God is able to make him stand." (Romans 14:4 KJ)*
Linking arms - unity. See puzzle pieces.
Living room - usually a family place of fellowship and activity.
Lotion - anointing. See syrup.
Magnet - the Lord's drawing power. *(Song of Solomon 1:4)*
Mail - a word from the Lord. Also a package would be a gift from Him.
Mail box - place of reception and expectancy for His news.
Mail man - messenger of God's Word.
Meat - a Word from Him that takes some chewing. Not quickly assimilated. *"But strong meat belongeth to them that are of full age, even those who by reason of use, have their senses exercised to discern both good and evil." (Hebrews 5:14 KJ)*
Merry-go-round - repeating old cycles, over and over.
Missile - weapon of the Lord. See arrow.
Motel - a place of refuge and rest, while on a journey of pursuit.
Mountain - symbol of power and strength in the Lord.

Music by ear (without written music) - communicating what the Holy Spirit is saying, without previous thought. Intercession. Tongues.

Nail - to attach firmly, secure, establish. *"And I will fasten him as a nail in a sure place." (Isaiah 22:23 KJ)*

Naked - without His enduement. Also see clothing. *"...that the shame of thy nakedness do not appear..." (Revelation 3:18 KJ)*

Number 1 - unity: from the Latin word Unus meaning one.

Number 2 - division: 2 separated entities instead of one. The number of witness. *(Matt 18:20)*

Number 3 - resurrection: raise the temple in 3 days. *(John 2:19-21)* Jonah raised from the whale in three days. *(Matthew 12:40)* Elisha prayed 3 times to raise the

Number 7 - perfection, completion: God finished His creation on the 7th day. *(Genesis 2:2)* Seven sabbaths shall be complete. *(Leviticus 23:15)* Sounding of the seventh angel-mystery of God is finished. *(Revelation 10:7)* The waters covered the earth in seven days. *(Genesis 7:10)*

Number 8 - new beginning: the first of a new series as in the week or in a musical scale.

Number 12 - rule, government, authority: 12 judges, 12 apostles, 12 gates, 12 months, 12 hours to the day, 12 to the night. *(Matthew 19:28)*

Number 40 - testing or tribulation: Jesus' testing was 40 days. *(Mark 1:12-13)* The Israelites were tested in the wilderness 40 years. *(Heb. 3:9)* Moses was on the mount 40 days. *(Ex. 24:18)*

Number 50 - inheritance. Jubilee the 50th year, gave the land inheritance back to the family. 50 days after Jesus' resurrection to heaven came Pentecost. Pente means 5. The Holy Spirit was then sent as a deposit towards our inheritance.

Number 666 - *Revelation 13:18* foretells the number of the beast.

Onion breath - offensive mouth. Carnality.

Open door - no obstacle. Way provided to walk through. *(Revelation 3:8)*

Pajamas - enduement or rest for a season. See clothing.

Peacock - being arrayed with the glory of God.

Perspiration - great inner exertion of will. Doing things in one's own strength. (Ezekiel 44:18)

Phone call - the Lord is calling.

Play (recreation) - pause and rest for the soul *"...and ye shall find rest for your soul." (Matthew 11:29 KJ)* Rest: [intermission, recreation, pause, rest (372 Gk)].

Point of a pencil - same as *Isaiah 49:2* polished shaft (see arrow).

Police - law. Schoolmaster. *"the law was our schoolmaster to bring us unto Christ..." (Galatians 3:24 KJ)*

Pots and pans - vessels and/or carriers of God's food.

Puzzle pieces - members of the body of Christ, each with his own gift to fit into a corporate whole. Can also be separate portions of food given from Him, that is meant to fit into a larger perspective. *"...Christ: from whom the whole body fitly joined together and compacted...every joint supplieth..." (Ephesians 4:16 KJ)* Also *1 Corinthians 12.*

Rain - the issuing forth of His Presence upon the earth. A time where He draws very close to us and He rains Himself upon us.

Reclining position - (chaise lounge, bed, couch etc.) a season of rest after a battle with the enemy. Resting upon His promises. *"But they that wait upon the Lord shall renew their strength..." (Isaiah 40:31 KJ) "Rest in the Lord, and wait patiently for Him." (Psalm 37:7 KJ)*

River - crossing over to new life. Or see swim.

Rocks - obstacles in our path. *"Cast up the highway, gather out the stones." (Isaiah 62:10 KJ)*

Rocking - see swinging.

Rowing boats - carrying the burden of ministry in the flesh through power and might, rather than being carried. *"Take my yoke upon you, and learn of me; for I am meek and lowly in heart: and ye shall find rest unto your souls. For my yoke is easy and my burden is light." (Matthew 11:29-30 KJ)* Light: [easy, smaller. Akin to rowing with oars. 1645/1640) Gk.]

School - place of growing and learning new things from Him. *(Galatians 3:24)* See police.

Seal-a-meal - the preservation of His Word.

Seeds - the Words and promises of the Lord.

Sew - to mend or fasten together *"... for the perfecting of saints..." (Ephesians 4:12 KJ)* Perfecting: [complete furnishing. (2677 Gk) From complete thoroughly, repair, adjust, fit, frame, mend, make perfectly, join together, prepare, restore. 2675 Gk]

Snow - a spiritual season of winter.

Snow - enemy obstacles in our path, towards our destination.

Snow - washed white as snow. Holiness, sanctification. *(Isaiah 1:18)*

Soap - washing in repentance. *"...for he is like a fuller's soap (Malachi 3:2 KJ)* Using too much soap can represent self condemnation.

Spot light - manifestation of something hidden.

Statue of liberty - recently restored, a testimony of freedom, light bearing. See sew.

Stork - carrying God's promise. See birthday. *(Jeremiah 8:7)*

Swinging (or rocking) - vacillating between two opinions. *"...how long halt ye between two opinions, if the Lord be God then follow Him..." (1 Kings 18:21 KJ)*

Swimming - growing to a place in the ministry of the spirit where one is immersed in His Spirit. (Growth of the living waters extending from the throne. *Genesis 7:10*) Swimming is also the spiritual process of "crossing over" to the other side.

Sword - sharpened instrument. See arrow.

Syrup - the sweetness of being immersed in the holy anointing oil of His Spirit. Anointing: [grease, ointment, fat things, olive oil, etc. 8081 Heb]

Telescope - viewing assignment of a watchman. *"...I have set thee a watchman...hear the word at my mouth and warn them for me..." (Ezekiel 33:7 KJ)* Watchman: [to lean forward. Peer into the distance (6822 Heb)]

Ten commandments (pulsating) - I saw them pulsating with light, like a heartbeat. He was saying His law was planted within my heart. *"...show the work of the law written in their hearts..." (Romans 2:15 KJ)*

Test at school - the proving of accountability *"... For unto whomsoever much is given, of him shall be much required." (Luke 12:48 KJ)*

Toll crossing - pay the price to cross over.

Tomahawk - sharpened instrument. See arrow.

Tooth - growing power.

Tree house - watchman's post.

Trigger - the power of decision, made through volition of will.

Trumpet - the mouthpiece or announcement of God's watchmen. *(Ezekiel 33:3-11)*

Tunnel - a passageway through an obstacle, usually a dark place.

Tying or untying a knot - (shoes, neck tie, ropes, etc.) To unravel a mystery. Daniel 5:12 Dissolving: [to free separate, unravel (8271 Heb) Dark sentences: [puzzle, trick, pun, problem (7001 Heb) From a word meaning to untie a knot. Doubts: [a knot, riddle (2330 Heb)]

Upside down - a place without security or control in one's environment. Loose things "fall away," sifting.

Under water - submerged under enemy influence, as in flooded.

U turn - turn around and cover old ground one more time.

Vacuum - intercession. The power that cleans debris from the pathway. *(Ephesians 6:18)*

Vaseline - anointing. See syrup.

Vulture - enemy predator sent to steal.

Waterfall - the power and refreshment of His coming rain.

Whirlwind - a place of turning around and around.

Window - a watchman's post. See telescope.

Wings - (bird, airplane, butterfly) being carried in His Spirit. Also breaking the day. *"But they that wait upon the Lord shall renew their strength; they shall mount up with wings as eagles..." (Isaiah 40:31 KJ)* Mount up: [ascend, be high, mount, dawn, break the day (5927 Heb)]

Yellow line - (on the road) the threshold of crossing over our conscience. *(Acts 24:16)*

101. HE SPEAKS THROUGH HIS ATTRIBUTES

Words that come from the Lord, no matter in what fashion, will always line up with Who He is. It is especially helpful to be grounded in the characteristics of God in order to know whether it is Him speaking to us.

The following is a list of the qualities and attributes of God and how they relate to the nature of His Words:

1. **God is Love.** God's Word to us is founded upon the characteristics of love.

    "Love endures long and is patient and kind; love never is envious nor boils over with jealousy; is not boastful or vainglorious, does not display itself haughtily. It is not conceited - arrogant and inflated with pride; it is not rude (unmannerly), and does not act unbecomingly. Love {God's love in us} does not insist on its own rights or its own way, for it is not self-seeking; it is not touchy or fretful or resentful; it takes no account of the evil done to it - pays no attention to a suffered wrong. It does not rejoice at injustice and unrighteousness, but rejoices when right and truth prevail. Love bears up under anything and everything that comes, is ever ready to believe the best of every person, its hopes are fadeless under all circumstances and it endures everything {without weakening}. Love never fails - never fades out or becomes obsolete or comes to an end..." (I Corinthians 13:4-8 AMP)

2. **God is Life.** When God speaks, it gives us strength, nourishment and fruitfulness; it gives us life.

    "...I have come that they might have life, and that they might have it more abundantly." (John 10:10 KJ) *"...The Words that I speak to you, are spirit, and they are life."* (John 6:63 NKJV)

3. **God is our Refuge.** He is our hiding place, shielding us from the fiery darts. Words from Him will carefully protect when uncovering a thorn.

    "He who dwells in the secret place of the Most High shall abide under the shadow of the Almighty. I will say of the Lord, He is my

refuge and my fortress: my God; in Him will I trust." (Psalm 91:1,2 NKJV)

4. **God is Peace**. There is no pushiness or driving anxiety in peace. Peace stills the storm. His Word to us will quiet our hearts when all is raging around us.
"..they cry unto the Lord in their trouble, and he bringeth them out of their distresses. He maketh the storm a calm, so the waves thereof are still. Then are they glad because they be quiet; so he bringeth them into their desired haven." (Psalm 107:28-30 KJ)

5. **God is Whole**. "I AM that I AM" is complete. When He speaks wholeness into our lives, we become well, whole, supplied and complete in Him.
"I AM that I AM" (Exodus 3:14 KJ) "That the man of God may be perfect, thoroughly furnished unto all good works." (2 Timothy 3:17 KJ) [Perfect = complete 739 Strong's]

6. **God is Discipline**. He disciplines us because He loves us and wants us to be partakers of His Holiness.
"For the Lord corrects and disciplines every one whom He loves, and He punishes, even scourges, every son whom He accepts and welcomes to His heart and cherishes...Moreover, we have had earthly fathers who disciplined us and we yielded {to them} and respected {them for training us}. Shall we not much more cheerfully submit to the Father of spirits, and so {truly} live? For {our earthly fathers} disciplined us for only a short period of time and chastised us as seemed proper and good to them, but He disciplines us for our certain good, that we may become sharers in His own holiness." (Hebrews 12:6-10 AMP)

7. **God is our Provider**. What He speaks into our lives, will provide everything we need.
"And Abraham said, My son, God will provide himself a lamb for a burnt offering..." (Genesis 22:8 KJ)

8. **God is the Bread of Life**. His Words will nourish us throughout our journey. They will strengthen, sustain and satisfy us.
"I am that bread of life. Your fathers did eat manna in the wilderness... I am the living bread which came down from heaven..." (John 6:48 KJ)

9. **God is our Strength**. His Words give strength to stand and strength

to rest.
"*The Lord is my strength and song...*" *(Exodus 15:2A KJ)*

10. **God is our Banner**. Words from Him are a sign that points the way to truth.
"*You have given a banner to those that fear You, that it may be displayed because of the truth.*" *(Psalm 60:4 NKJV)*

11. **God is our Counselor**. Words from the Holy Spirit will advise and guide us on the Lord's pathway. *[(Isaiah 9:6)* Counselor; to advise, deliberate, resolve, consult, determine, guide. 3289 Hebrew Strong's]
"*...when he, the Spirit of truth, is come, he will guide you into all truth...*" *(John 16:13 KJ)*

12. **God is Just**. His Words execute justice to the wicked and freedom to the wronged.
"*...for all his ways are judgment: for a God of truth and without iniquity, just and right is He.*" *(Deuteronomy 32:4B,C KJ)*

13. **God is Truth**. When He speaks, He does not lay heavy burdens upon our shoulders, rather He sets us free with truth.
"*...the Spirit of truth, which proceeds from the Father...*" *(John 15:26 KJ)* "*And you shall know the truth, and the truth shall make you free. If the Son therefore shall make you free, ye shall be free indeed.*" *(John 8:32,36 KJ)*

14. **God is a Deliverer**. When He speaks Words into our lives, they deliver us from the death of the evil one and sin. He speaks without condemnation.
"*For God did not send His son into the world to condemn the world; but that the world through Him might be saved. He who believes in Him is not condemned...*" *(John 3:17,18 NKJV)*

5. **God is our Shepherd**. The Lord's Words will be in one accord with a shepherd's care for his sheep.
"*I am the good shepherd. The good shepherd gives His life for the sheep.*" *(John 10:11 NKJV)*

16. **God is our Everlasting Father**. He gives good gifts to His children. His Words will be good gifts reflecting His Fatherhood. *(Isaiah 9:6 KJ)*
"*If ye then, being evil, know how to give good gifts to your children,*

how much more shall your Father which is in heaven, give good things to them that ask him?" (Matthew 7:11 KJ)

17. **God glorifies Jesus**. The Father glorifies His Name through glorifying His Son, Jesus. When He speaks Words into our lives, they point the way to and through Jesus, His Son.
"The Spirit of truth...He shall glorify me..." (John 16:13,14 KJ) "Father glorify thy name. Then came there a voice from heaven, saying, I have both glorified it, and will glorify it again. (John 12:28 KJ) I am the way, the truth, and the life: no man cometh unto the Father, but by me." (John 14:6 KJ)

18. **God is our Righteousness**. The Lord speaks His righteousness to cover our sins for we have no righteousness of our own.
"...and this is his name whereby he shall be called, The Lord Our Righteousness." (Jeremiah 23:6B KJ)

19. **God is Holy**. When He speaks, His Words are pure, clear, without spot and blemish. There is no mixture in His Words.
"...Every word of God is pure." (Proverbs 30:5 KJ) {Pure in the Hebrew means refined. 6884 Strong's}

20. **God is Merciful.** The Lord's Words are compassionate.
"And the Lord passed before him there, and proclaimed, "The Lord, the Lord God, merciful and gracious, longsuffering, and abounding in goodness and truth.." (Exodus 34:6 NKJV)

21. **God is Forgiving.** He speaks forgiveness for our sins.
"Keeping mercy for thousands, forgiving iniquity and transgression and sin..." (Exodus 34:7 NKJV)

22. **God is Comforting.** He speaks ease and consolation to our pain.
"As whom his mother comforts, so I will comfort you." (Isaiah 66:13 NKJV)

23. **God is Gracious.** The Lord shows us favor and pity.
"I will be gracious to whom I will be gracious..." (Exodus 33:19 NKJV)

24. **God is Wonderful.** His Words to us are extraordinary, filled with wonder and marvel.
"And His name shall be called Wonderful..." (Isaiah 9:6 NKJV)

25. **God is Omniscient**. God's Words reveal His secrets, for He knows all things.
   "Great is our Lord, and of great power: his understanding is infinite." (Psalm 147:5 KJ)

26. **God is Omnipresent**. His Words are present everywhere in life.
   "Where can I go from Your Spirit? or where can I flee from Your presence? If I ascend into heaven, You art there: if I make my bed in hell, behold You are there." (Psalm 139:7,8 NKJV)

27. **God is Omnipotent**. God's Words are all powerful.
   "There is none more powerful than He.....and thou reignest over all; and thine hand is power and might..." (1 Chronicles 29:12A,B)

1 Genesis 41:26
2 Romans 8:14 (KJ)
3 Isaiah 1:18 (KJ)
4 Isaiah 29:13
5 Genesis 40:8 (KJ)
6 Jeremiah 14:14

CHAPTER 10:
DISCERNMENT - SEPARATING THE WHITE, BLACK AND GRAY

"But solid food is for full-grown men, for those whose senses and mental faculties are trained by practice to discriminate and distinguish between what is morally good and noble and what is evil and contrary either to divine or human law." (Hebrews 5:14 AMP)

All that glitters, is not gold and Christians are not immune to fool's gold. Satan counterfeits all the ways one hears the Lord. Sometimes one can swallow a fish hook or take a wooden nickel because of ignorance, not realizing that he is NOT naturally immune just because he is a Christian. We cannot participate in this last day outpouring without accepting we have an enemy of our soul who does not want us to know God. We must resist and overcome this interference to know the Lord. The way has been provided, but it is not without obstacles.

We would like to bury our hearts in the Lord, and pretend the enemy lives on another planet. But it is interesting that the scriptures, *"Submit therefore to God. Resist the devil and he will flee from you. Draw near to God and He will draw near to you..."* are placed back to back. *(James 4:7-8 NASB)* As He pours forth His Holy Spirit upon mankind in a more intimate way, the enemy will be working overtime as well.

In these last days, the world is being exposed to the supernatural in a greater measure; the supernatural of God, and the supernatural of satan. Bible-believing Christians need to keep their eyes open. *"Behold, I send you out as **sheep in the midst** of wolves. Therefore be wise as serpents and harmless as doves." (Matthew 10:16 NKJV)*

God's supernatural outpouring:
"And it will come about after this that I will pour out My Spirit on all mankind; And your sons and daughters will prophesy, your old men will dream dreams, your young men will see visions. And even on the male and female servants I will pour out My Spirit in those days." (Joel 2:28,29 NASB)

False supernatural outpouring:
"For false Christ's and false prophets will arise and will show great signs and wonders, so as to mislead, if possible, even the elect." (Matthew 24:24 NASB) "Lord, Lord, did we not prophesy in Your name, and in Your name cast out demons, and in your name perform many miracles? And then I will declare to them, I never knew you; depart from Me, you who practice lawlessness." (Matthew 7:22,23 NASB)

PURSUING THE SUPERNATURAL

The Lord is using the supernatural to draw people to Him. We are told to earnestly desire spiritual gifts. *"But **covet earnestly** the best gifts: (1 Corinthians 12:31 KJ)* That word *covet earnestly* in the Greek is translated to be zealous and jealous over. It comes from words meaning to burn with zeal, to be heated or to boil.[1] He delights in giving us His good gifts and He wants us to pursue them.

There are some Christian songs that have lines in them about seeking the Lord's face, and not His hand. I used to think that was a good concept, because the supernatural has a lure all its own, and many run after "it" for the wrong reasons. "IT" is emphasized, because "it" is an experience and people can covet His gifts and not necessarily Him.

However I started thinking about a bride loving her husband. If she were to say, "My dear husband, I love who you are, but not what you give, not the work or your hands," then it is like saying I only love part of you. From that day on, I started singing the songs, "I seek Your face and Your hand!" If He is raining His supernatural upon us, then we need to crave every part of His good gifts and earnestly ask for them. We can enjoy the drawing power of His supernatural experiences, then run right into His arms. Yet it is always good to do a heart and motive check, as well as making sure that the luring, drawing power of the supernatural does not have us in its grip.

The Lord not only uses His good gifts to draw us to Him, but He also uses them as signs confirming His Word. In the next verse, notice the words "follow". This is the opposite of pursuing the supernatural experience because we are drawn by it. In this case, the supernatural follows us as a natural result of our Christian walk: *"And these signs shall follow them that believe; In my name shall they cast out devils; they shall speak with new tongues; they shall take up serpents; and if they drink any deadly thing, it shall not hurt them; they shall lay hands on the sick, and they shall recover... and they went forth, and preached everywhere, the Lord working with them, and confirming the word with signs following." (Mark 16:17-18,20 KJ)*

God intends to draw us with His good gifts, then make US His gifts. Being His gifts, we are meant to be given away. The gifts are not meant to exalt man as the vessel. Rather the Lord wants us to be gifted so that we may draw others into a deeper relationship with Himself. The supernatural is not just for show. It does display His awesome power, but He intends to go somewhere with it. And that intent is to show that He is a personal God and wants to be involved in our lives.

MAKING DECISIONS ABOUT THE SUPERNATURAL
Dicernment is learning to make careful decisions without being impulsve.

Part of the process of discernment is learning to make accurate decisions about what you are exposed to without being impulsive, rash, judgmental or critical: but with careful prayer, thought, consideration, and TIME. It is good to make a decision. The Lord has brought the earth to a season when it's TIME TO MAKE A DECISION. *(Joel 3:14)* We have arrived at the harvest time when both God and satan want a commitment one way or another.

Some people have been riding the yellow line for a long time, afraid to voice an opinion, or make a stand about what they believe. They have taken the middle of the road approach to avoid confrontations. The yellow line hasn't been a problem because there hasn't been much traffic. However, the traffic in both directions is now increasing and the guy in the middle is going to get crunched. The pace is accelerating.

"Behold, the days come, says the Lord, that the plowman shall overtake the reaper..." (Amos 9:13 KJ) Never on the face of this earth will humanity be exposed to so much, in so little time. This will happen

for two reasons: the pouring forth of His Presence, and His shaking of the earth. *(Hebrews 12:25-29)* Because everything that can be shaken will be shaken, Christians need a solid foundation of how God speaks and how to discern the supernatural.

The Lord's supernatural outpouring is breaking and shaking man's religious boxes as to Who He is. There are many ways man boxes God. One way is by interpreting the Bible to say God intended the supernatural to die with the early Apostles. Man will be confronted with a choice of removing the box and allowing God to reveal Himself as He chooses, or he may not be included in the blessings of the pouring forth of the latter rain of God's Spirit.

Have you ever been in a belly-gusher rain? One time we had a deep, very loud, and overwhelming downpour. The gutters overran and Cuddle's kitty pillow and blanket were drenched. I think it scared Cuddles, as after I washed and dried her bed (without offending soap or softeners) she would not come back and rest. She was sleeping somewhere else in the neighborhood and coming back to eat. It really bothered me and I kept praying that she would return and find her place of comfort.

Finally, I came up with an idea. Whenever John got her towel out and placed it on his lap, she came running! So, I told John to also get her clean blanket that was on top of her pillow, and sneak it in with the towel so she could get her smell on it. He did this and she loved her time with John. Then he placed her on her pillow with her blanket. The next day she was contentedly sleeping there.

The point of the allegory is that sometimes the supernatural rain of the Lord upsets our security because we are frail human beings. We become unstable and need to return to our resting place. The Lord wants to build in us a secure foundation. He understands and He will do His best to bring us to that place of security, that safe place of faith in Him.

People can go through a sifting process when they are learning to discern the supernatural. They really desire God and earnestly want to make the correct choices. However, the inability to make the decision causes the wavering to become intense. So many have already been sifted in their hearing and led astray because of lack of knowledge. To keep from being sifted, a firm foundation is needed in reading the Bible and understanding Who God is. The things that God speaks will always line up with Who He is, so if you earnestly desire God and come across something that shakes a box inside you, PRAY about it, and ask HIM. If you are insecure about what you've been exposed to, go to Him and He will establish you. He will help you find Him and help you make the correct decisions.

DISCERNING THE GIFTED VESSEL

In learning to discern a vessel we must be very careful not to esteem man, his natural gifts or his supernatural gifts out of proportion, and think of the person or experiences more highly than we ought. There is a common misconception that giftedness means God's approval of a vessel. The Word says, *"You have ascended on high, You have led captivity captive; You have received gifts among men, Even from the rebellious, That the LORD God might dwell there."* (Psalm 68:18 NKJV) For the gifts and calling of God are without repentance. (Romans 11:29 KJV) *"Many will say to Me in that day, 'Lord, Lord, have we not prophesied in Your name, cast out demons in Your name, and done many wonders in Your name?' And then I will declare to them, 'I never knew you; depart from Me, you who practice lawlessness!'* (Matthew 7:22 NKJV) The fact is, God honors His Word regardless of the vessel. Think of the many vessels that fell into sin in the Bible, yet God still performed His Word.

On the other hand, God's vessels need to be examples not only in what they say, but how they act when they are saying it. This is being accountable in word and deed. Consider the choices and communication skills of a wise parent:

1. A wise parent realizes if he yells at his children frequently, they begin to ignore and "tune him out" unless he is yelling. Soon they will become insensitive, deaf and hard of hearing even to the yelling.
2. A loving parent also realizes that controlling through pressure and coercion through his perspectives will only cause a wayward child to resist.
3. A sensible parent knows the best time to say a correcting word is in a teachable moment. When the child is striving, arguing, or defensive he is not teachable.
4. The astute parent resists an argument, for he knows only a downhill spiral will occur.
5. A loving parent will provide an atmosphere of believing and uplifting the child, rather than tearing the child down with criticism.

Should a preacher, a teacher, a servant, a friend, be any different in sharing God's message? *"God's people must not be quarrelsome; they must be gentle, patient teachers of those who are wrong. Be humble when you are trying to teach those who are mixed up concerning the truth. For if you talk meekly and courteously to them they are more likely, with God's help, to turn away from their wrong ideas and believe what is true."* (2 Timothy 2:24,25 TLB)

As delegates, the Lord's messengers represent His heart and

message. Purity of heart and motive are of extreme importance. I am reminded of the time when Moses was rebuked and not able to enter the promised land. (He struck the rock twice, and spoke a sentence of angry condemnation: *"Hear now, you rebels! Must we bring water for you out of this rock?" (Numbers 20:10 NKJV) "Then the Lord spoke to Moses and Aaron, Because you did not* **believe**[2] *me to* **hallow**[2] *Me in the eyes of the children of Israel, therefore you shall not bring this congregation into the land which I have given them." Numbers 20:12 NKJV)*

The above word *believe* (KJ) is an important concept describing the Father's character. It means: to build up or support, to foster as a parent or a nurse, render faithful, bring up, establish, be faithful of long continuance, nursing father, etc. Gesenius says *believe* is {to support with an arm, to carry a child, one who carries or cares for a child, who guards and brings up.} Hallow (sanctify KJ) means to pronounce clean.

Moses' action at the rock did not represent the Nursing Father, it represented Moses' exasperation and anger. It may appear as a small sin but because of his position, he was highly accountable. He carried great weight and authority: *"...And from everyone who has been given much, shall much be required; and to whom they entrusted much, of him they will ask all the more." (Luke 12:48 NASB)* Moses was chosen by God and led His people all the way to the door of their new beginning. But he was not allowed to enter. When representing the Lord today, it is important to remember Moses's example; <u>how</u> the message is delivered is just as important as the message.

God uses ANYTHING as a vessel for His message. (He even speaks through donkeys: Numbers 22:28) Unfortunately, vessels sometimes cause us to stumble in our ability to receive the message. We compare the vessel's personality with the Lord's, how the message is given, and then falter because of the weaknesses of the delivery of the message. God uses vessels to communicate even though marred by sin. **It is good to discern the vessel because one needs to discriminate between the impurity of flesh and the quickening power of the Spirit, but it is not good to be critical of the vessel.**

Divisions can occur among Christians when they are learning to discern. They happen when a threatened person says, "That person is hearing from satan, don't listen to him, he is from the devil." People are quick to categorize rashly and point the finger when they are insecure with what they do not understand. Because supernatural happenings come from the enemy as well as from the Lord, many actually do not know which side is which.

In learning the discerning process, we need to understand that DISCERNING IS A PROCESS. Not everyone is on the same level of perception. May we receive this needed understanding and have greater patience with ourselves and fellow Christians in their hearing. We need to treat others as God treats us: with understanding, forgiveness and love. Step by step, He imprints His image upon our lives, and that takes time. Meanwhile, He still needs vessels to impart His living Word. In learning to discern the vessel, the most important thing is to discern with love. He wants us to be wise as serpents, and harmless as doves.[3] When we are patient with man, love becomes the harmless part, taking the sting out of the discernment of evil and flesh.

Therefore, in our hearing and knowing the Lord through His people, we look to HIM Who is the Author, the Provider, the Creator, the SOURCE of perfect gifts, and let go of the part that does not represent Him. It is not that we let go of or turn our backs on humanity. Rather, **we simply separate the good gifts from the clutter, and gladly receive the good portion**. So, in getting to know and hear the Lord through His people, we receive His good and perfect gifts.

SEPARATING THE GRAY OF THE VESSEL

"But solid food is for the mature, who by constant use have trained themselves to distinguish good from evil." (Hebrews 5:14 AMP)

The process of discernment separates the words, receiving life from the good and dumping the waste. Identifying the source is the process of separation. The source has one of three choices: purity and white which is God, black and dark which is satan, or a mixture of both black and white, called gray. Distinguishing between the three, begins by pondering the qualities of God. If the message reflects these qualities, then He is the source. If the message is opposing God's character (Chapter 9), the source is the enemy. Most of the time, if it is the enemy, it is black and easy to throw out, unless the person is naive about God's character. The world is full of the mixture of white and black — GRAY, into which man has adapted. The gray area is where we stagger in discerning what we hear and that gray area is found in people.

The gray areas come through 1.) the flesh, or 2.) giants within the soul or personality. Giants are a term I use symbolically. It is derived from the giants in Joshua's promised land. The people were warned about allowing the foreigners and giants to stay in the land. When they entered into a forbidden marriage with them, they joined cultures, ideas, perspectives and beliefs. Union with them caused mutations, polluted worship and practices, and the corruption of God's separated and chosen people. Thus, I am using the term giants as a symbol of a forbidden intermarriage with the mixture of our flesh and the impurity of sin.

When one intermarries with a giant, its fruit causes a **mutated**

life pattern. These unions with sin, impure actions, thoughts, beliefs, motives or old wounds, are patterns or ruts of the personality that no matter how hard one tries, they just don't measure up to Jesus' image. They are continually repeated and acted out through the body, soul and spirit in spite of much effort to change. They are thorns and pricks left in the Christian's life and torment his freedom.

"And as for you, you shall make no covenant with the inhabitants of this land; you shall tear down their altars. But you have not obeyed Me; what is this you have done? Therefore I also said, 'I will not drive them out before you; but <u>they shall become as thorns in your sides, and their gods shall be a snare to you.</u>' And it came about when the angel of the LORD spoke these words to all the sons of Israel, that the people lifted up their voices and wept." (Judges 2:2-4 NASB) This speaks of Christians feeling remorse about their existence yet they have not been able to overcome.

Not everyone has the same giant patterns. Each person has his or her own unique personality and one person's hang-up may be another's strongest place of overcoming. Some of these giant "hang-ups" that do not glorify Jesus are listed below. As you read them, you may find weaknesses that fit yourself and others. If you have a weakness in one of these areas, it does not mean you have intermarried with a giant, but the weakness shows a vulnerability. <u>When one actually intermarries with something on the following list, he or she becomes snared by it, and it becomes a part of the person's makeup - namely personality</u>, decision making processes, actions, reactions and the overall life pattern of how that person lives life. It is the <u>pattern</u> of repeated weaknesses that expose an intermarriage with a giant.

This list not only contains giants but is also a list of the fruit of the flesh. The degree the flesh is nurtured in these areas determines whether one intermarries with such and thus causes a giant pattern and eventually a cankered wound. The choice of most words comes from King James. Scriptures are included as references to the general concept. Synonyms are listed to help identify the words.

GIANT AND FLESH LIST

Abuse .... Misuse, mistreat, maltreat. *(2 Corinthians 11:25)*
Accuse .... Charge, blame, incriminate. *(Luke 23:10)*
Adultery .... Infidelity, fornication. *(Matt 15:19)*
Ambition .... Overly enterprising, stepping on others, determined, goal oriented. *(Acts 8:19)*
Angry .... Violent passion, indignant, exasperated. *(Colossians 3:8)*
Anxious .... Exaggerated and distracted concern, apprehensive,

	uneasy, worried, dread and fear. *(Philippians 4:6)*
Apathetic	Indifferent, dull of feeling, passive. *(Revelation 3:16)*
Argumentative	Disputing, contending, hair splitting. *(2 Timothy 2:24)*
Betrayer	Double cross, trick. *(Matthew 26:25)*
Bitter	Resentful. *(Acts 8:23)*
Blasphemer	Irreverent, reviling. *(Matthew 15:19)*
Boast	Brag, proud, arrogant. *(2 Timothy 3:2)*
Co-dependent	Leaning on someone other than God. *(Deuteronomy 6:5)*
Compete	Ambitious, aggressive, contest, oppose. *(Mark 10:37)*
Complain	Grumble. *(Jude 16)*
Compromise	Bargain with evil. *(Genesis 19:8)*
Compulsive	Obsessive, driving passion. *(Matthew 12:45)*
Condemnation	False guilt. *(Romans 8:1)*
Control	Dominate, push, restrain. *(Acts 21:12)*
Covet	Desiring something that belongs to someone else, envy. *(Exodus 20:17)*
Coward	Fearful, lacking courage. *(Revelation 21:8)*
Critical	Disapprove, faultfinding. *(Galatians 5:15)*
Curse	To curse, doom, condemn evil upon. *(Matthew 26:74)*
Cursing	Swearing, profanity, filthy communication. *(Colossians 3:18)*
Deceive	Defraud, delude, dupe, mislead. *(Mark 7:22)*
Defensive	Justifying, guarding, shielding. *(Isaiah 45:9)*
Depressed	Despondent, downhearted, downcast, desolate. *(Proverbs 15:13)*
Desiring praise	Desiring esteem, admiration. *(John 12:43)*
Despise	Little regard for others, low opinion of, arrogant. *(2 Timothy 3:3)*
Discontent	Disgruntled, unsatisfied. *(Philippians 4:11)*
Disobedient	No submission or conformity. *(2 Timothy 3:2)*
Divination	Witchcraft. *(Leviticus 20:27)*
Double-minded	Vacillate between two opinions. *(James 1:8)*
Double-minded	Vacillate between two opinions. *(James 1:8)*
Double-tongued	Two stories. Saying a thing with the intent to deceive. *(1 Timothy 3:8)*
Doubter	Skeptic, unbeliever, mistrust, suspicion. *(Hebrews 11:6)*
Downcast	Low in spirit, depressed, joy withered away. *(Joel 1:12)*
Drunkard	Intoxication, insobriety. *(Luke 21:34)*
Emulation	Envious and contentious rivalry, competition, challenge. *Galatians 5:20)*
Envy	Jealousy, rivalry, competition. *(Galatians 5:21)*

Extortion .... Acquire deceitfully, defraud, blackmail. *(Leviticus 19:13)*
Evil thoughts ...... Unkind, tear down the person. *(2 Corinthians 10:5)*
False witness ...... False, deceitful testimony. *(Matthew 15:19)*
Fearful .... Timid, scared, lose courage. *(Revelation 21:8)*
Fierce .... Brutal, rough, savage, violent, wild. *(2 Timothy 3:3)*
Filthy speech ...... Foul speaking, low and obscene speech, vulgar language. *(Colossians 3:8)*
Filthy .... Defiling, dishonorable, dirty, wicked, vile, pornography, smut. *(James 1:21)*
Foolish .... Senseless, folly, reckless. *(Mark 7:22)*
Fornication .... Sexual immorality. *(Colossians 3:5)*
Gossip .... Spreading rumor, scuttlebutt, hearsay. *(1 Timothy 5:13)*
Greed .... Covet, hoard, grasp, possessive. *(Acts 5:2)*
Grievous .... Weighty, load, burdensome. *(1 John 5:3)*
Guilt .... Blame, fault, error, shame. *(1 John 2:1)*
Hatred .... Strife, detest, abhor, loathe. *(Proverbs 10:12)*
Heresy .... Disunion, dissension. *(Galatians 5:20)*
High-minded ...... Conceited, inflated. *(2 Timothy 3:4)*
Hopeless .... Despair, past hope. *(John 11:32)*
Homosexuality ... Vile affections against nature. *(Romans 1:26)*
Hypocrite .... Masquerades, faker. *(Matthew 23:15)*
Idolatry .... Infatuation, inordinately fond of. *(1 Corinthians 10:14)*
Impatient .... Restless, intolerant, resistant towards long suffering. *(Numbers 20:10 - 11)*
Impulsiveness .... No self control, unpremeditated, rash, impetuous, spontaneous. *(Proverbs 29:20)*
Inconsistent .... Erratic, discrepancy. *(James 1:6)*
Indifferent .... Unresponsive, detached, apathy, unconcern. *(Revelation 3:16)*
Jest .... Banter, wit, joke. *(Ephesians 5:4)*
Jealous .... Possessive, monopolize, envious. *(Proverbs 6:34)*
Knowledge lust .. Passion for knowledge for wrong motive. *(2 Timothy 4:3)*
Lazy .... Idle, slothful, indolent. *(Matthew 25:24-27)*
Liar .... Telling falsehoods, untruth. *(Revelation 21:8)*
Lewd .... Unbridled lust, shameless, indecent, sensual. *(Galatians 5:19)*
Love of pleasure ... Preferring pleasure to the things of God. *(2 Timothy 3:4)*
Lust .... Craving, an absorbing longing for, hunger, desire. *(1 John 2:16)*
Malice .... Desire to injure, animosity, spite. *(Colossians 3:8)*

Mock .... Scoff, ridicule, deride. *(Jude 18)*
Murder .... Kill with ones words as well as literally kill. *(Matthew 15:19)*
Murmuring .... One who discontentedly complains against God, grumble, mutter. *(Jude 16)*
Perverse .... Without natural affection. *(Romans 1:24)*
Phobias .... Irrational fear, avoidance, aversion. *(2 Timothy 1:7)*
Poverty .... Unproductive, insufficiency, shortage. *(Proverbs 15:19) (Romans 12:11)*
Possessive .... Controlling, grasping, selfish, cling. *(2 Samuel Chapter 11)*
Proud .... Arrogant, vain, self love. *(Proverbs 16:18)*
Procrastinate ...... Delay needlessly, put off. *(Proverbs 6:9-11)*
Presumptuous ..... Boldly arrogant, offensive, foolhardy. *(Psalm 19:13)*
Quarrelsome .... Contentious, ignites strife. *(Galatians 5:20)*
Regret .... Looking to past life or sins, not accepting the Lord's plan and His forgiveness. *(Luke 9:62)*
Reckless .... Heady, heedless, careless, rash. *(2 Timothy 3:4)*
Rejection .... Feeling discarded. *(Genesis 29:30-32)*
Resentment .... Offense, umbrage, embittered, hostile. *(Genesis 4:4-8)*
Reveling .... Drunken carousing, rioting. *(Galatians 5:21)*
Revenge .... Taking things into ones' own hands instead of waiting for God, retaliate. *(Romans 12:19)*
Revile .... Slander, rail. *(1 Corinthians 5:11)*
Sanctimonious ... Hypocritically devout. *(Matthew 23:14)*
Seduce .... Entice, decoy, lure. *(1 Timothy 4:1)*
Sedition .... Dissension, divisions, sects. *(Galatians 5:20)*
Self willed .... Arrogant, stubborn. *(2 Peter 2:10)*
Sensuality .... Sensory pleasures. *(Jude 18)*
Self pity .... Self sympathy. *(Jonah 4:8)*
Skeptic .... Doubter, unbeliever, cynic. *(John 20:25)*
Slander .... Defame, dishonor. *(Proverbs 10:18)*
Sodomy .... Sexual perversion. *(Genesis 19:4-5)*
Strife .... Bitter conflict, selfish or self promoting which causes quarrels, division and dissension. *(Galatians 5:20)*
Striving .... Disputing, contending, arguing. *(Romans 9:20)*
Talebearer .... Telling secrets, spreading gossip or rumor. *(Proverbs 11:13)*
Theft .... Steal, rob. *(Matthew 15:19)*
Traitor .... A betrayer, treacherous. *(2 Timothy 3:4)*
Truce breaker ..... Irreconcilable, impossible to appease. *(2 Timothy 3:3)*
Unbelief .... No faith. *(Matthew 17:17)*

Uncleanness .... Impurity of thought, motive or deed. *(Colossians 3:5)*
Unforgiveness .... Refusing to pardon. *(Matthew 6:14)*
Unholy .... Sacrilegious, blasphemous, irreverent, ungodly, profane. *(Leviticus 10:10)*
Unjust .... Wrongful, dishonest, unfair. *(Proverbs 22:16)*
Unmerciful .... Without leniency, unsparing. *(Matthew 18:33)*
Unstable .... Unbalanced, uncertain, fluctuating, fickle, changeable. *(Ephesians 4:14)*
Unthankful .... Without gratefulness. *(2 Timothy 3:2)*
Violent .... Cruel, fierce, vehement. *(Psalm 7:16)*
Wavering .... Vacillating, doubting, hesitating, fluctuating, instability. *(James 1:6)*
Wickedness .... Depravity, malice, iniquity. *(Mark 7:22)*
Witchcraft .... The use of drugs - see Strong's #5331, medications, magic, sorcery, witchcraft. *(Galatians 5:20)*
Wantonness .... Self indulgence, self gratification. *(James 5:5)*
Wrath .... Fury. *(Colossians 3:8)*

Giants influence how we hear the Lord. Their influence is like a wound in a tree. The rings of the tree become warped and twisted as it wraps around the wounded area. In time, the circled areas may eventually even out, but when in close proximity to that wound, the rings are twisted, warped, perverted and bent out of shape. This analogy is the same with people who have giant wounds. When God's Word comes close to their wound, there is a crooked emotional reaction that is blown out of proportion. What is heard, is twisted, misunderstood, taken out of context, or interpreted completely backwards.

Learning to identify giants is helpful in the discernment process. Sometimes one will struggle with a rhema "Word or message" and be unable to discern whether it is from the Lord, because of his own giants. What may be happening is the message is from Him, but the receiver's inner self wrestles because he is intermarried with a giant pattern and is not free of its warped perspective. For instance, if one is suffering under a giant of condemnation, it is very difficult to receive God's praise for a job well done. If the giant is rejection the person finds it very difficult to receive God's love. If one was wounded by abuse in the past he may perceive the Lord as an angry God.

It is also possible to hear a message given through another who has a giant and thus you will doubt and stagger over what is shared. If you become aware of the potential for giants and understand them, you will quickly be able to recognize the impurity of messages and motives spoken through another. I heard a preacher who was a dynamic speaker. He exalted Jesus Christ with the Holy Spirit evident in his meeting. Yet he had a mutated giant of control from a wound in his past, and the Holy Spirit within me became deeply grieved at something he said, as well as the attitude behind it. I struggled with it and took it to the Lord. Without my asking, three people came to me, mentioning how this man "ran" his church. It became very obvious he was bound by the giant of control and this did not glorify Jesus' image. I was then able to separate God's pure message from the controlling statement. As a result, the man's ministry, his giftedness and his impurities no longer were a stumbling block to me. I was able to hear the Lord through him in spite of his wounded flesh.

Giants and their wounds disfigure the purity of God and canker perspectives. They will always distort the character of God. Giants affect our thought life, our understanding of God's message, and our ability to receive His Words in that area. Examples of how they influence us are coming up in following sections.

GIANTS, THOUGHTS AND THE ENEMY

Scientists tell us we need to think about something a number of times, before it becomes "grooved" in our brains via the axons, dendrites and synaptic junctions, thus forming new brain patterns. The process of thinking about something repeatedly, plants seeds and nurtures them to grow in our "heart." This process happens good unto good, and evil unto evil.

Christian warfare begins in the thought life. Jesus said, *"But I say to you, that everyone who looks on a woman to lust for her has committed adultery with her already in his heart."* (Matthew 5:28 NASB) The lust in the heart begins as a thought and is nurtured instead of resisted. Through a process of nurturing thoughts, the seed of lust is allowed to grow until it becomes a weed. Thus a mere sight or thought triggers the weed response.

People who are vulnerable to the giants of self pity, resentment, anger, lust, unforgiveness, etc., are easy prey to suggestive thoughts the enemy puts in their mind. Just the mere suggestion of a random thought causes a giant pattern to be stroked. Then old patterns pursue the direction of the wandering mind. The enemy quickly binds the thoughts and emotions, and the person becomes a victim, in captivity to that particular thought and its emotion, resulting in unrest.

Take for example someone who has intermarried with unforgiveness. The union took place because somewhere in the past this person was offended many times. In the process, the person never forgave the offenders. Throughout the years, issues built up that would not have been so difficult to deal with, within the normal set of events. But because of this unforgiving pattern, a giant of unforgiveness was finally set in place in the heart. So now the enemy comes along and "inspires" a random thought about a person. Immediately the mind wrestles with all kinds of issues, perhaps critical feelings or feelings of disapproval of what the person is doing, or any other number of feelings. These issues may not be emotional issues in themselves, but because of the giant of unforgiveness, now they become blown out of proportion. Thus the enemy has succeeded in bringing the person's thoughts into captivity and there is a loss of peace.

Thoughts are also susceptible to wounds that crave to be healed. When wounded, one is inclined to grasp at things to survive. And receiving thoughts that stroke one's pain is an instinctive part of that survival of the flesh. In the example of unforgiveness, nursing old grudges or offenses are a perverted way of self comfort.

There are two ways man is vulnerable to enemy thoughts: through our thoughts and to our thoughts. Through our thoughts happens subjectively with the involvement of the personality and giants. The way the enemy battles us through our thoughts is to "inspire" them. Thoughts that stroke giant patterns have "drawing" power and inspire the thought life to center around issues that exalt the giant to be number one in perspective. We are a part of the involvement by "nurturing" these thoughts. We hold onto them for false comfort. But in reality, giant thoughts will always find a way to distort the purity and character of God, feeding unrest and anxiety.

Giant patterns also make us vulnerable in hearing the enemy. We can become entrapped into hearing the wrong source when we do not recognize our own giants. We need to know our weaknesses — the enemy does, and he is adept at using them against us. Examples would be hearing something that sounds Biblically correct by way of principles etc. and yet it feeds pride, or lust, or ambition, or greed or desiring man's approval, or self pity, or fear, etc. Since he cannot create a good and perfect gift, he will try to make one as close as possible. One way of doing that is to stroke the giants in our personalities.

REBUKING ENEMY THOUGHTS

"For though we walk in the flesh, we do not war according to the flesh, for the weapons of our warfare are not of the flesh, but divinely powerful for the destruction of fortresses. We are destroying speculations and every lofty thing raised up against the knowledge of God, and we are taking every thought captive to the obedience of Christ." (2 Corinthians 10:4,5 NASB)

For many years, I swallowed the lie that the enemy could not hear my thoughts. Because of this, I prayed silently. It was only after the Lord started teaching me about spiritual warfare and using His authority against obstacles, that I realized most of the warfare is seeded into our thoughts. I discovered this when I would take a quiet time to pray and listen to the Lord, then suddenly I would get an interruption by hearing a spirit speak. Sometimes it would be in response to what I was thinking. Then when I would rebuke it in Jesus' Name, (still within my thoughts) it would give a rebellious reply as it was leaving. Boy was I surprised. Actually I was shocked at first, but then it gave me more strength to fight the battle, because I KNEW I was making a difference. The bottom line to this example is that the realm of God is spirit, and so is satan's. They don't need our open mouths to hear us.

When the enemy speaks directly to your thoughts, you are hearing a thought that does not originate from yourself as mentioned above, and is the counterfeit of the Lord's voice. The problem is that because it is a thought, it has no voice inflection and "sounds" the same as the Lord's voice. If you have some doubts that what you are hearing may not be the Lord, be alert to His bringing warnings to you. He may use another Christian. You may be directly admonished, or perhaps the person's body language will hint what was said or done was offensive. In a group situation, the leader might ignore your input as if you hadn't said it. Test yourself. Is what I'm hearing out of joint with the body of Christ? Does it bring strife? Does it point the finger, bringing guilt and condemnation, or does it build up and edify?

If you hear the enemy occasionally, do not be anxious, or feel guilty. It wasn't your idea to hear him or listen to what he said. Your place is simply to recognize him and resist his attempt to snare. He must flee in Jesus Name. *(James 4:7)* There are two reasons the enemy is allowed to touch us: intentional sin and the Lord's purpose. In these last days, the Lord has even more of a purpose for us to overcome the enemy. We will be called to recognize the darkness and leave it behind. There will come a day when darkness will be under our feet and we will rule and reign with Him.[4]

If you recognize the enemy either through or to your thoughts as a pattern, start resisting in Jesus' Name over and over again. Do not be concerned that you will grieve the Holy Spirit of God by mistaking Him for the enemy. Obviously, the Lord knows and understands your plight, especially in learning to discern. He wants you stable and established in hearing HIM. God will work with you to get His will accomplished in your hearing Him.

Every time you come up against the foreign thought, rebuke it in Jesus' Name. If you belong to Jesus, you WILL OVERCOME. No weapon formed against you shall prosper. *(Isaiah 54:17)* Do not fret or fear this, simply take an active part in renouncing the thought in Jesus'

Name. Set your face like flint and rebuke as often as you need to until you are no longer harassed. You have the authority of Jesus' Name, and the devil hates and fears His Name. You can stand in the Lord and resist all that comes against you.

DISCERNING COUNTERFEIT SPIRITS

Familiar spirits have the power to counterfeit any manner of hearing described in this book. They can speak to and through one's thoughts. They can answer fleeces, give visions and pictures, etc. Familiar spirits are literally divining demons and the Lord came across very strongly about it in Old Testament law: *"A man or a woman who is a medium or has a familiar spirit or is a wizard, shall surely be put to death..."* (Leviticus 20:27 KJ) Their assignment from the enemy is the exact counterfeit of prophesy. Divination is the practice of securing secret knowledge, especially about the future.

Divination is satan's counterfeit to God's guidance. People who have toyed with anything regarding occult activity do not realize it is not a game. The forces behind those seemingly harmless pursuits are deadly. If children or adults could see the real issues behind the scenes they would never choose that road for a simple amusing diversion. That road leads to death and hell. Doors open to the demonic is many ways:

• Participation in the following practices: Acupuncture, Aerobics or physical fitness based upon other religions, Amulets, Astral projection, Astrology, Automatic handwriting, Fantasy Books, Card Reading, Channeling, Charms (good luck pieces), Clairvoyance, Conjuring, Consulter of the dead, Crystal ball, New Age Crystals, Deliverances (non-scriptural exorcisms), Dispatching demons, Divination, Diviner, Dreamer, Charms, Clairvoyance, Communication with the dead (necromancy), Conjuration, Crystals, Dream catcher, Drugs, Dungeons & Dragons, Eight ball, Enchanter, ESP, Fetishes (good luck pieces), Fortune Telling, Gypsy, Hallucinations, Handwriting analysis, Harry Potter, Horoscopes, Horror movies, Hypnosis, I Ching, Incantation, Indian burial grounds objects, Indian Jewelry, Indian artifacts, KKK, Magic, - Black, White, Yellow, Gray, Good luck charms, (St Christophers, rabbit's foot, clovers, crickets), Healing through psychic healer, Higher levels of martial arts, Household gods and idols from other countries (including Buddha and Japanese Bogota, shrines), Pictures and statues of Jesus, Pictures and statues of angels, Pictures and statues of cupids, Pictures and statues of Mary and saints, Witchcraft paraphernalia, Mediums, Blood covenantors, Horror & occult (movies TV, books, computer games, toys), Psychic hot line, Incantations, New Age Incense, Life or reincarnation reading, Magic games, Mantras, Medium, Mental telepathy, Mind control, Mind reader, Music (heavy metal), Necromancy (talking with the dead), New Age, Non-Christian exorcism, Occult, Ouija board, Pagan objects (Buddha, Tiki), Pagan temples, Palm reading, Palmistry, Past life readings, Pendulum divination, Pokemon, Potions, Psychic healing, Psychic predicating, Pyramids, Ritualism, Rock music (secular or Christian), Role playing games (like Dungeons/ Dragons & Kabala), Satanism, Science fantasy (movies, books, games, etc) Séances, Soothsayer, Sorcery, Sorcery games, Spell or hex, casting, Spirit guide(s), Spiritism, Spiritist, Table lifting, Tarot cards, Tea leaves, Toys of magic including E.T., Transcendental Meditation, Voodoo, Warlock, Water witching, White magic, Wicca, Witchcraft, Yoga.

• Having unclean objects within one's house that give glory to the works of the devil. All paraphernalia having to do with the above list, including books, games, toys, magic, crystals, art, music, and thousands of other items.

• Keeping gifts or remembrances from past unclean relationships. This is called unclean soul ties, such as past lovers or even sinful relationships.

• Keepsakes from travel in foreign lands. Many cultures believe demons live inside their objects of worship. Whether they are inside, they certainly are attached. Foreigners also place curses upon many of their souvenirs so that tourists will be drawn to purchase them. American Indians of the past often prayed to their gods for protection over their items and art.

• Past generational curses are passed down by way of demons to the 3rd and 4th generations. These curses come through ancestral sins and practices, including secret vows of the Masonic orders, and cults.

• Lusting for supernatural knowledge leaves doors open to the demonic. Lust for knowledge in a Christian most often is found in one who finds ways to demand answers from God. This is like a lust of itching ears.

• An absorbing desire to learn about the supernatural will open the door. Also a lust to experience the supernatural experiences will open doors to the demonic. There is only one door, Jesus Christ.[5] We do not want to stumble in desiring the EXPERIENCE of the supernatural, we want to desire HIM. *"But let him who glories <u>glory in this, That he understands and knows Me</u>, That I am the LORD, exercising lovingkindness, judgment, and righteousness in the earth. For in these I delight," says the LORD."* (Jeremiah 9:24 NKJV)

• Looking for signs makes one vulnerable. One way of looking for signs is to lay fleeces before the Lord on a continuing basis. Fleeces,[6] if used at all, should be used with extreme caution as unto the fear and respect for the Lord.

PRAYER OVER UNCLEAN PRACTICES AND PARAPHERNALIA

Lord I repent of my sins of participating in _____. I turn my back upon and denounce this behavior and sever all ties with it in Jesus Name. Lord, I ask Your forgiveness for participating in _____. I also ask Your forgiveness for the sins of my ancestors who practiced _____. Please cover these sins under the blood of Jesus Christ, cleanse my bloodlines and deliver us from the curses of these sins. Thank You Lord for hearing me, and answering this prayer, not by my own righteousness, but by Your accepting Jesus Christ in my stead.

And now I stand as a forgiven child of God, with the authority He has given me to bind and loose. I bind all demonic forces behind every curse, hex, spell, vex, voodoo, witchcraft, satanic ritual, unclean practice and vow sent to me in the Name of Jesus. And now that these demonic powers are bound, I break every assignment they have sent my way, whether they have been caused by my ancestors, my enemies, or my own foolish behavior. These broken assignments are now null and void and sent to the feet of Jesus Christ.

Lord if there is anything left in my life that I am ignorant of, that is keeping the door open to the demonic, please deliver me from spiritual blindness and open my eyes. Reveal them to me by the power of Your Holy Spirit, and I promise to obey You and renounce the unclean thing in Jesus Name. Amen.

Note: If you have had association with witches or anything stronger you need to seek deliverance through an appointed gift. This is a strong warning. If you do not denounce these things, you will find yourself yoked[7] into hearing a familiar spirit and following its road. You will lose your hedge of protection and be severely cut back[8] so as not to lose your soul. [For those interested in deliverance, I have written a book called, "Ministering Deliverance." See the back of this book for order info.]

DISCERNING ENEMY DREAMS AND VISIONS

The characteristics of dreams from the enemy are usually full of twisted accusations and darts that wound. Sometimes a dream will have knives, darts, sharp cutting instruments that inflict and cause pain. The purpose is to dump fear, remorse, guilt, torment, and barriers to one's relationship with the Lord. The dream can be resisted and stopped by thinking "In Jesus' Name" during the dream. If you unable to do this, pray that the Lord will help you to stand in your dreams and the Holy Spirit will remind you to do this while you are sleeping.

Also many times enemy visions and dreams will have a numbing, immobilizing or even paralyzing influence over man's will. This can happen with an inability to speak or move the body, or have a lack of freedom in exercising the will. Another characteristic of an enemy dream is the inability to wake up. Because the sleep is so deep, when the person does wake up in the middle of it, there is such a lethargic state that it is very difficult to stay awake. Frequently, there is the tendency to fall right back to sleep into the same enemy onslaught. I have learned to truly fight myself awake and then stay awake to do adequate warfare and gain the peace of the Lord before I go back to sleep. If you suffer this, always remember that thinking or speaking the Name of Jesus will break the enemy restraint. His Name is a very powerful weapon.

The Lord continually mentions in the Bible, we shall find Him when we search for Him with all our heart. He is to be our first love. He is a rewarder of those that diligently seek Him. Seeking Him is not a mellow, "What will be, will be," attitude. It is a pursuit, and it goes upstream against the current. Christians are not immune to enemy experiences.

Enemy conflict is a current sent against us for two reasons. Both are because THE LORD ALLOWS IT. First, intentional sin lifts the hedge. The Word says, *"herein do I exercise myself, to have always a conscience void of offense toward God, and toward man...give none occasion to the adversary to speak reproachfully....Whatsoever is not of faith, is sin."* (Acts 24:16 KJ, I Timothy. 5:14B KJ, Romans 14:23B KJ) When I disobey the training of my conscience, I give the enemy cause to speak reproach, the hedge of protection is lifted and I get "dumped on." Most often when I get dumped on by a nightmare or bad dream, He reminds me of those three verses. [The more mature we become in the Lord, the more sensitive our conscience becomes to very slight details in a day. An example would be attitudes that grieve the Holy Spirit, like being critical of others in our thoughts.]

I can always tell an enemy dream because it is almost always a personal accusation to that particular day. The problem with enemy dreams is that there is always a measure of truth in them. So after I take heed to the partial truth, I must then overcome guilt and condemnation and remember that I am covered by the blood of Jesus. I must also remember it is His righteousness that keeps me, not my own. The Lord does not want us buried in guilt that puts another layer between ourselves and His love.

The second reason the Lord allows enemy conflict is that the Lord wants us to become an overcomer. Satan puts many things in our path to try to get us off course, discouraged and tired, waylaid and delayed, all the while hoping we will give up. The Lord allows this to help us to grow, overcome darkness, and find HIM. We cannot find Him without resistance. The two go hand in hand.

We have entered a last days war between good and evil. The witches gather at midnight and send curses, etc upon the Christians from 12 AM - 3 AM. Much of a Christian's warfare at night is due to this united onslaught. Start taking authority over your sleep and bind the forces of witchcraft sent against you and your loved ones in Jesus Name.

DISCERNING MISUNDERSTANDING

Years ago, my son drew an elephant in a bathing suit, and gave it to me. In my female mindset, I interpreted it to be me... bulging. Later I tuned into a car radio sermon and heard: "If you see an elephant, don't interpret it to be a snake!" The preacher said, "In other words, if it makes normal sense, then it's good sense, so don't make NONSENSE." Giggling, I listened to the sermon which was about not twisting God's Word (a good gift) into something weird.

When we begin to realize we are hearing from the Lord, understanding is so important. There are three main causes of misunderstanding. The first is the enemy. The second are giants in a personality. And last, it could be the Lord's purpose for us having a temporary misunderstanding.

The enemy causes havoc in influencing our interpretation of the Lord's Word. Paul said, *"O full of all deceit and all fraud, you son of the devil, you enemy of all righteousness, will you not cease perverting[9] the straight ways of the Lord? (Acts 13:10 KJ)* The truth is turned around so that truth is twisted to say the opposite. An example might be one who receives a picture from the Lord of a bulb in the ground. He perceives he is the bulb, which is what the Lord intended. However the enemy twists the truth around so the person thinks the Lord is not pleased with him because he is in the dark not knowing what is going on and not being fruitful in that state.

The most frequent cause of misunderstanding in a Christian's life are the giants within the personality causing warped and twisted understandings. As mentioned before, giants create silent decay, generating wounds and vulnerabilities that stimulate one to hear through those wounds. This is why discernment of giants in what we are hearing is so important. Remember, giants are crooked patterns within personalities that do not reflect Jesus' image.

They ruin interpretations of His message causing misunderstandings. For example, when one receives a Word of encouragement he twists it and ends up in self pity. For many years he succumbed to this kind of pattern because of difficult circumstances and did not experience any outside comfort or relief. The unhealed giant wounds of self pity from the past are momentarily touched through the word of encouragement. Now the old pattern of attempting to comfort himself in this manner is triggered. Rather than receiving encouragement and being lifted up, the person uncovers an unhealed wound, beginning the cycles of self pity. The exhortation is twisted, becoming a reason to become self-centered instead of God-centered. The person feels worse than he did before.

Or perhaps one has been bound by the giant of ambition, another may have a giant of desiring man's approval. Both are stroked by comments from man, and they might think the Lord is giving His approval to be involved in certain programs, which in truth He has not sanctioned.

The third reason for misunderstanding is it may be the Lord's purpose![10] Eli misunderstood Hannah praying in the temple. He thought she was drunken, and because he misunderstood, he came over to rebuke her. She said it was not so and explained her plight. The truth was manifested to him and his heart was moved to give forth a prophesy and blessing.[11] God also allowed a misunderstanding about Jesus dying and rising again. *"But we speak the wisdom of God in a mystery, even the hidden wisdom, which God ordained before the world unto our glory: which none of the princes of this world knew: for HAD THEY KNOWN IT, THEY WOULD NOT HAVE CRUCIFIED THE LORD of glory." (1 Corinthians 2:7,8 KJ)*

I went through a time when I wavered back and forth between truth and misunderstanding. The Lord desired this, for I had a lesson to learn and needed a proper foundation built in my communication with Him.

As a review of the concept I have shared throughout this book, when the Lord began to speak to me by way of dreams, visions and pictures at night, He began to teach me a new language. It was built one night at a time, word upon word, until an extensive vocabulary was constructed. *"I will bless the Lord Who has given me counsel; yes, my heart instructs me in the night seasons." (Psalm 16:7 AMP, 17:3)* Each night I heard from Him, all the while growing in vocabulary. Then the milk changed into chewable food. It was food that wasn't just swallowed and assimilated. It had to be chewed and pondered during the day.

Sometimes it would take several days, even weeks for me to

chew and swallow. And sometimes, I didn't like it and spit it out! One time, for several weeks, the Lord kept reiterating upon one subject. I would stumble upon the exact interpretation, and immediately spit it out, saying, "No way! It can't be!" He fed it to me over and over again. Each time I approached that door of understanding, my flesh would recoil and I would retreat.

During this time, I was having a very difficult time feeding my three year old his meat. I had cooked a soft and tender roast, and throughout the daily leftovers the "appearance" of that pot roast would change! He'd spit it out every time. Finally, the last day of the roast I ground it up, pulverized it in the blender and mixed it with miracle whip as a sandwich spread. This was a day of victory. He ate it!

That very day someone asked me if I had considered "such n' such?" You guessed it, the subject was the "meat" He had served me over and over. Maybe I wasn't so far off after all... Just maybe, just perhaps it could be so. Before I went to sleep I said, "Is it really so Lord?" That night He gave me a picture of that roast on my son's plate and said, *"I changed the form so you would swallow it!"*

Coming to the chewable stage of His manna I had yet to learn this important lesson. I went through a whole season, hearing very clearly, knowing He was speaking; but everything I heard could be interpreted two ways in drastic contrast. I had no way of knowing which of the two He was speaking. They were always in opposition. I was on a spiritual swing-set, going back and forth, wavering, and vacillating between two opinions. What an exhausting season! I ended upside down like a turtle with my feet anywhere but on solid ground. I had no stability, no hope of ever understanding God, no confidence; I was a zero.

I needed that season of weakness to know my limitations and my need for His help in understanding Him. He had so carefully built our language and vocabulary. He would speak, and I could hear. But interpretation is just like revelation — it can not happen without HIM. I learned that particular season how important the Holy Spirit is in understanding what the Lord speaks.

DISCERNING THE MESSAGE

Much of discernment is a matter of logical deduction but is not meant to be without Biblical knowledge and the Holy Spirit's help. The enemy has a subtle strategy of adding his lies to something that is recognized as truth. He knows we are too smart to listen to something that is drastically opposed to our understanding of the Lord. Because of that, we need to be equipped with a good foundation of the entire Bible, both the Old and the New Testament. We need to know it in context as well as understanding the types, shadows and symbolism. *"Now all these things happened unto them for ensamples: and they are written for our admonition, upon whom the ends of the world are come." (1 Corinthians 10:11 KJ) "For had ye believed Moses, ye would have believed me: for he wrote of me." (John 5:46 KJ) "For whatsoever things were written aforetime were written for our learning, that we through patience and comfort of the scriptures might have hope." (Romans 15:4 KJ)* Obviously we can not know all this at once, it is a lifetime pursuit, but as our Biblical knowledge increases, so will our discernment. We need to rely on the Holy Spirit to give us discernment in everything that comes our way. In every instance, do not rely on your own power, just pray and ask the Lord for help! He understands your plight and your concerns.

In the beginning of the discerning process, there are times when the message seems true to our understanding of the Lord, yet our spirit will be repulsed. That is a wonderful help when it happens, but even that needs discernment, to separate our flesh from our spirit. Our flesh can be threatened by hearing the Lord confront with truth. Sometimes we will hear something subtly correct and have no feeling in our spirit at all. That is when the discernment of a message and the understanding of our own giants is so important. If it is the Lord and we remain repulsed, He will continue to bring the same message to us in other ways until we receive it!

He loves us very much and understands our struggles. The Lord brings us through the journey of discernment, and understands our struggles to separate and receive only Him. He knows our heart in wanting to fight the battle in overcoming darkness.

Here are some basic things to remember when discerning a message:

1) Quickening

Remember to <u>always</u> apply the quickening test to anything heard. His Words to us will be a quickened message to our hearts, and they will always bring us life. *(John 6:63)* If it isn't quickened then let it go. Life is too short to waste ourselves on words that speak nothing and go nowhere. The concept of quickening is the most basic test of all that is heard, and it is also the simplest. It is easy to forget this while trying to wade knee-deep through the discernment process.

If it is God's Word, it will fit. His Words to us are like a puzzle. He gives them to us a piece at a time, and they'll find a place that fits perfectly with all the other Words He has been sharing. It takes time to work a puzzle, some pieces come to us upside down and backwards. Yet if it is HIS message, it will prosper no matter what the enemy has tried to do with it. His Word will turn and find the place that fits in perfect connection with other quickened Words that have found their niche (been confirmed and made secure). This takes time. His desire is for us to be planted in a sure place. *"And I will fasten him as a nail in a sure place; and he shall be for a glorious throne to his father's house."* *(Isaiah 22:23 KJ)*

When one is searching, the enemy may bring puzzle pieces that appear to be the right color, shape, or size. But only God's piece will fit perfectly. The enemy's attempt to snare will cause a distortion of the picture. We are not immune to taking something the enemy has planted and trying to make it fit.

It is like forcing a puzzle piece that has been cut the same shape but not quite the same size. When placing the two together, there will either be a gap between the pieces, or the fit will be such a squeeze a "bump" will occur. This may delay the puzzle and disrupt its unity. The more pieces of God's Word that come together, the more the enemy's puzzle piece will look alien. This takes time.

2) The good and perfect gift

Only God gives good and perfect gifts, which are a reflection of Himself. *"Every good gift and every perfect gift is from above, and comes down from the Father of lights, with whom there is no variation or shadow of turning."* *(James 1:17 NKJV)* The enemy cannot give a good and perfect gift. But he tries to disguise his so called gift to look like one. Ask yourself some questions about what you've heard; how did it make you feel? Did you receive peace, joy, or comfort? Or did it create a division in your relationship with the Lord, for instance: feelings of guilt, confusion, fear, remorse, anxiousness, etc.?

A good verse to test what is heard is: *"Finally, brethren, whatever things are true, whatever things are noble, whatever things are just, whatever things are pure, whatever things are lovely, whatever things are of good report, if there is any virtue and if there is anything praiseworthy — meditate on these things."* *(Philippians 4:8 NKJV)* Ask yourself, if the thought you heard lined up with the qualities of that verse.

3) In Jesus' Likeness

It is the Lord's desire to bring us into Jesus' full image and stature of maturity. *"Unto a perfect man, unto the measure of the stature of the fullness of Christ."* *(Ephesians 4:13 KJ)* What He speaks will build us towards that direction. Did what you hear build you up into Jesus' image - did it sound like something Jesus Christ would have said? Satan cannot exalt Jesus as Lord and Savior. The enemy's purpose will be to display power and control, especially glorifying man and self-image, which is the exact opposite of exalting Jesus Christ.

4) The nature of His Words

A message from the Lord will always reflect His character. The list in Chapter 9 "Understanding What He Speaks," gives Biblical foundations as to Who God is and defines His attributes. Its summary is applied here as a checklist:

- Does the thought reflect the qualities of love?
- Check for a mixed message; note its purity, and life giving qualities.
- Make sure it doesn't condemn, does glorify Jesus, has the motive for building wholeness, provides peace and refuge.
- Watch that it reflects His Fatherhood, disciplines in love, guides into His truth, feeds and sustains, provides, covers and protects.
- Check that it strengthens, nurtures, is righteous and just, reflects that He is all powerful, all present, and all knowing.

In summary, His Words to us always speak, *"And you shall know the truth, and the truth shall make you free."* (John 8:32 NKJV) And for the most part, understanding discernment is that simple. The thought can be easily discerned simply by lining it up with the qualities of God and the Bible. It can be a process of choice through **logical checks and balances of His character, balanced with His quickening power**. If the message lines up with Jesus Christ and His Word, is quickened by His Spirit to give life, then the message can be swallowed.

No matter what, use discernment in what you see, hear and understand, concerning any message, not only yours, but from others as well. If you have heard a message and it does not reflect the goodness of God, then the message is impure. If you hear a word through an appointed gift of God, and it does not reflect His qualities, the message is impure. Do not esteem the reputation of man and ministry over the discernment of the message. If you hear anything from the various ways described in this book, even if they are true but do not reflect Him and His character, then discern the message and the source.

SUMMARY OF HOW TO DISCERN GOD IS SPEAKING

When you hear something, no matter what form it is in, test it. Ask yourself these questions:

KNOW THE BIBLE
DOES IT AGREE WITH THE BIBLE?

DOES IT:
1. Validate Jesus Christ is King of kings and Lord of lords?
2. Recognize Jesus Christ is the door?
3. Recognize Biblical sin?
4. Certify the attributes of God?
5. Synchronize with the Biblical message?
6. Build Jesus' image?

KNOW THE HOLY SPIRIT
DOES IT VERIFY HIS PURPOSE?

DOES IT:
7. Quicken with relevance?
8. Fit the puzzle together?
9. Identify the Holy Spirit is grieved?
10. Reveal a misunderstanding of God's purpose?
11. Manifest His Presence?
12. Refresh your soul, body and spirit?
13. Bring you closer to Him?
14. Identify the Gifts of the Holy Spirit?
15. Make darkness manifest?
16. Give a good and perfect gift? James 1:17
17. Nurture purity? Philippians 4:8
18. Encourage walking in holiness?

IDENTIFY THE FLESH
ARE YOU SEPARATING THE DIFFERENCE?

DO YOU:
19. Know God's Word is more faithful than the vessel?
20. Distinguish the personality of the vessel?

21   Make decisions with love and patience about the vessel?
22   Take your own thoughts captive?
23   Understand nurturing thoughts?
24   Feel wary of fleeces?
25   Recognize when your flesh is repulsed?

IDENTIFY GIANTS
DO YOU RECOGNIZE GIANTS?

DO YOU:
26   Identify your own giants?
27   Understand your own weakness towards opening the door to giants?
28   Recognize giant decay in yourself and others?
29   Recognize giant patterns in others?
30   Understand giants pervert truth?
31   Distinguish what strokes a giant wound?
32   Separate strong meat spoken from a giant's influence?

SEPARATE THE ENEMY
DO YOU RECOGNIZE ENEMY TACTICS?

DOES IT:
33   Hate Jesus Christ?
34   Hate light?
35   Identify occult practices?
36   Bind, hinder, numb and chain the ability and personal will?
37   Lie and deceive?
38   Cover over truth
39   Hide from exposure?
40   Portray a grievous message or heavy feeling?
41   Divide people?
42   Scatter people from God's source?
43   Oppose God's character?
44   Display power with control, manipulation, pushiness, force over your personal will, coercion?
45   Warp and pervert the message?
46   Accuse and condemn?
47   Distort the attributes of God?

KNOW THE TIMES
DOES IT FIT WITH THE TIMES?

DO YOU:
48 Define it as the outpouring of the supernatural?
49 Recognize the counter culture, counterfeit and activities of the occult?
50 Perceive the lust for supernatural knowledge and itching ears?
51 Understand the process of overcoming in this time in history?

UNDERSTAND GOD'S CYCLES
DO YOU ALLOW TIME?

DO YOU:
52 Accept discernment is a process, not necessarily an experience?
53 Understand wavering faith?
54 Recognize sifted faith?
55 Pray through sifting?
56 Acknowledge God speaks in circles?
57 Recognize the application of His Word is larger tomorrow than it is today?
58 Wait for 2 or 3 witnesses for confirmation?
59 Wait for understanding?

1   Covet: 2206 Greek, from 2205 and 2204. Strong's Exhaustive Concordance
2   Believed - describes the Father's character; Build up or support, to foster as a parent or a nurse, render faithful, bring up, establish, be faithful of long continuance, nursing father, etc. [539 Hebrew Strong's] Gesenius says {to support with an arm, to carry a child, one who carries or cares for a child, who guards and brings up.} Hallow (Sanctify KJ): pronounce clean. [6942 Hebrew Strong's]
3   Wise yet harmless: (Matthew 10:16)
4   Rule: (Romans 16:20; Revelation 2:26,27; 3:21; Hebrews 2:7,8; 2 Corinthians 10:6)
5   Door: John 10:1 and Revelation 3:20
6   Fleeces: chapter 8
7   Yoke: Isaiah 8:19, 29:4
8   Cut back: Isaiah 5:4,5
9   Pervert: distort, misinterpret, corrupt, turn away. From through twisting, turning around. 1294 from 1223 and 4762 Greek from the Strong's Exhaustive Concordance
10 Isaiah 45:7, Isaiah 54:16
11 I Samuel 1:13-20

The Lord is our Perfect Father and He gives good and perfect gifts. The degree we hear will be directly related to the proportion of yieldedness we offer Him with complete trust. He is a Perfect Gentleman. The Lord never takes or robs man of free will. He needs man's will to cooperate and companion with Him, in all ways, including hearing from Him. We have a choice in the portion we hear.

It helps to be reminded of the many ways He can speak to us. It helps to desire to hear Him more. In the process, our faith grows just like a language, one step at a time. (Not one leap at a time.) Be willing for God to increase your faith in hearing Him and your hearing will become 100 fold.

How do I know if the Lord is speaking to me? First, I have 101+ ways He has spoken before. Of all those mentioned, the most important are quickening and revelation. The Holy Spirit must punch it with relevance and the Holy Spirit must "dawn" upon my mind He has just spoken.

A PRAYER FOR YOU

Heavenly Father, I ask a special blessing for the person that has read this book. Please bring the many ways to hear You back to memory while he or she is out living life. Lord I know You want to reach us at the place we are, not necessarily where we want to be. Regardless of whether we think we are in the "right" place with You, please open our ears to hear You right where we are at this moment in time. I ask that all who read this book will begin to hear You in all the ways mentioned, and even more. I pray this book will make a difference in their lives and those they love, and I pray You will bring them refreshment by a rekindled relationship with You. In Jesus Precious Name, quicken Your Words, one by one. Amen.

Words to Ponder

Words to Ponder, volumes 1 & 2 are a collection of prophetically inspired writings. Conveying the heart of the Father, they reveal a mosaic of His purpose. Throughout its separate threads weaves a story of where His people have been and where they are going. Together, they portray a timely message for this hour. Be encouraged as you find understanding in what He is accomplishing in your life.

- A collection of over 200 Words of inspiration
- Written over a period of 15 years
- They have been tested and confirmed
- They give understanding, hope, encouragement, comfort and direction

TO ORDER:
MAIL:
SOS Publications
PO Box 7096
Eugene, OR 97401

EMAIL:
swauthor@usa.net

WEBSITE:
www.thequickenedword.com

THE QUICKENED WORD
Website

www.thequickenedword.com

WEBSITE MINISTRY:
PROPHETIC RHEMA AROUND THE WORLD

*Quickened Words for Hungry
and Searching Hearts*

This Websight offers several thousand pages of quickened rhema Words birthed out of a living communication with Jesus Christ.

Our goal is to encourage faith in readers as they study common denominators in which the Lord is speaking to His people. The files are built in themes and contain rhema from people all around the world and hopefully this format will give readers an understanding of the times and seasons in which we live, thus understanding the Lord's perspective.

We hope this sight will be a blessing to you as you seek to hear Him!

Facilitator,
Sandy Warner
swauthor@usa.net

THE QUICKENED WORD
Newsletter

FREE E-MAIL NEWSLETTER
to subscribe, send a blank email to:
Subscribe-thequickenedword@MyInJesus.com

The Quickened Word newsletter shares timely prophetic insights through a variety of means: Visions · Dreams · Still Small Voice · Words to Ponder · Articles · Scriptural Studies ·

In 1984 Sandy had a personal visitation from Jesus Christ in which He handed her a solid gold pen. He planted within her an anointing and passion to encourage a hurting world and to teach others how to hear the Lord.

PONDERWORD
Devotional Words to Ponder

FREE E-MAIL WORDS TO PONDERS
to subscribe, send a blank email to:
Subscribe-PonderWord@MyInJesus.com

PonderWord...
is one short Word to Ponder sent via email about 3 days a week. Words to Ponder are prophetically inspired and written from rhema containing visions, dreams, His still small voice and prophetic revelation. In essence, Words to Ponder are summaries and interpretations of rhema, punched with the word of wisdom and written under inspiration.

BOOKS AND BOOKLETS OFFERED

Books:
1]   101+ Ways God Speaks (And How To Hear Him)
2]   Words to Ponder Volume 1
3]   Words to Ponder Volume 2
4]   Discernment - Separating the Holy from the Profane
5]   Ministering Deliverance
6]   Annie's Visions - Books 1 & 2 combined
7]   Annie's Visions - Books 3 & 4 combined

Booklets:
8]   Intercessors Arise & Finding Your Authority
9]   Rain & Glory - The Last Day Joel 2 Rain
10] Gold Fever! - Visions, Dreams & Testimonies of Gold Glitter & Teeth
11] All Aboard His Glory Train!
12] The Baptism of the Holy Spirit - Why Speak in Tongues?

FOR MORE INFORMATION:

WEBSITE:
www.thequickenedword.com

EMAIL:
swauthor@usa.net

MAIL:
SOS Publications
PO Box 7096
Eugene, OR 97401